THE TWENTIETH CENTURY

A THEOLOGICAL OVERVIEW

THE TWENTIETH CENTURY

A THEOLOGICAL OVERVIEW

Edited by
Gregory Baum

ORBIS BOOKS
Maryknoll, New York

NOVALIS

**GEOFFREY
CHAPMAN**

Published in the United States by Orbis Books, PO Box 308, Maryknoll, New York 10545-0308.

Published in Great Britain by Geoffrey Chapman, a Cassell imprint, Wellington House, 125 Strand, London WC2R 0BB, England.

Published in Canada by Novalis, Saint Paul University, 223 Main Street, Ottawa, Ontario K1S 1C4.

Manufactured in the United States of America.

Copy editing and typesetting by Joan Weber Laflamme.

Library of Congress Catalogue Card No: 99-23295

British Library Cataloguing-in-Publication Data
A catalogue record for this book is available from the British Library.

Canadian Library Catalogue Card No: 99-901029-8

ORBIS/ISBN — 1-57075-282-6
CASSELL/ISBN — 0-225-66880-7
NOVALIS/ISBN — 2-89507-015-6

Contents

Introduction

The idea for this book came from Robert Ellsberg, editor-in-chief of Orbis Books. He felt that it would be important at the end of the twentieth century to reflect on the events of the last hundred years from a theological perspective. He invited me to edit a book that would reveal how theologians of the twentieth century were influenced by the historical events that affected their society and, secondly, how contemporary theologians reflecting on the past evaluate the cultural and religious movements of this century. The title, *The Twentieth Century: A Theological Overview*, is therefore not meant to suggest that the book offers a theological evaluation of the twentieth century. Rather, the essays in this book offer an overview of events and movements that have had, and possibly still have, theological significance. They reveal the creativity and, in some instances, the betrayal of theology.

The book falls naturally into two parts. Part 1 examines the impact of major historical events of the twentieth century on the interpretation theologians have given of the Christian message. These events include World War I, the Russian Revolution, the Great Depression, Nazi Germany, the Holocaust, post–World War II welfare capitalism, the emergence of the World Church, and the globalization of the free market economy. Because Catholic theologians prior to Vatican Council II were more affected by events taking place in their own church, rather than by social and political upheavals, this collection includes an article by a church historian on the impact on Catholic theology of the papal condemnation of modernism pronounced in the early years of the twentieth century.

Part 2 offers theological reflections from a contemporary perspective upon important cultural and religious developments of the twentieth century. Included are reflections on the process of secularization, the ecumenical movement represented by the World Council of Churches, Christian dialogue with Marxism, the achievements of Christian feminism, Christian voices speaking from the margins of U.S. society, the environmental movement, and the postmodern debate. The two parts of the book are followed by concluding reflections offered by the editor.

This volume is an ecumenical undertaking. Some of the articles are written from a Catholic perspective, others from a Protestant one, and others again from a Christian vantage point that does not reveal the author's confessional background.

While the topics treated in this collection cover a wide territory, it does not claim to be comprehensive. Unattended remain several contextual theologies produced in particular historical circumstances that, in spite of their particularity, have universal significance. I am thinking, for instance, of Christian theology struggling against the apartheid regime in South Africa and Protestant theology moving in a new direction in communist East Germany. The book does not look at all at Christian thought in the Eastern part of Europe. Latin American liberation theology, which has had a powerful influence upon theologians in all parts of the world, and the emerging African and Asian theologies are briefly treated in a single article on the coming pluri-centered World Church, yet there has been no space to include longer reflections on these original theological developments. Nor does the German political theology of Johann-Baptist Metz, Jürgen Moltmann, and Dorothee Soelle receive appropriate attention. Nor does this book report the wrestling of theologians with the remarkable evolution of science and technology in the latter part of the twentieth century. Christian theology is such a rich and diversified field that a single volume on theological responses to the major events of the twentieth century cannot aspire to completeness.

Still, this collection documents in a persuasive manner that theologians have reacted in a creative manner to the challenges posed by the historical events and the cultural movements of the twentieth century. They have produced insights and developed critical perspectives that will continue to enlighten the churches in the coming age. Despite certain episodes of betrayal, the story of twentieth-century theology is one of fidelity and anguish—fidelity to God's revealed word under changing historical conditions, and anguish over the unanswered questions and the powerlessness of truth in a sinful world.

—GREGORY BAUM

Part I

THE IMPACT OF HISTORICAL EVENTS ON THEOLOGY

1

"The Great War" and the Theologians

DOUGLAS JOHN HALL

Optimism and Disillusionment

"The nineteenth century ended on August 1, 1914." So Paul Tillich, year after year, announced to his puzzled North American students. Though many of us had had our childhood prior to 1939 and therefore had learned to call the war of 1914-18 "the Great War," the impact of that event upon us and our parents as citizens of the "New World" was evidently not so pronounced as to render its onset, as it was for the European Tillich, the decisive and specifically datable end of an epoch. Besides, we had lived through another war, greater than the "Great" one, a war in which some of our fellow-students had actually fought; and since World War II had ended, the Korean War and a number of other dramatic conflicts had already demonstrated to us that even victories as conclusive as the Allied triumph of 1945 guaranteed nothing with respect to world peace.

If already in the 1950s it was hard for young North Americans to appreciate the effect of World War I on the spirits of those who experienced it firsthand, the difficulty has only increased with the passage of the decades. At the end of a century saturated with war (some two hundred of them since the end of World War II!), it requires more than the usual historical knowledge to grasp something of the shock and outrage that greeted the outbreak of war on August 1, 1914. Despite our knowledge of the devastations of modern warfare, and indeed of the impossibility of ever really *winning* a war, given the nature of contemporary weaponry, we have become inured to global conflict, hot or cold. We lack the credulity (I will not say innocence) of our grandparents and great-grandparents—that is, the sincerity of their belief in progress and the perfectibility of human nature and human society.

At least by present standards, the mood of Western society at the beginning of the twentieth century was exceptionally positive. This was to be the period in which all the promises of nineteenth-century industry, inventiveness, and culture would be realized. Enthusiastic, world-missionizing Christians announced that it would be "the Christian century," and an important journal, still in existence, was launched under that nomenclature. It was also to be the century in which democracy, as exemplified in the United States of America particularly, would spread to all corners of the earth. Canadians were encouraged to believe that the new century would belong, in a special way, to this immense and as yet unpopulous and unexploited nation. In London, England, it was possible to rent a box in the famous Albert Hall for 999 years, and many wealthy patrons of the arts did so.

Barbara Tuchman opens her splendid analysis of the first weeks of World War I with a description of the public event that most captures the optimism of European civilization just prior to the outbreak of hostilities: the funeral, in May 1910, of the most popular monarch of the age, Edward VII of England. It was a magnificent occasion. All the reigning heads of the nations walked behind the imperial casket, robed in their ceremonial best and among them none was more admired by the crowd, "waiting in hushed and black-clad awe," than the nephew of the dead king and grandson of Queen Victoria, Kaiser Wilhelm II, who rode at the side of the new king, George V, and of whom *The Times* said "[he] has never lost his popularity amongst us."[1] Though Wilhelm had in fact come to England in high spirits to bury the man whom he regarded, naively, as the chief architect of the alleged "encirclement" *(Einkreisung)* of Germany (the rhetorical cause of Germany's war initiative), the English, long accustomed to their German connection, felt no need to interpret his deportment as anything other than that of a dutiful nephew.

Besides, despite fears in high places that a war was on the horizon, the general opinion was that such a thing was quite improbable. In fact, a new and very popular book by Norman Angell, *The Great Illusion*, demonstrated that war was virtually "impossible":

> Already translated into eleven languages, *The Great Illusion* had become a cult. At the universities, in Manchester, Glasgow, and other industrial cities, more than forty study groups of true believers had formed, devoted to propagating its dogma. Angell's most earnest disciple was a man of great influence on military policy, the King's friend and adviser, Viscount Esher, chairman of the War Committee assigned to remaking the British Army after the shock of its performance in the Boer War. Lord Esher delivered lectures on the lesson of *The Great Illusion* at Cambridge and the Sorbonne, wherein he showed how "new economic factors clearly prove the inanity of aggressive wars." A twentieth century war would be on such a scale, he said, that its inevitable consequences of "commercial disaster, financial ruin and individual suffering" would be "so pregnant with restraining influences" as to make war unthinkable.[2]

The story that circulated in Prussian-led Germany, however, was significantly different. There, the rhetoric of Germany's "victimization" by other
European powers (notably France and Britain) combined with theories of
the "necessity" of war and of ethnic superiority to create an atmosphere of
eager anticipation that spread from the military to many other quarters of
society. While Angell and Esher were busy proving the impossibility of war,
General von Bernhardi was composing his famous book *Germany and the
Next War*, in which he demonstrated that war was not only "a biological
necessity" but that Germany, which is "at the head of all progress in culture" but impossibly "compressed into narrow, unnatural limits," *must* make
war, and indeed has a positive, historic duty to do so.

That this kind of "German war theology"[3] had, in the end, a very wide
appeal, is shown by the manner in which young, well-educated and even
pacifist-inclined Germans like Paul Tillich immediately volunteered for duty
in the armed services of the Fatherland. There is a world of unspecified
nationalistic fervor in the following sentences from Tillich's later autobiographical reflections:

> The First World War was the end of my period of preparation. To-
> gether with my whole generation, I was grasped by the overwhelming
> experience of a nation-wide community—of the end of a merely indi-
> vidualistic and predominantly theoretical existence. I volunteered, and
> was asked to serve as a war chaplain, which I did from September,
> 1914, to September, 1918.[4]

Enthusiasm for the war, however, was short-lived in the experience of
such sensitive Germans. If prewar British optimism assumed the form of a
naive belief in war's impossibility, German optimism expressed itself in the
equally naive if more deadly belief that a war undertaken by so formidable
a *Volk* as the German nation would be a very short one. Long before
Germany's ignominious defeat in 1918, the first great Battle of the Marne,
occurring less than six weeks after the war began, robbed Tillich and many
of his contemporaries of any zeal they might have had for battle:

> The first weeks had not passed before one's original enthusiasm dis-
> appeared; after a few months I became convinced that the war would
> last indefinitely and ruin all Europe. Above all, I saw that the unity of
> the first weeks was an illusion, that the nation was split into classes,
> and that the industrial masses considered the Church as an unques-
> tioned ally of the ruling groups.[5]

Within the year, Tillich felt compelled to question not only the capitalist
roots of the war but much of the cultural and theological tradition in which
he had been educated:

The real transformation happened at the Battle of Champagne in 1915. A night attack came, and all night long I moved among the wounded and dying as they were brought in—many of them my close friends. All that horrible, long night I walked along the rows of dying men, and much of my German classical philosophy broke down that night—the belief that man could master cognitively the essence of his being, the belief in the identity of essence and existence. . . .

I well remember sitting in the woods in France reading Nietzsche's *Thus Spake Zarathustra*, as many other German soldiers did, in a continuous state of exaltation. This was the final liberation from heteronomy. European nihilism carried Nietzsche's prophetic word that "God is dead." Well, the traditional concept of God was dead.[6]

By the end of the war in 1918, the disillusionment experienced by the twenty-eight-year-old German chaplain was extensive enough to include most of the victors as well as the vanquished. Tuchman writes:

When at last it was over, the war had many diverse results and one dominant one transcending all others: disillusion. "All the great words were cancelled out for that generation," wrote D. H. Lawrence in simple summary for his contemporaries. If any of them remembered, with a twinge of pain, like Emil Verhaeren, "the man I used to be," it was because he knew the great words and beliefs of the time before 1914 could never be restored.

After the Marne the war grew and spread until it drew in the nations of both hemispheres and entangled them in a pattern of world conflict no peace treaty could dissolve. The Battle of the Marne was one of the decisive battles of the world not because it determined that Germany would ultimately lose or the Allies ultimately win the war but because it determined that the war would go on. There was no looking back. . . . The nations were caught in a trap, a trap made during the first thirty days out of battles that failed to be decisive, a trap from which there was, *and has been*, no exit.[7]

Christianity's Failure to Confront the Illusion

World War I was the shock that it was—the beginning, as one could say, of that whole phenomenon of "future shock" that has been the great and abiding malaise of the twentieth century—because the violence and viciousness that it revealed lying just beneath the urbane surface of the West's high culture had been so successfully repressed by that culture. If at the end of the war "disillusion" was "the one dominant result transcending all others," it was because so much of what had come to be by the end of the nineteenth century was sheer illusion: the illusion of unimpeded progress,

of the moral neutrality of science and technology, of the essential goodness
of the human spirit, of humanity's rightful mastery over nature, of the victory of rationality over ignorance and superstition, of the socially beneficial
character of individual pursuit of wealth and power, and so on. So uncondi-
tionally positive were the expectations of the leading classes of European
and North American societies that the experience of negation—and especially of a negation as bloody as "the Great War" proved to be—could only
overwhelm.

Serious Christians throughout the present century have had to reflect
upon the fact that it was Christianity, and Christianity in its apparently most
"advanced" expressions, that provided the necessary *cultic* support for this
cultural optimism. Undoubtedly the countering of the dark side of existence always entails some recourse to religion, broadly conceived. But what
must be said of a religion that helped an entire civilization, already in the
throes of decline according to many of its keenest observers (Spengler,
Schopenhauer, Nietzsche, Kafka, et al.), to indulge in so grand an act of
societal repression as to persuade itself that the future could only "grow
ever lighter" (Buber)?

Of course, one does not speak here of all Christians or even of Christianity as such. If one were required actually to name the faith that so aided and
abetted the birth of the positive outlook of modernity, one could do no
better than to call it, as the late political philosopher George P. Grant did,
the "religion of progress."[8] But that Christianity, and specifically the form
of Christianity that regarded itself and was generally regarded as the cutting edge of the faith, had a heavy hand in the production of that religion
cannot be denied. It was perhaps inevitable that this would be the case.
With the breakdown of purely "legal" forms of Christian establishment,
Christian institutions found it increasingly necessary to accommodate themselves to the dominant spirit of their host culture in order to retain their
hold upon the latter. Thus when modern Western civilization began to pursue the theme of human autonomy and the mastery of nature and history,
many Christians found it within themselves to accentuate whatever in Christian teaching seemed favorably disposed to such an *imago hominis*, and to
discard what did not.

To be sure, Christian liberalism, which is the name by which history designates this type of apologetic, was and (where it still exists) is neither
monolithic nor uniform. One cannot put into one basket the great work of
Friedrich Schleiermacher, *The Christian Faith*, and the sermons of Norman
Vincent Peale—or even of Harry Emerson Fosdick. Like most other such
categories (evangelicalism, for instance), liberalism covers a spectrum. It
may be said to include everything from the learned and (relatively speaking) conservative reflections of scholarly theologians like Schleiermacher,
Ritschl, Adolf von Harnack, Wilhelm Hermann, and Walter Rauschenbusch
to the more secular productions of the ethical culturalists and frankly radical modernists like Shailer Mathews or Henry Nelson Wieman. In all of its

expressions, however, with the possible exception of the Social Gospel, Christian liberalism wished to make itself amenable to what was, after all, an exceptionally expectant image of human being and society; therefore it tended to soften, if not altogether to dispense with, all those aspects of traditional Christian doctrine that came into conflict with such a conception of human nature and destiny. Following this apologetic principle, the Christianity that allowed many to believe that war was a twentieth-century impossibility itself became so enmeshed in illusion that it was incapable of responding to the reality of war when it actually occurred. If in the process of the war all the high-minded words of our civilization were "cancelled out," as D. H. Lawrence said, it was at least in part because, long before the war, Christianity itself intentionally had dispensed with other and different "great words"—words that could have helped people not only to comprehend the war but perhaps to avert it. With such concepts as sin, the demonic, spiritual death, divine wrath, and the like having been set aside in the Christian scramble to be culturally acceptable, the liberal Christianity in which Tillich, Barth, the Niebuhrs, Bultmann, and their cohort of theologians were reared had little or nothing left with which to comprehend the material and spiritual devastations laid open by the war, let alone with which to comfort its myriad victims.

Christian Liberalism

It was the opinion of the eminent British theologian and historian Alec R. Vidler that there may be no better description of liberal theology "in its various forms" than that offered by H. Richard Niebuhr "in his description of what American Liberal Protestantism added up to in the end":

> The romantic conception of the kingdom of God involved no discontinuities, no crises, no tragedies, or sacrifices, no loss of all things, no cross, and resurrection. In ethics it reconciled the interests of the individual with those of society by means of faith in a natural identity of interests or in the benevolent, altruistic character of man. In politics and economics it slurred over national and class divisions, seeing only the growth of unity and ignoring the increase of self-assertion and exploitation. In religion it reconciled God and man by deifying the latter and humanizing the former. . . . Christ the Redeemer became Jesus the teacher or the spiritual genius in whom the religious capacities of mankind were fully developed. . . . Evolution, growth, development, the culture of the religious life, the nurture of the kindly sentiments, the extension of humanitarian ideals, and the progress of civilization took the place of the Christian revolution. . . . A God without wrath brought men without sin into a kingdom without judgement through the ministrations of a Christ without a cross.[9]

This characterization may describe North American better than it does European liberalism, but, perhaps for that very reason, it goes to the heart of the *problem* of liberalism with an admirable kind of directness. The leading German liberals, the complexities of their dialectics notwithstanding, failed as miserably as did the less theoretically inclined liberal teachers of the New World to give adequate direction to their students. Whether nuanced or simplistic, Christian liberalism simply did not prepare its adherents for the realities of the new century.[10]

Though it is not without virtues, the problem with Christian liberalism, as H. R. Niebuhr's characterization of it graphically depicts, is its premature identification of apparent historical gains in human well-being with the progressive redemption of the world by a predictably benevolent deity. Whether it originates in Europe or America, whether it is clothed in the language and concerns of the nineteenth or of the twentieth century, theological liberalism tends to overlook the likelihood that new achievements, such as modern technology, become the occasions for new problems, and that what seems gain for some may prove loss and detriment to others. Committed to a stained-glass version of the modern secular reduction of *Providentia Dei* to "the religion of progress," liberalism is forever confused by the reality of evil, suffering, and other intimations of creaturely deviation or deprivation. This may explain why, its long associations with democratic America notwithstanding, such liberal Christianity as still exists "is a minority religious movement in America, and it is likely to remain in that position for the foreseeable future."[11] For in the meantime, the *Nihil* has manifested itself also in North American society and life.

The "New Theology"

There can be no doubt that it was "the Great War" that drove the young theologians of the first part of the twentieth century to abandon the more extravagant hopes of their liberal mentors and to find alternative cartographers of their night in such rejected nineteenth-century figures as Nietzsche, Kierkegaard, Dostoevsky, and Karl Marx. On the very day that the war broke out, Karl Barth and many others were astonished to find in their newspapers "a terrible manifesto," in which "ninety-three German intellectuals" publicly identified themselves with the war policies of Kaiser Wilhelm II. Among the signatories were Harnack, Hermann, Rade, Eucken, and other leading liberal theologians. "It was like the twilight of the gods," wrote Barth. "To me they seemed to have been hopelessly compromised by what I regarded as their failure in the face of the ideology of war. . . . A whole world of exegesis, ethics, dogmatics and preaching, which I had hitherto held to be essentially trustworthy, was shaken to the foundations."[12]

Nevertheless, it is possible to locate the causes of the new theology that emerged at this time too one-sidedly in the war. In a real sense, World War

I only *punctuated* what was already becoming evident to perceptive Christians before its occurrence, namely, the sheer inadequacy of a faith that had adapted itself too easily to the happy assumptions of modernity.

It is for this reason that the central figure of the theological revival that began to occur in the second decade of the century, Karl Barth, consistently refused to identify "the crisis" to which his so-called theology of crisis referred with the war as such.[13] The crisis (*krisis*=judgment) had for him as much to do with the supposedly positive values of his society as with its upheavals. Beneath the thin surface of apparent social well-being and progress a tumult of dissatisfaction over human inequality and systemic injustice was ready to erupt—and did erupt, of course, in the midst of the war itself, with the introduction of Marxism-Leninism in Russia. Already from 1911 onward, Barth as a young pastor had encountered intimations of a serious gap between the theology he had imbibed and the social and economic realities of life in his small Swiss town, Safenwil—a gap strikingly similar to that experienced, a decade later, by the young Reinhold Niebuhr in the burgeoning industrial city of Detroit. As Barth recounted:

> Class warfare, which was going on in my parish, before my very eyes, introduced me almost for the first time to the real problems of real life. The result of this was that my main study was now directed towards factory legislation, insurance, trade union affairs and so on, and my energies were taken up in disputes sparked off by my support for the workers, not only in the neighbourhood but in the canton.[14]

The socialist alternative that Pastor Barth began seriously to embrace[15] in the light of these "real problems of real life" presented itself forcibly to many Christians as the church began finally to take notice of the immense changes that had been introduced by the Industrial Revolution. As Emil Brunner writes in his "Intellectual Autobiography":

> "Religious Socialism" was the *avantgarde* of this church which was just becoming sensitive to the appalling plight of the industrial laborer. Hermann Kutter's book, *Sie müssen* (*They Must*, 1904), which appeared in numerous editions and languages, proved to be a rude awakening for the church in that it portrayed the Social Democrats, in spite of their atheistic leanings, as true bearers of the message of the Kingdom of God in our time. Leonhard Ragaz and a number of Swiss pastors then joined the Social Democratic party in order to demonstrate their solidarity with the workers, whose predominant concern was the struggle for social justice.[16]

It is unfortunate that so many, especially in North America, have failed to grasp the political—to be precise, the socialistic—component of the theological renewal that was inaugurated by these disillusioned younger theologians of the first half of the twentieth century. Conservative Christians who admire the reputed orthodoxy of Barth, Brunner, and other representatives of the so-called Neo-orthodox movement but either ignore or reject its socialist-influenced analysis and ethic, almost invariably distort its theology as well. For this is not just a return to the orthodox doctrine of divine transcendence—the God who is *totaliter aliter* (R. Otto); it is a testimony to a redeeming God who wills to "change the world" (Karl Marx!).What troubled these theologians was not merely a doctrinal concern for the purity of biblical and Reformation faith, but a theological-ethical concern for the world beloved—and therefore judged (*krisis*)—by God. What was wrong with that world, in their view, was not only that power-driven nations were ready to shed the blood of millions to sustain their preeminence, but that within *all* the nations those who were being served by war were the same persons and classes who were served by the social arrangement that passed for peace. Walter Rauschenbusch, the leading figure of the American Social Gospel, could be heard to speak for most of these theologians when, in his 1917 Taylor Lectures at Yale University, he insisted that "the ultimate cause of the war was the same lust for easy and unearned gain which has created the internal social evils under which every nation has suffered. The social problem and the war problem are fundamentally one problem."[17] If Karl Barth's *Römerbrief*—the document that signaled the great sea change in twentieth-century Christian theology— "fell like a bomb on the playground of the theologians," as Roman Catholic theologian Karl Adam said of it,[18] it did so not only because of its critical theology but also because of its sociopolitical critique—and the two are inseparable.

Conclusions

The theology that had its beginnings in the catastrophic and unanticipated ending of the nineteenth century has been called, variously, theology of crisis, dialectical theology, Neo-Reformation theology, and Neo-orthodoxy. None of these terms adequately captures the phenomenon in question, though each may be said to denote an aspect of what was involved. Wilhelm Pauck, in a remarkably lucid essay on Emil Brunner, summarizes the position taken by these thinkers, despite their quite differing ways of expressing it, in five observations: (1) their common accentuation of divine revelation as faith's point of departure: "Instead of asking: What has modern man to say about the gospel? the theologians now concerned themselves with the question: What does the gospel say to modern man?"; (2) their renewed emphasis on the scriptures, an emphasis quite distinct from both fundamentalist and liberal approaches to the Bible; (3) their historical consciousness, including the denial of any supra-historical access to truth as well as their recognition of the abiding relevance of liberal insights; (4)

their renewal of Reformation concerns and study; and (5) the ecumenical character of their conception of Christian faith.[19]

The latter feature of this movement deserves, in the present context, to be stressed. If "the Great War" demonstrated to all thoughtful citizens of the planet the necessity of finding some viable alternative to war as conflict resolution, it made sensitive Christians conscious at long last of the *dangerous* as well as the contradictory character of their dividedness. That Christian peoples could face one another as deadly enemies, each claiming the Christian God for its "side," made clearer than ever before that a religion aligned with nationalism and racism could only end in self-contradiction and violence. The ecumenical movement, which many regard as the greatest achievement of Christianity in the modern epoch, and which during the present century has grown to include all of the historic branches of divided Christendom, may perhaps be said to be the most positive outcome of the terrible human conflicts that have threatened civilization ever since the opening salvoes of "the guns of August." Christianity may no longer pretend to dominate the course of our secularized and pluralistic planet, but from a position outside the realms of worldly power and prestige it *may* have greater influence for worldly good than it ever possessed as Christendom.

Notes

[1] Barbara Tuchman, *The Guns of August* (New York: Dell Publishing Co., 1962), 16.

[2] Ibid., 24-25.

[3] Karl Barth, in a letter to his friend Eduard Thurneysen (James D. Smart, ed., *Revolutionary Theology in the Making: Barth-Thurneysen Correspondence, 1914-1925* [Richmond, Va.: John Knox Press, 1964], 26).

[4] Charles W. Kegley and Robert W. Bretall, eds., *The Theology of Paul Tillich* (New York: Macmillan, 1952), 12.

[5] Ibid., 12.

[6] Paul Tillich, as reported in *Time* 73, no. 11 (March 16, 1959), 47. The soldiers were able to read Nietzsche even on the battlefield for a very good reason: Kaiser Wilhelm had caused thousands of copies of *Thus Spake Zarathustra* to be circulated to the troops in an abridged and pocket-sized edition, thus demonstrating that Nietzsche's ideas were powerfully at work long before Hitler made such devastating uses of them.

[7] Tuchman, *The Guns of August*, 489 (emphasis added).

[8] For example: "Like all civilizations the West is based on a great religion—the religion of progress. This is the belief that the conquest of human and non-human nature will give existence meaning. Western civilization is now universal so that this religion is nearly everywhere dominant. To question the dominant world religion is indeed to invite an alienation far greater than the simply political" (George P. Grant, *Technology and Empire: Perspectives on North America* [Toronto: House of Anansi, 1969], 77).

[9] H. Richard Niebuhr, *The Kingdom of God in America* (New York: Harper Torchbook, 1959<1937>), 191f. Quoted by Alec R. Vidler in *The Church in an Age of Revolution*, The Pelican History of the Church, vol. 5 (Harmondsworth: Penguin Books, 1961).

[10] In fact, as Sydney E. Ahlstrom points out, the influence of German liberalism upon the American Christianity of the period was so direct that, when at last the United States

entered the fray in 1917, many Christian educators drew upon the thought of German theologians to justify and promote the war against Germany!

For a full century before the coming of war Germany had been America's tutor in the arts and sciences as well as in philosophy and theology. . . . So deep did this influence penetrate that the president of the Hartford Seminary Foundation resorted to Wilhelm Hermann's *Ethics* and Johann Kaspar Bluntschli's theory of military force to justify the United States entering the conflict (Sydney E. Ahlstrom, *A Religious History of the American People* [Garden City, N.Y: Image Books, 1975<1972>], 2:365f.).

[11] This is part of the interesting thesis of Joseph C. Hough Jr. in his essay, "The Loss of Optimism as a Problem for Liberal Christian Faith," in *Liberal Protestantism: Realities and Possibilities*, ed. Robert S. Michaelsen and Wade Clark Roof (New York: The Pilgrim Press, 1986), 145ff.

[12] Karl Barth, quoted in Eberhard Busch, *Karl Barth: His Life from Letters and Autobiographical Texts*, trans. John Bowden (London: S.C.M. Press, 1975), 81.

[13] "The concept of crisis in this theology may not be regarded as an independent theme, but can be rightly understood only when it is seen in indissoluble relationship with the grace and light of God. This makes clear why Barth has always been opposed to every interpretation of his theology which represented it as stemming from the mood inspired by World War I. He has been unwilling to acknowledge the legitimacy of the view which identified him with the No of cultural and historical pessimism rather than with the saying Yes of God" (G. C. Berkouwer, *The Triumph of Grace in the Theology of Karl Barth*, trans. Harry R. Boer [Grand Rapids, Mich.: Eerdmans, 1956], 25).

[14] Busch, *Karl Barth,* 69.

[15] By 1913, Barth was being pressed to become a Social Democrat candidate for the Great Council, though he did not join the Social Democratic Party until 1915 (ibid., 71).

[16] Emil Brunner, quoted in Charles W. Kegley and Robert W. Bretall, *The Theology of Emil Brunner* (New York: Macmillan, 1962), 5. Brunner himself had been drawn into the movement of religious socialism early in his life through the influence upon his parents of Christoph Blumhardt and his pupils Hermann Kutter and Leonhard Ragaz. Of Kutter in particular Karl Barth would write later: "It was this 'prophetic thinker and preacher' . . . who at that time, with a force unrivalled by any of his contemporaries, represented the insight that the sphere of God's power really is greater than the sphere of the church and that from time to time it has pleased God, and still pleases him, to warn and to comfort his church through the figures and events of secular world history" (Busch, *Karl Barth,* 76).

[17] Ahlstrom, *A Religious History of the American People,* 372.

[18] John McConnachie, *The Significance of Karl Barth* (London: Hodder and Stoughton, 1931), 43.

[19] Kegley and Bretall, *The Theology of Emil Brunner,* 3:25-38. See also Douglas John Hall, *Remembered Voices: Reclaiming the Legacy of "Neo-Orthodoxy"* (Louisville, Ky.: Westminster/John Knox Press, 1998), "Conclusions."

2

The Condemnation of Modernism and the Survival of Catholic Theology

VICTOR CONSEMIUS

Overview

On July 3, 1907, the Holy Office published the decree *Lamentabili sane exitu*, sanctioned the following day by Pope Pius X. Patterned on the 1864 Syllabus, the document rejected sixty-five theses, excerpted preponderantly from the writings of French exegete Alfred Loisy and bearing on the emancipation of exegesis from official church teaching; the inspiration and inerrancy of Sacred Scripture; the concepts of revelation, faith, and dogma; the sacraments; the constitution of the church; and the immutability of Christian truth. The encyclical *Pascendi dominici gregis* followed on September 8 of the same year. It cast the summary rejections of the preceding decree in a systematic form and coined for the condemned propositions the concept of modernism.[1] Those who adhered to these propositions were, accordingly, labeled modernists.

The papal encyclical saw the source of the new errors—scored as the "receptacle of all heresies"—in agnosticism and religious immanentism. The rejection of rational demonstrations in the religious field and the reduction of religious truths to feelings and needs were regarded as evacuating the rational defense of the Christian faith. Likewise rejected were modern biblical criticism and demands for reforms of church structures. As a remedy, the obligatory study of scholastic philosophy and theology was imposed in the seminaries, along with an intensified supervision of the writings emerging from those institutions and the establishment of vigilance councils—a kind of ecclesiastical spy system.

The encyclical and its forerunner, the decree *Lamentabili,* can be credited with locating the focal point of the conflict between faith and reason. The content of some of the theses has remained a matter of discussion throughout the twentieth century, including the post–Vatican II decades.

However, scarcely a single theologian accused of modernism actually represented wholly or even preponderantly the theses denounced in the papal documents. At most, one or another proposition can be laid to the account of certain theologians. The encyclical limits itself by and large to a negative account of the problems mentioned, spelling out the conflicts between traditional church doctrine and modern philosophical and religious ideas. It does not settle the question of how the faith is to be expressed positively in light of the growth of critical knowledge.

The modernist crisis—orchestrated by the placing of certain works on the Index of Forbidden Books, by disciplinary measures, and by occasional tumultuous dismissals—had its greatest impact in France and Italy, also affecting certain intellectuals from England. Catholics in Germany were not usually affected. Why did the crisis concern especially the two Romance countries, France and Italy, and not Catholic Germany, which, according to general Roman assessment, was in permanent and acute danger of contagion by a dominant Protestant culture?

German theology was subjected to a vigorous shock prior to and during Vatican Council I when Ignaz von Döllinger (1789-1890) and other theologians criticized Ultramontanism and what they thought were exaggerated and historically unwarranted claims of the papacy. Döllinger and some other theologians were eventually excommunicated. When the *Kulturkampf*—the government's effort to restrict the influence of Catholicism—subsided at the end of the century, German theology turned again to historical scholarship, especially in ecclesiastical history, avoiding, to a large extent, the consideration of explosive issues. As late as 1908, as the controversy over modernism was reaching its climax, Protestant religious sociologist Ernst Troeltsch complained that the best of the German Catholic theologians confined themselves to historical research in innocent areas. There was no actual dogmatic modernism with these thinkers, Troeltsch went on, for the most intelligent were keeping their thoughts to themselves.[2]

The starting position of the French theologians after the collapse of the Gallican church in 1790 was the secularizing impact of the Revolution. Catholics complained of the decline of theology in the erstwhile classic Catholic country. When Ernest Renan published his *Life of Jesus* in 1863, it became the most popular book of the century in France. Renan transmitted to the educated middle class of his time plausible pictures of Jesus and the church, free from aspects that no longer seemed to make sense and hence were offensive. His book lent wings to the battle waged by the Third Republic against the Catholic church. Catholic theology was gradually ejected from the University of Paris and French schools. In response to this, Catholic universities were founded from 1875 on; a few years later they were obliged by the state to be renamed "Instituts Catholiques." It is significant that at these institutes the first conflicts emerged in the area of ecclesiastical history, especially regarding the beginning of the papacy and the regional and local church history of France. Well remembered are Louis Duchesne

(1843-1922), who managed to avoid ecclesiastical censures, and Pierre Battifol (1861-1929), who lost his position as rector of the Institut Catholique at Toulouse and whose book on the eucharist was put on the Index.

Catholic biblical studies received a substantial thrust through the founding of the École Biblique in Jerusalem. In contrast with the École's founder, Marie Joseph Lagrange (1855-1938), was Alfred Loisy (1857-1940), who was a student of Renan yet rejected his scientism. Loisy was removed from his position as professor of exegesis at the Institut Catholique in Paris because of his idea that the scriptures were historically conditioned. In 1902 his book *L'Évangile et l'Église (The Gospel and the Church)* was published. In this volume he refuted Adolph von Harnack's position denying the abiding significance of the church for the transmission of the faith and won his epithet, "father of modernism." In 1903 five of his books were placed on the Index. When he attacked the encyclical *Pascendi* with biting irony and superior arguments, all of his writings were placed on the Index (March 7, 1908).

Loisy's original approach was in line with the renewal taking place in the philosophy and the psychology of religion. Maurice Blondel (1861-1949) in his chef d'oeuvre *L'action* (1893), demonstrated against all forms of objectivism, including neo-scholasticism, that knowledge and the revelation of being were bound up with subjectivity. For Blondel, the contrast between immanence and transcendence achieved its synthesis in "action"—"the self-realization of being"—in which immanence revealed itself as transcendent. His student Lucien Laberthonnière came down even more emphatically on the side of an immanent philosophy of religion. The binding force of a religious doctrine depends, he said, on the extent to which the believer assimilates it as his or her personal law of life. Thus the ethical challenge of Catholic dogma is to offer binding guidelines for moral and religious life. Both Blondel and Laberthonnière were accused of immanentism and fell under suspicion of modernism. In 1913, Oratorian Laberthonnière received an admonition from the Holy Office. Blondel, a member of the laity, escaped ecclesiastical censures, and, as rediscoverer of the human being's natural striving for the vision of God and new theoretician of the relationship between theology and grace, exercised a formative influence on the theology that led to Vatican II, that is, on the "new theology" of Henri de Lubac, the school of Joseph Maréchal, and the theology of M. Dominique Chenu and Karl Rahner.

After France, Italy was most strongly affected by the modernist crisis. Here it was not primarily the debates over biblical criticism that inspired the reform movement, but the necessity of finding a viable modus vivendi with the Italian lay state of 1870 and of initiating social reform. The 1871 prohibition of the Roman Curia (only abrogated by Benedict XV) forbidding Catholics to run for parliamentary office or to vote for candidates for such offices ("ne eletti ne elettori") provided no feasible solution. The ensuing polarization hardened the attitude of the intransigent ecclesiastical camp and embittered the anticlericals.

The principal concerns of reform-minded Italian Catholics were the social problems that middle-class political liberalism refused to recognize. Two personages in particular represented a pragmatic openness to social democracy, the priest Luigi Sturzo (1871-1959) and a friend of his, Romolo Murri (1870-1944). Sturzo was able to introduce progressive community administrations and to support a social movement that, after World War I, created a non-confessional people's party, Partito Populare, from which, after World War II, Christian Democracy emerged. By contrast, Romolo Murri developed a more radical reform program for society and the church, which resulted in his excommunication in 1909. A number of Italian theologians suffered ecclesiastical penalties, and Antonio Fogazzaro's novel *Il Santo*, critical of the church, was put on the Index, yet on the whole the renewal movements in Italy—and to some extent in France—dealt with social issues and did not coincide with theological modernism.

In England, philosopher of religion Baron von Hügel (1852-1925), an independent scholar, created international connections among thinkers who sympathized with modernism. He escaped the Index owing to his lay status. By contrast, the Jesuit George Tyrell, a short-lived comet of modernist thought, was expelled from the Jesuits in 1910 and excommunicated by the pope. Yet the new critical consciousness did not affect English Catholicism, which had been unable to accept even the theology of John Henry Newman (1800-90). While influential in France and later in Germany, and honored as a bridge to modern theology, Newman remained suspect in his own country, even though he was created a cardinal in 1879.

Two points clearly emerge: first, the infectious hysteria created by the suspicion of modernism; and second, the difficulty of specifying what precisely modernism represented. Since the encyclical *Pascendi* had failed to offer a clear concept of modernism, simply characterizing it as an attitude of mind, the door was opened to suspicions, libels, denunciations, character assassinations, and arbitrary church censures. Despite these destructive events, it would be a mistake to suggest that Catholic theology died during the modernist crisis.

A glance at the Catholic University of Louvain illustrates this point. This university not only avoided the crisis of modernism but sought and found, in disciplines like philosophy, psychology, and social sciences, connections for new developments. Founded in 1888 by Désiré Mercier, later archbishop of Mechelin, the Institute for Philosophy contributed to the rebirth of Thomism on an international scale.[3] Characteristic of the Louvain school was its historical orientation, which was particularly fruitful in church history, the history of philosophy, and Oriental studies.

Catholics in Germany had a similar experience. Here the Görres Society, founded in 1876 during the *Kulturkampf* for the purpose of overcoming Catholic intellectual inferiority, also assigned priority to the historical sciences. It is noteworthy that there was no theology department in the Görres Society. Theology was regarded as an affair of seminaries and theological faculties at universities. After the publication of the encyclical *Pascendi,* the German bishops wrote in a pastoral letter of December 10, 1907, that no lay person or cleric in Germany defended the system of thought and its ultimate consequences condemned by the encyclical. In this manner the bishops were able to sidestep Rome's recommended preventive measures and avoid a conflict over modernism. German theological faculties were spared the oath against modernism, which from 1910 to 1967 all teachers of theology and all candidates for theological degrees had to swear.[4]

The German bishops' assessment was basically correct. In Germany, neo-scholastic theology had no monopoly; it was one school of thought among others. Yet this did not prevent a few individual theologians, like Albert Erhard of Strasbourg and Vienna and the fundamental theologian Hermann Schell of Würzburg, from being suspected of modernism. We note, however, that the liturgical movement, which had its beginning at this time and which was to play such an important role in the Catholic church, was only peripherally, if at all, affected by the modernist crisis.

Roman anti-modernism cannot be equated with political conservatism. This can be seen in the personality of Pius X, who has been designated an anti-modernist or even "retrograde," as he is sometimes called. Pius X was by no means an anti-modernist across the board. He set important modernization processes in motion, for example, the renewal of catechesis, the reform of the minor and major seminaries, the consolidation of Catholic Action, and the codification of canon law. Yet in other areas, such as fundamental theology and biblical studies, Pius X, concerned for the faith of the simple believers, reacted in conservative fashion to the new questions of science and philosophy and dealt with them through repressive juridical measures. In individual instances these measures may have been justified. They did, however, open the door to less qualified watchdogs of the faith, damaging the reputation and careers of theologians who were loyal to the church. Pope John XXIII's journal, *Journal of a Soul,* affords an insight into this climate of suspicion that poisoned the atmosphere in the circles of theologians between 1910 and 1914. Yet the problems posed by modern thought could not be solved with rulings from the magisterium. The most negative legacy of the anti-modernist campaign was the indiscriminate use of the reproach of modernism by timorous minds. It was often applied to conceal important new sets of problems. Timid spirits recoiled and took refuge in anti-modernist security.

The Survival of Catholic Theology

The aim of our overview has been to locate theology in the life of the Catholic church between 1900 and 1950. As we noted, the disciplining of so-called modernist thinkers did not mean the end of Catholic theology.

World War I altered the situation of Catholics in various countries. The national loyalty of Catholics, repeatedly called into question in Romance and German-speaking countries, was sealed in their bloody sacrifice in the trenches of World War I. The canonization of Joan of Arc in 1920 and the restoration of France's diplomatic relations with the Vatican, which shortly ensued, attenuated, in foreign affairs, the rigid secularism of the Republic. It is worthy of note that devotion to Carmelite Thérèse of Lisieux (1873-1897), whose message had brought such consolation to soldiers, found sympathy even in circles other than explicitly ecclesial ones. The reaction against scientism and materialism, which had set in about 1890 and led to the conversion of artists and writers to the Catholic church, maintained its currency even in the spiritual shocks produced by the war.[5] In particular, philosopher Jacques Maritain (1882-1973) initiated a Thomistic renaissance and sketched, over against the Enlightenment, an alternative concept of the modern world that boded fair for the rebirth of an intellectual spirituality. Maritain's "anti-modern" stance was actually "ultramodern," designating spiritual support for the specific conditions and potentialities of the present. Maritain manifested a particular interest in the areas of aesthetics, political ethics, and mysticism; he influenced the formulation of Christian Democratic programs in Latin America and Italy; and he encouraged a broader Roman Catholic acceptance of the principles of religious freedom, for which John Courtney Murray, S.J., subsequently engaged himself at Vatican Council II.

Despite inner struggles over direction, French Catholicism succeeded in exercising considerable attraction for intellectuals and students, manifest in numerous pastoral initiatives. French Catholics of the time between the two wars were characterized by a pastoral sensitivity that found expression in the creation of a variety of ministerial projects. A key ministerial and pastoral concept was "le témoignage" (bearing witness). Questions that had arisen in the intense debates over modernism and were later no longer addressed, such as the experience of God and the psychology of religion, now received serious treatment in periodicals like *La Vie Spirituelle* (1920) or *Études Carmélitaines*. Abbé Henri Brémond's *Histoire du sentiment religieux* (12 vols., 1906-36), a history of seventeenth-century spirituality, became part and parcel of the French literary tradition.

French liturgical scholarship in the 1930s developed a fruitful equilibrium between basic scientific work and the liturgical education of the faithful. A similar phenomenon occurred with the availability of the Bible for the Catholic people. It was true, of course, that a fearful avoidance of modern questions was at work in scholarly exegesis. Placed on the Index were, in 1924, the handbook, *Manuel biblique*, in common use in France, and actually very cautious; in 1929, a study on Messianism; and in 1932, a work on primitive biblical history. The Pontifical Biblical Commission, founded by Leo XIII in 1902, held tightly to traditional standards in the first forty years of its existence and was a hindrance to genuine research. Lucien Cerfaux liberated the methods of form criticism developed by Protestant scholars from the elements that had rendered it suspect in Rome. Only with the encyclical *Divino afflante spiritu* (1943) could Catholic exegetes, until then working under heavy restrictions, draw a breath of fresh air. Many of them had not dared to publish their research, having the threat of Roman censure constantly hanging over them like a sword of Damocles. Reserve with regard to paleontologist Pierre Teilhard de Chardin, S.J. (1881-1954), who pleaded for a consistent consideration of the theory of evolution, is situated in this context. The results of his investigations could be published only posthumously.

The symbiosis of scholarly research, pastoral sensitivity, and alert objectivity in the observation of societal processes in the world is probably represented most impressively by Dominican Marie-Dominique Chenu (1895-1990). In 1930 he founded, with Etienne Gilson, the Institute for Medieval Studies in Toronto. His plea for the historical method in theology resulted in his being placed on the Index in 1937, and he was later subjected to disciplinary measures in the course of the debate over worker-priests. Chenu bore up without leaving his order or giving up the church. The influence that he exerted within the Dominican Order, as well as in the implementation of pastoral initiatives (Mission de France, 1941; Mission de Paris, 1942), marks him as one of the most important forerunners of Vatican Council II. His influence appeared less in the work of the conciliar committees than in the general orientation of the bishops to world problems, especially those of the Third World. His confrere and student Yves M.-J. Congar (1904-95) adopted his historical method, applying it to his own foundational investigations in ecclesiology, the theology of the laity, and the hermeneutics of a church reform without schism and with ecumenical impact. He and those who spread his stimulating ideas, especially in Romance countries, revealed French Catholicism as the inspiring trailblazer and supplier of ideas for Vatican Council II.

The conviction of assisting at a new departure that marked French Catholicism after World War I and culminated in the "renouveau catholique" impinged on German Catholicism as well. The conditions of this period were better for Catholics than they had been in the German empire: the church had an improved status under the 1919 Weimar Constitution, Catholics had easier access to public offices and institutions, and the Center Party became a leading political force until 1933. The political change was accompanied by a revival of religious and theological energies. The Prussian-Protestant-liberal hegemony seemed to have broken, and a rapprochement between Catholicism and German humanist culture was in the air. As in France, it was a time of great conversions and returns to the church: Theodor Haecker, Gertrud von Le Fort, Hugo Ball, Alfred Döblin, Sigrid Undset, Erich Peterson, Heinrich Schlier, and others. The philosophical ideas of this time—the phenomenology of Edmund Husserl (1859-1938) and the value philosophy of Max Scheler (1874-1928)—also nourished hopes for a bridge between the human sciences and the Catholic interpretation of the Christian message.

Romano Guardini (1885-1968), the most universal mind of this era, spoke of the "awakening of the church" in souls as the fundamental mood of the time. An ecclesiological euphoria gripped the spirit of the epoch. It expressed itself particularly in the youth movement. Here Guardini assumed a leading pedagogical role, especially in the areas of personality formation and liturgical spirituality. At stake was not a return to modernist themes but a response to a new situation, inspired in part by elevated yet illusory notions in regard to future achievements of Catholicism.

Romano Guardini distanced himself from modernist echoes. In his student years at Tübingen he attended the lectures of dogmatic theologian Wilhelm Koch, who had been under suspicion of modernism. In his autobiographical retrospective Guardini writes that Koch was the first to inquire into the meaning of dogmas for real-life situations—inadequately, it is true, and with short-lived usefulness, but significant nevertheless. There was a barrenness in Koch's being, Guardini goes on. Earnest to a fault, conscientious in the extreme, smitten with a fixation on the really real, he still lacked theological depth. He had too much respect for science, as then conceived, and too little awareness of revelation as bestowing fact and force to make revelation the source of theology and proclaim the new creation.[6]

Guardini settled his own work in a space marked out by the new feeling for life known as sense of community. His flair for seizing upon philosophical questions of life and existence of the time between and after the world wars, and illustrating them with literary themes or with great figures of the faith, enabled theology in its Catholic form to remain a dialogue partner in the academic world. This scholar, moreover, who bound church loyalty to critical openness, bestowed on academic Catholic youth an orientation that protected it from the corruption threatening it from 1933 onward at the hands of National Socialism. He penetrated areas shunned by scholastic theology. It was not in a technical theological sense but rather through a new mood of openness that Guardini made an important contribution to the movement that prepared the way to Vatican Council II. Systematic theology, which acknowledged him grudgingly in the spirit of "we know better," turned much later to the themes Guardini had been the first to examine.

Guardini was not the only one to attempt to break open scholastic theology's conceptual armor and, from the rediscovery of his own tradition, build a bridge to the present. Tübingen dogmatic theologian Karl Adam, in his *The Spirit of Catholicism* (1924), developed an understanding of the institutional church, the sacraments and the lifestyle of Catholics in the light of the idea of the body of Christ. He held that the church is the whole of humanity leavened with the yeast of God's grace, developing in a slow yet relentless process that embraces the human family in need of salvation in the supra-personal unity of the body of Christ.[7] Thanks to numerous translations of his books on Jesus, *Christus unser Bruder* (1929) and *Jesus Christus* (1933), in which he emphasized Christ's human nature, he reached a wide audience, far beyond the world of the German language.

The most successful handbook of dogmatics was *Katholische Dogmatik* (5 vols., 1938-41), written by Michael Schmaus of Munich. Schmaus laid more stress than did previous scholastic handbooks on Sacred Scripture and the Fathers of the church and entering into questions of the philosophy of life and existential concerns. In doing so, he did not neglect the accent on historical theology and its research, developed by his teacher, Martin Grabmann, a scholar of the history of medieval theology. Through the foundation of the Martin Grabmann Institute he gave historical theology a solid place in the training and continuing education of theologians.

The advantage of this scholarly direction, which bound historical continuity with the power of interpretation, was that it formed an instrument of communication with theologians of other languages whose scholastic conceptual apparatus was strong. This stood his students in good stead, especially the young conciliar theologian Joseph Ratzinger, who had established his footing in theology with his books on Augustine's doctrine of the church and Bonaventure's theory of history.

Catholic theology in Germany, even in the generation of the council, continued its historical preoccupation. It would not do justice to this orientation if it were seen primarily as a flight from the urgent problems of the day. Primary attention must always be given to the exploration of the Christian tradition to avoid premature generalizations and parallel conceptual constructs. Acquaintance with history is the prerequisite for subsequent possibilities of dialogue. This has been verified by the detailed investigations in early church history by the Bonn historian of religion and culture, Franz Dölger. Another strong example of this principle is the book *Missarum Sollemnia* (1948), an investigation of the liturgy of the mass, spanning a long period of time, by Innsbruck scholar Josef Jungmann, S.J. His work provided the historical foundation of the reform of the liturgy at Vatican II, for which Romano Guardini, on the basis of his own approach, had provided a comprehensive understanding of symbols and insights drawn from the psychology of religion. Speaking in 1957, Jungmann still believed that the liturgy of the church contained a powerful potential for human guidance—for Christian life-orientation and life-mastery—a potential that has been very imperfectly actualized. To what extent modern persons at the close of the millennium are still capable of being gripped by liturgy is another question. Guardini himself had doubts in this regard toward the end of his life. It would seem, nonetheless, that the human need for rituals has continued in both totalitarian dictatorships and today's post-Christian societies.

At the time of National Socialism, a retreat into historical research was for many theologians the only opportunity to continue their scholarship. Scholars who sought to address topical issues or who cultivated an openness to the new were in danger of being lured by the ideology of National Socialism. Alongside Karl Adam and Michael Schmaus, church historian Josef Lortz, over a short period (1933-34), worked at building a bridge to the new state.[8] Later, in his two-volume work *Die Reformation in Deutschland* (1939), Lortz succeeded in transcending Catholic self-justification as well as exaggerated self-incrimination and grasped the Reformation as a deeply rooted religious event. Lortz was one of the first Catholic theologians able to mount a positive appreciation of Martin Luther's importance and religious depth, even if contrasting Luther's subjectivism with Catholic objectivism. That was the concession he had to make in order to have Luther and the events of the Reformation discussed on the Catholic side without the traditional confessionally conditioned and dogmatically carved-out stereotypes of demarcation. Lortz's work achieved a breakthrough, even beyond German-speaking lands. He bestowed a new thrust on the ecumenical movement and a deeper understanding of Luther.

It was reserved to brothers Hugo (1900-68) and Karl (1904-84) Rahner, both Jesuits, to take up themes, in their complementary life work, that led to Vatican Council II and beyond. Hugo was a historian, a scholar of the Fathers of the church and meticulous interpreter of the history of religious orders and the life of faith. Karl, the systematician, probed theology's classic themes and concepts in many distinct investigations. He used a language that refused to anticipate the answers in the very questions. What bound question and answer, constituting the specific element of their synergy, was the adherence to the church's mission of proclamation, the synthesis of theological research with existential attachment to the faith: theology as *theologia cordis*, the birth of God in the heart. Hugo, who stood somewhat in the shadow of his younger brother, demonstrated that the symbolic theology of the Fathers of the church does not belong on the back shelves of antiquity. Instead, it transmits a manner of reflection on and contemplation of divine revelation that resembles the spirit of Sacred Scripture. In *Symbole der Kirche* (1964) he uncovered the power of symbols in the transmission of the deposit of faith. His other chef d'oeuvre, *Griechische Mythen in christlicher Deutung* (1945), uses the example of Hellas and the theology of the Fathers to shed light on the encounter with the non-Christian religions. He does this not by encouraging an arbitrary syncretism but rather by retrieving pre-Christian wisdom and knowledge of God in the light of Christ. As the lamps of antiquity anticipate the coming *helios*, the sun of justice, so it is in order to bring the deposit of truth dwelling in the non-Christian religions into a dialogic relationship with the Christian deposit of faith.

With an original interpretation of transcendental and existential philosophy, Karl Rahner succeeded in challenging and breaking up the largely ossified formal world of the neo-scholastic linguistic and conceptual tradition. To call him a disciple of Heidegger (Rahner did study under Heidegger in Freiburg) does not characterize correctly his philosophical direction.

Rahner found the major inspiration and starting point for his thought in two theologians of his own order, Pierre Rousselot (1878-1915) and Joseph Maréchal (1878-1954). While he never studied with them, their publications opened his eyes to the possibility of interpreting the texts of Thomas Aquinas in a manner that had a vital connection with modern thought. Here, too, came into play the Blondelian approach, which recognized a transcendental foundation in people's search for self-realization and hence their implicit relationship to divine revelation. Rahner's thinking has its spiritual center in the affirmation of the experience of grace. The structural moments of his theology are derived from the spiritual tradition and its patristic, medieval, and Ignatian interpretation. The integration of tradition into his theology explains the wide acceptance of his work, set down especially in his *Theological Investigations* (22 vols., 1954–). This international reception occasioned suspicion on the part of colleagues whose methods were more deeply indebted to scholasticism. The suspicions spread all the way to Roman ecclesiastics, who sought, unsuccessfully, to exclude Rahner from a consultative participation at the Second Vatican Council.

In other writings Karl Rahner called attention to the need for reform in the Catholic church—a concern for which he pleaded in concert with his colleague Hans Urs von Balthasar of Basel, who left the Jesuit Order in 1955. Von Balthasar, too, was under suspicion in the intermediate and higher ranks of the curial hierarchy, especially because he pleaded as effectively as Rahner for a departure from the ecclesiastical ghetto (*Schleifung der Bastionen*, 1953). Unlike Rahner, who wrote no synthesis of his dogmatics, von Balthasar, in his magnificent principal work, *Herrlichkeit* (9 vols., 1961-87), created a synthesis of imposing consistency and completeness in the triad of theological aesthetics, theodramatics, and logic. Von Balthasar's work is beholden to the inspiration of French theology, to which his versatile teacher, Henri de Lubac, S.J., had introduced him. In addition to his activity as a writer and his restless commitment to spiritual direction and the preaching of retreats, von Balthasar assumed the mission of mediating between French and German intellectual culture. A cloud of suspicion hung over the trio of de Lubac, Rahner, and von Balthasar during the best years of their lives. However, Rahner was appointed a theologian of the council, while de Lubac and von Balthasar went on to become cardinals.

Conclusion

As we examine the theological debates over modernism, we find that they reflect the transition of the church into the paradigm of a new age. Just as liberal Catholicism can only be defined with reference to Ultramontanism, so the content of Catholic modernism can only be determined with reference to its opponent, anti-modernism. But the latter is identical neither with theological traditionalism nor with political conservatism. It is rather of a selective nature—an anti-modernism a la carte. It balks at ideas that at first glance seem to shake the foundations of the faith and employs the rich arsenal of ecclesiastical disciplinary measures to stave off this danger. The temporal lag of the state of theological consciousness in different cultural spheres contributes as much to the sharpening of the conflict as the inclination, anchored in the nature of the Roman Catholic Church, to resolve church crises through official measures. In juridical disputes, this method may be appropriate, indeed may even succeed. Yet as an authoritarian disciplinary measure, it is incapable of guiding the problem of change and development, to which even dogmas and church definitions are subject. The intervention of the magisterium may effect a certain postponement that will allow the new problem to be examined in its various facets, and in this way clarifications and the integration of new insight may be attained. It would be too easy, in retrospect, when critique and integration had finally been achieved, to assume that the capacity for integration had existed at the very beginning. Taking history seriously in a consistent manner means for the believing theologian not only the task of relativizing dogmas but also the effort to appreciate the historicity of ecclesiastical developments across the board. "Les troupes de la victoire" (the winning troops) the French historian Augustin Thierry said, can be recognized only after the battle has been waged. In the conflict over the configuration of faith that corresponds to a given time the issue is not choosing between winners and losers but engaging in the painful process of assimilating the new. This task can be accomplished by trusting the faith of the whole church, not by the bridling of chargers, scholarship on one side and papal encyclicals and curial decrees on the other.

—TRANSLATED FROM GERMAN BY ROBERT R. BARR

Notes

[1] Literature on modernism is available under that word in the theological reference works, *Religion in Geschichte und Gegenwart*, *Lexikon für Theologie und Kirche*, *Theologische Realenzyklopädie*, and others. The best overview in terms of historical theology remains that of Roger Aubert, *Handbuch für Kirchengeschichte*, ed. Hubert Jedin (Freiburg: Herder, 1973), vol. 6/2; or idem, *Geschichte der Kirche* (Benziger, 1976), vol. 5/1. An overview of the state of research today is presented by Otto Weiss in the collection *Antimodernismus und Modernismus in der katholischen Kirche*, ed. Hubert Wolf (Paderborn: F. Schoningh, 1998). A view from a philosophical perspective is offered by Pierre Colin, *L'audace et le soupçon: La crise moderniste dans le catholicisme Français* (Paris, 1997).

[2] F. W. Graf, in Wolf, *Antimodernismus und Modernismus*, 87.

[3] See Roger Aubert, *Le Cardinal Mercier (1851-1926): Un prélat d'avant-garde* (Louvain-la-Neuve, 1995).

[4] For modernism in Germany, see Norbert Trippen, *Theologie und Lehramt im Konflikt: die kirchlichen Massnahmen gegen den Modernismus im Jahr 1907 und ihre Auswirkungen in Deutschland* (Freiburg: Herder, 1977). See also Otto Weiss, *Der Modernismus in*

Deutschland: Ein Beitrag zur Theologiegeschichte (Regensburg, 1955). I do not share Weiss's overly broad concept of modernism.

[5] Pierre Colin, ed., *Intellectuels chrétiens et esprit des annés 1920* (Paris: Cerf, 1997).

[6] Romano Guardini, *Berichte über mein Leben: Autobiographische Aufzeichnungen* (Düsseldorf: Patmos, 1984).

[7] In Albert Raffelt, *Geschichte des Christentums*, vol. 12 (Freiburg: Herder).

[8] See Victor Consemius, "Joseph Lortz: Ein Kirchenhistoriker als Brückenbauer," *Geschichte und Gegenwart* 9 (1990), 247-78.

3

After the Bolshevik Revolution

Theologians in the Russian Diaspora

BERNARD DUPUIS

The Russians who left their country after the Revolution of 1917 and took up residence in Sofia, Prague, and finally in Paris, regarded themselves at first as temporary refugees, not as émigrés. They had been the primary moving spirits of the "religious renaissance" arising in Russia around the 1900s under the inspiration of Vladimir Soloviev, Serge Bulgakov, and Nicholas Berdiaev. They had preserved the inspiration of their renaissance amid the Revolution and nourished the hope of a return to their country. It was only with time that they came to make a choice that they had not at first foreseen and adopted the citizenship of other countries—France, England, America—entered into their institutions, and established themselves there for a long duration, eventually conceiving of a "symbiosis" of the spiritual tradition of the East with that of the West.

These displaced persons were almost all laity and philosophers, not clerics and theologians, although some among them eventually took up the service of the priesthood. No sooner had they arrived than they acquainted the world with the adventure, at once spiritual and tragic, that they had been living, and with the enterprise of religious philosophy that had been represented in 1909 in *Veki*, the collection in the name of which they criticized communism in its Leninist version. Thereby they took their place, immediately and solidly, in the current of ideas of the age—without engaging, as we shall see, especially after 1945, in a polemical discussion with Western Christianity, Catholic or Protestant.

Post-Revolution Currents of Thought: Berdiaev and Bulgakov

Nicholas Berdiaev is doubtless the philosopher who, in the 1920s, best incarnated this current of Russian thought. Neither academician, nor politician (like certain Eurasians who felt themselves strangers to the West on principle, regarding it as corrupt), nor official person of the church (the periodical, *Put'*, directed by him, was not aligned with any religious obedience, either Muscovite or exarchal), he caused a sensation with the profundity of his analyses, which addressed, from a very high vantage, the social and political problems stirred by the revolution. He testified to the enormous legacy of life, humanism, and freedom residing in the Orthodox tradition; but he spoke, without question, in the name of the church as such—the indivisible church, as over against Christianity's contemporary deviations. The genius of his intuition was inspired at every moment by the Christian experience of the communion of saints, prophets, the outraged, those persecuted for justice's sake—those he called the "creators" as over against the "smotherers of the spirit." Upon entrance into the group of French philosophers of Meudon, with their guiding spirit Jacques Maritain, he made this memorable declaration: "One says 'sweet France,' 'perfidious Albion,' but 'holy Russia.'"

This survivor, however, so strong in his convictions, had not himself sought to flee the communist regime taking over his country. During the February Revolution he had played a role of peacemaker, becoming a deputy of the short-lived Council of the Republic. The anarchism of the Bolshevik Revolution, in which he had seen the shadow of the Grand Inquisitor looming, had inspired his cry of indignation, but, accepting realities, he had sought, at his risk and peril (two years of prison), to promote a spirit of liberty. For the church, he aspired to a renewed Christianity, whose expression he found with a *starets*, the married priest Alexei Metchev. As vice president of the Writers' Society, he was called to Moscow in 1920 to be professor at the university (his lectures would become the books *Le sense de l'histoire* and *L'espirit de Dostoyevski*). But in 1922 he was declared an "ideological adversary" of communism, and he joined the group of displaced persons on the famous "boatload of intellectuals" sent abroad by Lenin.

In Russia itself, his indicted thought, now become secret, had begun to bear its fruits, which ripened sixty years later and contributed to the collapse of the colossus of clay feet. It was a collapse less economic and political than spiritual, for its diagnosis and key word in the face of communism was and would remain *spirit*. His thought is intended as "creation" (the theme of his first book, "creation" is seen as a reality at once mysteriously divine and human). He sees himself as on a quest. (The name of the periodical *Put'* means "path"—not a "route" known in advance.) For him, today's combat is but an episode in a story that, in the next millennium, will come to formulate the "ultimate questions."

Berdiaev is the opposite of a systematic thinker, and this is what stupefied and fascinated his French interlocutors, distinguished and civilized disciples of Hegel or Bergson. Like him, the Russians who came to France speaking philosophically of incarnation of the spirit, transfiguration, and eschatology took that country by surprise, but they could not but be welcomed by that Catholic milieu, which flocked to hear them. They were mighty witnesses of the Christian tradition in a universe in quest of sources after the confusions of rationalism and the impasses of Kantianism. The awaited renewal would come through them.

Berdiaev, Bulgakov, and Zander were not traditionalists. Besides Soloviev and Florensky, their pedagogues in thought, they built on Léon Bloy, Schelling, even Boehme, which caused them to be labeled gnostics by their opponents. Berdiaev wrote, in *Esprit et liberté:*

> I would commune with Joan of Arc, but not with the bishop Cauchon who burned her. I would join myself to Francis of Assisi, but not with the churchmen who persecuted him. I can commune with Jacob Boehme, that great mystic with childlike simplicity of heart, but I cannot join myself to the Lutheran clergy who sentenced him. Thus it is in everything, and everywhere. In the enterprise of reunion of the Christian world, a mystical, in-depth penetration of Christianity must play an essential role.[1]

In this spirit the Institut Saint-Serge of Paris was formed, a school marked by great openness of spirit and a vital drive to theological research. It insisted on philosophical anthropology. It sought to promote an encounter of East and West by developing a Christianity that would be at once more mystical and more social. It contributed to the inspiration of the personalist movement, which found its moving forces in the work of Jacques Maritain and Emmanuel Mounier. In 1930, Berdiaev participated in the foundational meeting of the periodical *Esprit,* which thereupon referred to him constantly, and he was to contribute again in 1946 to the celebrated special issue of this periodical entitled "Monde chrétien, monde moderne."

For the Russian school of Paris, knowledge could not be an activity in itself, divorced from life. It constitutes a function of life. It steps back from the empirical world, where separation and constraint reign, and which does not exhaust the real. Theology is more than a set of symbols of the spiritual life. The depth of the existential comes to light only in the experience of saints, prophets, creators of life. Humanism must be promoted, but it remains ever ambiguous, for it can lead to death by the objectivization of the human as well as to life by the spiritual experience that it implies. Such is the condition of the "spiritual realism" that leads one to engage in the "existential dialectic of the divine and the human," that leads one to the experience of liberty that, ultimately, opens out to the "sense of history."

Père Serge Bulgakov, who became rector of the Institut Saint-Serge, sought to furnish this theory of knowledge with a theological foundation. His view was that the Fathers of the church rarely recognized the principle of knowledge that modern Christianity discerns under the name of wisdom. He proclaimed a "quest for the path that leads to Orthodoxy by way of the modern spirit." However, this path is the object not of speculation, but of vision, as Soloviev had already posited. Sophia, which is not to be taken as a new divine person, exists first in God, who has conceived it, and it presents itself to us with a personal face. It is the idea of the world eternally present in God that is to realize itself in time. To the divine Sophia corresponds the "Sophia of the created world," and, by this idea of Sophia, which ensures the autonomy of creation, Bulgakov's thought manifests affinities with the cabala.

Bulgakov's work is not only an effort to conceive, by sophiology, humanity in divinity. It is also an effort to conceive divinity in humanity. Ever since the manifestation of revelation in the world, especially in the humanity of Christ, humanity is no longer the same. For Bulgakov, the nature of the human being has been transformed in its very naturality. If ancient pagan naturalism was an illusion in itself, modern pagan naturalism, which is opposed to Christianity, exists only by its ignorance of Christian naturalism. This is what ancient gnosis was ignorant of, failing as it did to recognize the Incarnation. But when Christ arrived, "the great Pan was dead," and all humanity entered into the expectation of the resurrection of the flesh. In "rendering his spirit" Jesus left to the world the water and blood that have flowed from his body (Jn 19:34). His dead body had not only "swooned," been cast into a deep sleep, it was truly dead, since its blood had left it. But it did not become a corpse. It was in a kind of anabiosis, in expectation of the Resurrection. Now this blood and this water, although they had flowed forth into the world, are risen with him. They are the sacred heart of humanity. They are the inextinguishable image of the "spilled blood that, from Abel to the end of history, inundates the earth." Thus, the event of Golgotha did not occur only between Jesus and the divinity; it also took place between Jesus and humanity. It inaugurated a mystical path and progress of the world toward the reign of God, toward a transfigured world, and it delivered humanity from guilt in freeing it from the myth of original sin. The expectation of the reign is not simply a hope on the part of the human being. It places the world, even now, beyond this world. From this viewpoint, human beings' bond with the body and blood of Christ is not reducible, for Bulgakov, to the sacrament of the eucharist, nor the church to the earthly institution. And it is not surprising that this theme, which has escaped Christian dogmatics, should have found refuge in the liturgy and in literature; it is the testimony of the medieval legend of the Grail.[2]

Père Bulgakov's theology sought to be typically Orthodox, and indeed it was welcomed by the Christians of the Russian emigration. It presented itself as "God's life" under the inspiration of wisdom, which ever maintains the divine and the human under one sole regard. While Catholicism would be the guardian authority of truth in history by its organization, and Protestantism a service of the revealed word, Orthodoxy would be first and foremost praise in mystery: the church as the "numen" of the external sacramental life. Faithful to his idealist origins, Bulgakov suggested that the hierarchy, not being the adequate and absolute manifestation of the church, would be only its historical organization, its "phenomenon." Hence his tendency to relativize the temporal and "householding" aspect of the church, and to place absolute emphasis only on the divine and eschatological aspect. Bulgakov attaches the faith of the church less to its discursive teaching, catechetical or academic, than to the vision at hand in the liturgical act. He also sought to integrate an understanding of Judaism in these perspectives.

This Orthodox "religious renaissance" entailed the nostalgia for a "free theocracy," a mystical, Johannine church, in which, one day, all would be priests and prophets, where the sacraments would but express the depth of beings and things, where the church would appear as an ontology of the mystery yet to come.[3] "We live in an age," Bulgakov had already written in 1910, "in which one should not pronounce excommunications, but should make beings feel their attachment to the church."[4] Religion is not an abstraction. "Life itself must be transformed into Eucharist." "For us, true religion is a mystique in which the Word shines forth." "One must show Christ to human beings, for they have forgotten what Christianity is. They no longer know it. Their consciousness, most often, while not anti-Christian, is, as it were, pre-Christian."[5]

Reaction: Lossky

These stimulating but daring theses provoked a reaction. It came first from Vladimir Lossky, who took a firm and harsh position against sophiology. Lossky, too, had been on the "boat of 1922." Arriving in Paris, he joined the school of Étienne Gilson and began to study Thomas Aquinas, then Meister Eckart, to know them well in order the better to criticize them. Contrary to the majority of representatives of the sophianic tendency, who wrote only in Russian, Lossky published exclusively in French. He even envisaged the institution of a French Orthodoxy. Over against the typically Russian "confraternity of Sophia," created by Bulgakov at the Institut Saint-Serge, he created a "confraternity of Saint Photius," which, unlike the other, drew on the Greek tradition. He sought an Orthodox theology that would be dogmatic and rigorous, and he criticized the books of Père Bulgakov to the point of having them condemned in 1934 by Metropolitan Sergius of Moscow.

But, if he warned against the dangers of the first "Russian school of Paris," Vladimir Lossky was nevertheless very close to it. It was against the facile and widespread tendency of our age to a sentimental dogmatism that he rose up, against a dogmatism that can in no way lead to the rapprochement between the churches but only to the worst confusions. Where Bulgakov invokes Christian gnosis, Lossky appeals to dogma and to a renewal of dogma. Dogma, for him, is a "narrow gate" through which the intellect must pass by a "death-resurrection" in order to receive a metalogical light. A Christian doctrine that would claim to be a perfect explanation of revealed mystery would inevitably be a false one. By the very fact of pretend-ing to the plenitude of knowledge, it opposes itself to the plenitude in which one partially recognizes truth. Faith is not conceptual. Dogma purifies our concepts; it in some way shatters their sufficiency, not by contempt for in-tellectual rigor, but by posing, where heresies create oppositions, a "distinction-identity." Dogma, at once antinomic and apophatic, crucifies the intellect and obliges it to exceed itself. Distinction-identity, on which Lossky insisted without respite, is the key to the dogma of Chalcedon: we believe in the union of two natures in one person; but the "how" of this union is far too deep for us to sound, just as is the love that seeks the lost sheep, the love determined to save all of humanity and each individual one among us.

Between the extremes of the tendencies perpetually dividing Russian thought—strict copy or obsessive rejection of the West—Lossky aimed to sketch the royal way of a theology that would be nonspeculative, creative, and yet traditional. One must return to the Fathers of the church rather than establish their insufficiencies. One must meditate anew on the word of St. John, the Greek writings of Evagrius, of Gregory of Nazianzus, and those inspired by the Syrian tradition, of Simeon the New Theologian, who, so to speak, "chant" the ineffable. At the heart of theology, the presence and logical structure of apophasis must be manifested.

In order to arrive at this, Lossky, thanks to Meister Eckart, emphasizes that, when we speak of the things of God, we must avoid diminishing them by using our human logic; we must refrain from speaking of the divine Persons as we speak of human persons. "God is inobjectivizable" is Lossky's *leitmotiv,* as it has already been that of Berdiaev. Lossky loves to stress the limits, even the necessary *failure* of theological thought. The latter must never claim to be a system. The true theologians are those who crush sys-tems: "If the God of the philosophers is not the living God, that of the theologians is only half such, as the last projection, the last *dépassement,* has not been made."

Lossky recognizes the significance of the dialectical (historical) inspira-tion of contemporary Protestantism. But he serves it notice that one must, at the end of the analogy of faith, abstain from conceptualizing God's own being by an interplay of opposition. One must say with Karl Barth that God is the utterly other; but one must likewise say, with Nicholas of Cusa, "Deus non est aliud," God is not something other. True, God is utterly distinct, but nothing in creation, not even nothingness, can be opposed to God. In other words, nothingness cannot, as certain modern philosophers claim, be substantiated; creation has no subsistence of its own, and hence cannot be conceptualized separately, parallel to the Creator. Nothingness is but a limit concept—the very limit of concept.

With Lossky, then, we have a little of the dream that, by the encounter of the Christian East and West, Orthodoxy in diaspora could become a center of lucidity and a focus of Christian regeneration, and that Europe, scarred by wars and de-Christianization, could be a new land of Christian life, "the land of the last apostles, proclaimed by the Virgin of La Salette."[6]

This openness to the culture and history of the West, acquired in the school of Étienne Gilson, helped Vladimir Lossky to accord a value of concrete universality to the message of Orthodoxy, recognized as a message of the undivided church. This invitation was to be transmitted, after the Second World War, through the periodical *Dieu Vivant.* Lossky offered a new understanding of the Greco-Russian Orthodox tradition as testimonial of the original and the ancient, in an encounter with the Roman West understood especially as impatience for the ultimate. Then the truths acquired on either side in the course of history would transcend their as yet unperceived limitations—would entail a withdrawal from sclerotic traditionalisms to engage the whole church in the infinite dynamism of an "epecstasis," which, from the Cappadocians onward, underlies the authentic sense of history.

Post–World War II

In the following period, after 1945, Russian Orthodoxy would tend to abandon its first inspiration in favor of what has been called, pejoratively, it is true, a "neo-patristic synthesis." Its most outstanding exponent was Père Georges Florovsky, experienced ecclesiologist and patrologist, but rather removed from politics and the preoccupations of history. He had presented his critical rereading of the Russian theocracy at the First Athens Congress of Theology, in 1930, and after the war became rector of the Institut Saint-Serge in Paris and then of the Saint Vladimir Institute in New York. Succeeding Père Bulgakov, Florovsky, just as his successors Alexander Schmemann and John Meyendorff, was in the forefront of the ecumenical movement; together they represented the voice of Orthodoxy. But with the passage of time it seemed clear, as Alexander Schmemann put it, that there were two successive, different attitudes in Orthodoxy toward ecumenism:

> On the one hand, we find theologians who acknowledge the Ecumenical Movement as, in a way, an ontological new phenomenon in Christian history requiring a deep rethinking and reevaluation of Orthodox ecclesiology as shaped during the "pre-ecumenical" era. Representative names here are those of Sergius Bulgakov, Leo Zander, Nicholas Zernov and Paul Evdokimov. This tendency is opposed by those who, without denying the need for ecumenical dialogue and defending the necessity of participation in the Ecumenical Movement, reject the very possibility of any ecclesiological revision or adjustment and who view the Ecumenical Movement mainly as a possibility of an Orthodox witness in the West. This tendency finds its most articulate expression in the writings of Georges Florovsky.[7]

It would be correct to judge that the two theological tendencies of modern Orthodoxy form the poles of a pendular movement. There is no way to predict the path that Russian thought will take in the years to come. At present, it is still clearly the second tendency that prevails, with an acute concern for the defense of the specificity of the Orthodox faith in confrontation with Western Christianity, and without subscribing to the expectation of unity expressed by Christianity, whether the voice of Rome or that of the ecumenical movement. But the quest for a balance between the two tendencies is becoming more and more salient through the testimonial and writings of more recent theologians such as Olivier Clément and Nicolas Lossky.

—TRANSLATED BY ROBERT R. BARR

Notes

[1] Nicholas Berdiaev, *Esprit et liberté*, new ed. (Paris, 1984 <1933>), 301.

[2] "Le Saint Graal, Jean 19, 3," *Contacts* 27, no. 91 (1975), 181-218.

[3] Père Bulgakov, *La nouvelle conscience religieuse et la réalité sociale* (Paris, 1985 <in Russian 1907>), 193-228.

[4] Ibid., 202.

[5] Père Bulgakov, "Le destin de la culture," in *Le Roseau d'or* (Paris: Plon, 1926), 73-100. Republished as *La crise spirituelle de l'intelligentsia* (Paris, 1986), 5.

[6] Vladimir Lossky, *Sept jours sur les routes de France* (Paris: Cerf, 1998).

[7] Alexander Schmemann, *Russian Theology 1920-1972,* lecture, Union Theological Seminary in Virginia (1969), 29-30.

4

Returning from Exile

Catholic Theology in the 1930s

JOSEPH A. KOMONCHAK

"That's where it all began," Marie-Dominique Chenu remarked. He was talking about a series of developments that led to a more engaged Catholicism and displayed their fruits most visibly at the Second Vatican Council, and he was claiming that they all began in the 1930s.[1] That was, of course, a decade of crisis, marked and determined from beginning to end by the Great Depression, which seemed to prove the internal contradictions of liberal capitalism and to vindicate socialist alternatives. It also saw the disappointment of the great hopes that World War I, "the war to end all wars," would make the world "safe for democracy" and that the League of Nations would provide a framework of international community and cooperation. Instead, by the end of the decade totalitarian regimes were in power in Russia, Italy, and Germany; liberal democracies were in crisis elsewhere; a revival of imperialist colonialism had led Italy to invade Ethiopia; and the Spanish Civil War had proven to be a dress rehearsal for a second world war. A literature of crisis appeared, initiated by Spengler's *Decline of the West* (1918-22) and illustrated by such diverse works as Freud's *Civilization and Its Discontents* (1930), Benda's *La trahison des clercs* (1930), Ortega y Gasset's *The Revolt of the Masses* (1930), Huizinga's *The Crisis of Civilization* (1935), and Husserl's *Die Krisis der europäischen Wissenschaften* (1936).[2]

Pius XI reigned as pope during most of the decade, offering a grand project and a new practical orientation that were both responses to the general crisis. The goal was "the peace of Christ in the reign of Christ," the return of Western society and culture to their roots in the truths and values of Christ as mediated by the Catholic church. The pope shared the view common since the French Revolution that the cause of the problems of modernity lay in the abandonment of the faith that had inspired and directed the great achievement of medieval Christendom, which remained for him the ideal embodiment of Christ's authority over society and culture.[3] To promote "the social reign of Christ," a common slogan of the time, he published a number of encyclicals that set out a critique both of liberal modernity, particularly in its economic consequences (*Quadragesimo anno*, 1931), and of the new threat represented by the rise of totalitarianism (*Non abbiamo bisogno*, 1931; *Mit brennender Sorge*, 1937; *Divini Redemptoris*, 1937); to inspire Catholics in the pursuit of that goal, he established the feast of Christ the King (1925).[4] As a practical means for achieving his purpose, he placed much less faith in the organization of Catholics into political parties than in the new forms of Christian engagement in the world represented by Catholic Action, instruments of what was then known as the "lay apostolate." Pius XI's vision and practice were to inspire two generations of Catholics in the years ahead.

In France, according to René Rémond, the 1930s were the first of two "golden ages" of Catholic intellectual life.[5] In literature the great names were those of Charles Péguy, Paul Claudel, Georges Bernanos, and François Mauriac. In philosophy, while Maurice Blondel was bringing his lifework to fulfillment, Jacques Maritain, Étienne Gilson, Gabriel Marcel, and Emmanuel Mounier were beginning or extending their influence. In theology the work of a younger generation began to become known: Teilhard de Chardin, M.-D. Chenu, Yves Congar, Henri de Lubac, Gaston Fessard. What contrasted most notably with the work of the previous generation, particularly in philosophy and theology, was the movement toward active and critical engagement with a society and culture in crisis that three decades later would make Vatican II possible.

This revival was enabled and encouraged, first, by the relaxation of tensions between the church and the Third Republic and, second, by two developments in the life of the church. The bitter hostility that had characterized relations after the Law of Separation (1905) had been eased by the fervent participation of Catholics in World War I and by the government's gradual move away from anticlericalism in the 1920s. The *ralliement* to the Republic that Leo XIII had unsuccessfully urged on French Catholics now seemed to be occurring, except, of course, among the ranks of Catholics linked to Action française. But in 1926 Pius XI forbade Catholic participation in that movement, largely because of its extreme nationalism and its subordination of the religious to the political (*politique d'abord*). His action, traumatic as it was for many bishops and intellectuals, spared the new generation of French intellectuals the crises of conscience that had divided their elders and enabled them to conceive of their work, not as a principled rejection of modernity, but as an effort to discriminate among its achievements and to work for a reconciliation of the church and the modern world.

The second ecclesiastical factor was the waning of the anti-modernist zealotry that had nearly smothered Catholic intellectual life in the two decades after the condemnation of 1907. In theology the new atmosphere was illustrated in two courageous articles published at the beginning of the 1930s in comment on Jean Rivière's *Le modernisme dans l'Église* (1929). Bruno de Solages found in the poverty of ecclesiastical instruction both the cause and the consequence of the modernist crisis and argued that only improvement in clerical education could prevent a recurrence of the problem.[6] Marie-Dominique Chenu so departed from the common apocalyptic interpretation of the crisis that he could offer an analysis of modernism as "a normal crisis of growth," "a normal effect of the intellectual growth of Christian society," comparable to and no more surprising or to be feared than the crises that had marked two earlier moments which had proven to be very fruitful for the life of the church and the quality of theology: the renaissances of the Carolingian period and of the twelfth and thirteenth centuries. As the introduction of grammar had marked the first and the introduction of philosophical dialectics the second, so the rise of historical consciousness occasioned the modernist crisis. Since Christianity is not simply a set of timeless doctrines but faith in historical events, theology could not be content to be a "sacred metaphysics but would have to engage the challenge represented by modern history while avoiding the two extremes of historicism and theologism. If these extremes had dominated the modernist crisis, it was now time for a mediating position inspired by and modelled after the work of Thomas Aquinas in the thirteenth-century disputes.[7]

The political, cultural, and ecclesiastical situation in France, then, had greatly changed, and Catholics embarked upon an engagement with the events of the decade that contrasted greatly with the bitter alienation of the first decade of the century. If French Catholics remained divided in their political allegiances, at least they were no longer sitting on the sidelines, sullenly muttering their "*Non possumus.*" An impressive number of new journals became forums for vigorous Catholic debates on public questions (*La Vie intellectuelle, Sept, Esprit,* and others). The 1930s were also the era of manifestos by Catholic intellectuals that responded to successive controversies over rearmament, nationalism, the threat of communism, the social question (corporatism and workers' rights), the Italian invasion of Ethiopia, and the Spanish Civil War. Obviously there were problems enough throughout the decade and, toward its end, a growing sense of looming crisis, and French Catholics were full participants in the general debates.

The impact of these developments on the development of Catholic intellectual life, particularly in philosophy and theology, is the subject of this chapter. I will illustrate it by brief discussions of three important figures, Jacques Maritain, M.-D. Chenu, and Henri de Lubac.

Jacques Maritain

Maritain's conversion to Catholicism had been mediated by a Dominican priest, Humbert Clérissac, who, along with another Dominican mentor,

Reginald Garrigou-Lagrange, steered him in the direction of Action française, in which they thought they found a politics in accord with Aquinas' philosophy. Maritain's early books are typified by the title he gave to one of them: *Antimoderne*. But he accepted Pius XI's condemnation of Catholic participation in the movement and even became one of the most prolific defenders of the papal action. His early defenses attempted to place the pope's condemnation in the context of the classic doctrine of the indirect power of the papacy in temporal matters, exercised *ratione peccati*. But soon, perhaps in response to criticisms, he began to interpret it rather as an exercise of the properly spiritual authority to teach.[8]

More significantly, Maritain began to construct a theory of relations between church and society that, while it derived an inspiration from the Christian Middle Ages, found only an "analogous" ideal in them and recognized that any desirable "new Christendom" would have to be constructed in a different world, under different cultural "skies." Among the features of this new situation, now positively evaluated as indications of a coming of age, were a greater sense of humanity's historic self-responsibility, the just claim for human rights reflected in democratic political orders, whose roots he traced to Christian principles, and the inevitability of religious and cultural pluralism. The sacral, theocentric Christendom was gone forever, he argued, and a new concrete historical ideal had to be pursued, a secular, anthropocentric Christendom. A "humanism of the incarnation" was to be constructed in opposition to both the bourgeois humanism of capitalism and the revolutionary humanism of atheistic communism. In the inevitable conditions of pluralism the state would cease to be the secular arm of the church and, respecting the autonomy and rights of conscience, would not use the coercive power to defend or restore religious uniformity that in countries Maritain dismissed as "decoratively Christian" too often had inhibited the construction of a genuinely Christian society. Accompanying this political analysis were critiques both of capitalism and of socialism and of the tendency, common to both, to counterpose individual and society, a dichotomy that Maritain replaced by a non-adversarial theory of person and community.[9]

Maritain's was one of the earliest and certainly the most famous and most influential of proposals for a "new Christendom."[10] The term *Christendom* is ambiguous, of course, not least of all because of the close links between religious and secular power that characterized medieval Christendom.[11] These linkages, on the one hand, would lead Catholics of the right, particularly in Italy, Spain, parts of Latin America, and Canada, to conclude that what was new in Maritain's historical ideal—democracy, human rights, and a lay state—disqualified it as a "Christendom" and reduced it to "integral naturalism." On the other hand, they also led Emmanuel Mounier, who was much more critical than Maritain of the "established disorder" of capitalism and the Third Republic, to reject the idea of a new Christendom in favor of what he called a "personalist and communitarian revolution." But the term continued to be invoked by an impressive number of Catholic thinkers who meant by it something like the concrete social, political, and cultural difference Christianity can and ought to make in the world.[12] Understood thus generally, they were unanimous in the view that there can and must be many "Christendoms" precisely because worlds and times differ. The large body of material that can be cited under this rubric thus represents various efforts to rethink the relationship between Christianity and modernity and to enable Catholic thought redemptively to re-enter the public, history-shaping discussions from which it had largely been kept absent and to which the dominant intransigent attitude and strategy had kept it alien. But this effort to rejoin the debate would require that theology also would have to return from exile, and illustrations of this effort to promote this restoration of a publicly significant theology are found in two figures who represent two of the main lines of the twentieth-century renewal of their discipline.

M.-D. Chenu

Already apparent in Chenu's analysis of the modernist crisis, cited above, was the historical sensitivity that led him to establish a program in the history of doctrines at Le Saulchoir and to embark upon a type of historical inquiry into medieval theology, particularly that of St. Thomas, that would have close links with the *Annales* school of historiography. The great works of medieval theology would be studied in the context of and as an engagement with the economic, social, and cultural changes that constituted the renaissance of the twelfth and thirteenth centuries. It was not surprising, then, that at the same time the "other Chenu" would begin to propose that a theology faithful, as was required, to Aquinas would have also to engage the no less powerful transformations taking place in his own time. Historical consciousness would acquire a second sense: "presence to one's own times."

In 1937 Chenu published "Dimension nouvelle de la Chrétienté," an article written for chaplains of the Jeunesse ouvrière chrétienne (Jocists), with whom he had closely associated himself.[13] This Catholic Action movement, founded by Canon Joseph Cardijn, exemplified the apostolate of milieu to milieu in which Pius XI was placing so much confidence. Chenu regarded it as one of the many signs that the church was abandoning "the state of siege" during which "the Church was, it seems, 'irrelevant' (*inactuelle*), always falling short of the present moment, without imagination in face of the future, without effective control over contemporary institutions and developments, and, what is worse, without that constant newness which inexhaustible and deep resources of discovery bring to a society. It seemed that history would be made without the church."

What was the world into whose course the church was now inserting itself? It was one marked by the overcoming of liberal individualism in a growing awareness of collective interdependencies in nearly every area of human life and, more particularly, the insight gained from Karl Marx of the dehumanizing effect of the collective organization of modern labor.[14] This consciousness of communal solidarities represented a new appreciation of a dimension of the human condition, unfolding according to natural laws and dynamics. To this new phenomenon Chenu applied the analogy of the Incarnation, in which all that was human was taken up into union with the divine Word. The law of Incarnation now required the church to take up this newly appreciated collective dimension, "to incarnate the life of grace in social 'milieux.'" To be content with the salvation of the individual, without the salvation of society, would be to frustrate the law, logic, and dynamism of the Incarnation.[15]

> For too long a magnificent apostolic zeal was designed to "protect" the Christian from his milieu, to create an artificial milieu for him in which he could take refuge and live in a Christian way in the pious atmosphere of a closed-off group, apart from a pagan or perverse ambience. It was, perhaps, inevitable at a particular moment, but its narrow empiricism led us to a Christianity of *émigrés*, cut off from life, from its daily reality, from its states, its classes, and thus to a Christianity that had no bite and no boldness, a disincarnate Christianity, . . . abandoning to its misery the damned and disgraceful mass of a paganized proletariat.[16]

The Jocists had broken with this strategy. They represented an effort to realize a new Christendom, particularly by inserting themselves into the collectivity of the masses that had so often crushed and dehumanized workers and there undertaking an apostolate of their milieu. This new apostolic method, which supplemented the traditional parish-centered apostolate, too tied to earlier forms of social aggregation, displayed the church's incarnational adaptability to the emergence of social classes and was in that respect analogous to the new methods introduced by the mendicant orders in response to similarly transformative developments in the twelfth and thirteenth centuries.

This book ended with Chenu's expression of deference to the chaplains with whom he often conversed at Le Saulchoir, deference not only for friendship's sake but "the deference of a theologian for the Christian fact (*le donné chrétien*) on which he reflects, whose religious intelligibility he seeks." In the Jocists, Chenu saw Christendom in travail, laboring toward a new incarnation. The life of the church is the first object of the theologian: "There it is that he finds his proper and immediately inspiring matter: to do theology is to be present to the revelation given in the present life of the church and the present experience of Christendom. . . . The theologian keeps his eyes upon Christendom in travail. This is how he is *present* to his time; this is the very law of his knowledge" (350-51).

In 1937 Chenu published for circulation in Dominican circles a little book describing the structure and logic of studies at Le Saulchoir.[17] At almost every point he contrasted the work being done there in historical studies, in philosophy, and in theology to the ahistorical, systematized, and deductivistic methods common elsewhere, and especially, as it was not hard to conclude, in Rome, which showed its displeasure by placing the book on the Index in 1942. The law of Incarnation once again played a great role, visible also in Chenu's notion of tradition, not as a set of formulas, but as the life and experience of a church that is present to its time, and in his emphasis upon the role of discovery (*invention*) in theology. A brief description of contemporary developments set out what he would later call signs of the times. The church's missionary expansion in an age when colonialism was in decline was bringing a new sense of wider dimensions of the world, of its solidarities and autonomies, of the pluralism of civilizations reflecting "the divine suppleness of grace," and, in particular, of the treasures of Eastern Christianity. Beneath a nascent ecumenical movement lay a new appreciation of the unity of the church. In society the masses were coming to self-consciousness, posing not only practical problems, but also "the great problem of a new Christendom in gestation, a mystical body in which work will attain its spiritual status and the person his human condition between wealth and misery." And in all this, the militant church "is finding again in this new world a new youth, by a new method of conquest, in which lay people share in the hierarchical apostolate, bringing in their milieux the witness and life of Christ: a prolonged incarnation, in which all the density of human society, in its professions and classes, is taken up into the institutions that are the specialized movements, the typical structure of this new Christendom." "These are theological *loci 'en acte,'*" he concluded, "for the doctrine of grace, of the incarnation, of redemption. . . . Poor theologians are they who, buried away in their folios and their scholastic disputes, are not open to these remarkable developments, and not only in the pious fervor of their hearts, but formally, in their science: here is a very profitable theological datum, in the *presence* of the Spirit."[18]

There are visible in Chenu's approach not only his own irrepressible optimism and enthusiasm but also a strong theological basis in the doctrine of the Incarnation and a methodological orientation, borrowed from Aquinas, that Chenu believed was the only one appropriate to the world disclosed by that great and defining fact. The most intimate and complete union with God did not destroy or even compromise but rather elevated and integrated the humanity of Christ, and any theology faithful to the logic of Incarnation had to respect the integrity of the human in all its dimensions—personal, communal, and social. There are few words that appear more often in these writings of Chenu than the word *autonomy*. There was not only the autonomy of the created order, having its own substance and density, following its own laws, but also the autonomy of the sciences and disciplines that study it, which is not to be compromised by facile efforts at concordism or by premature and undifferentiated theological explanations.

Given his own role in the renewal of Catholic theology in the twentieth century, it is worth noting how Chenu's student and colleague, Yves Congar, in one of his first essays, echoed Chenu's analysis when he offered a theological analysis of the responses given to a poll on the causes of unbelief in France:

> We believe we have not betrayed either the truth or the responses to the survey in finding the most general reason for present unbelief in a certain hiatus between faith and life, a hiatus that affects the faith in one of its essential properties and determines collective conditions unfavorable to belief. The constitution of a spiritual and even religious world, of a *total* human life outside of Christianity, on the one hand, the contraction of the Church, its self-withdrawal into a special world and the fatal defensive attitudes it has adopted, on the other hand: two major and correlative facts that have together created this hiatus between faith and life and made Catholicism appear as *a part* of the world, a group apart, and even, in the eyes of some, as a sect or a party. Thus the very conditions in which the faith is presented to the modern world constitute a difficulty and almost a contradiction.

Congar's solution was also similar to Chenu's:

> The faith has to become humanly present, as Christ was. A policy of presence; not a policy of prestige on behalf of some sort of ecclesiastical imperialism, but a policy of the presence of the faith in all that is human, in order to take up every human value and thus to manifest the total value of faith with regard to human life.[19]

Henri de Lubac

At roughly the same time that Chenu published his analysis of the modernist crisis, Henri de Lubac, in one of his first published articles, offered an analysis of the state of theology and a proposal to restore its original task. For the young French Jesuit, the problem was the separation of theology and apologetics, particularly when the latter is conceived as a positivistic demonstration uninterested in the links between grace and nature and the former as a set of separate truths to be understood in themselves.

> What a shabby theology it is that treats the object of faith as an object of science, that does not know how to discern religion in its inner and universal reality and so sees it only as a system of truths and precepts,

imposing themselves only on the basis of a certain number of facts! It confines dogma to the extremities of knowledge, in a distant province, out of touch with other provinces. It makes dogma a kind of "superstructure," believing that, if it is to remain "supernatural," it must be "superficial" and thinking that by cutting it off from all human roots, it is making dogma all the more divine. As if God were not the author of both nature and grace, and of nature in view of grace.[20]

A "shabby theology," he called it, unfaithful to the tradition of the Fathers and Aquinas, a "separated theology tagging behind a separated philosophy" itself unworthy of the line of Justin, Augustine, Aquinas, and Pascal. Theology should not be conceived as simply "the science of revealed truths," simply an understanding *of* the faith; what is needed is an understanding of all reality *by means of faith*, an integrated fundamental theology in which the invitation to faith is mediated, not by extrinsic demonstration, but by an exposition of how revelation and grace illumine and empower the human mystery.

It is indicative that in this essay de Lubac anticipated that his proposal would be criticized either for naturalizing the supernatural or for supernaturalizing the natural. The same criticisms had been addressed to the man from whom he had begun to learn the need for a more integrated Christian anthropology than the one then reigning in Catholic theology. De Lubac would later recall his debts to Maurice Blondel and the influence of the dispute between Blondel and Pedro Descoqs over Catholic allegiance to Action française. A compartmentalized anthropology had permitted Descoqs and many other theologians to accept the agnostic and positivistic social analysis of Maurras, to which the supernatural was simply added as a necessary but extrinsic complement. For Blondel, as also for de Lubac, this theory legitimized authoritarian views both of society and of the church and inhibited the ability of Christians to bring the light and power of the faith to bear upon the whole of reality in an integral Catholicism that could inspire respect for democracy and the struggle for social justice. The recovery of the dynamic links between nature and grace, between Christianity and history, would be the aim of a good part of de Lubac's work during the 1930s, resulting in his two great books, *Catholicisme* and *Surnaturel*.[21]

The first of these set out to restore to Catholic consciousness what he called in its subtitle "the social aspects of dogma."[22] Drawing in particular on the thought of the Fathers of the church, de Lubac sought to overcome the widespread perception expressed in two quotations, one saying of the Christian that "in his blessedness he passes through the battlefields with a rose in his hand," the other Renan's comment that "Christianity is a religion made for the inner consolation of a few chosen souls." In the early chapters he set out a Christian vision of creation and history focused on the theme of unity. God had created the human race as one; sin had splintered that unity; the redemption wrought by Christ consisted in the restoration of that unity, finally in the kingdom of God but already anticipated in history in the reconciling and integrating work of a genuinely catholic church. In a chapter entitled "Person and Society," de Lubac insisted that, unlike many modern theories, the Catholic understanding did not require one to choose society over the person, the collectivity over the individual. Catholic inclusiveness insists upon and exalts both Person and the Whole.

If *Catholicisme* set out the objective, communal, and historical framework of the Christian response to the dissociating effects of sin, *Surnaturel* attempted to explain how it happened that Christian thought came in the modern world to be marginalized and lost its ability to influence the course of its history.[23] Responsibility for this, de Lubac argued, lay not only with the secularizing of Western thought, but also with the capitulation of theologians to a naturalistic anthropology that so dwelt upon the natural powers and finality of human nature that an appeal to the supernatural powers and finality of grace had almost inevitably to appear as an extrinsic and almost arbitrary addition. "There was," he would later write, "a sort of unconscious conspiracy between the movement which led to secularism and a certain theology, and while the supernatural was exiled and proscribed, we began to think that the supernatural was thus placed beyond the reach of nature, in the only realm where it is to reign."[24] The dynamism of human spirit, unsatisfied short of the vision of God, was lost from view. The fulfillment of natural powers and desires could be left to the masters of the human order, while theologians could be left to tend their walled-off supernatural garden. An integrated view of the only order that exists—an order with an intrinsic supernatural destiny—was rendered impossible. In *Surnaturel* de Lubac sketched an anthropology to match the cosmic, historical, and ecclesial vision of *Catholicisme.*

During the 1930s de Lubac also published various essays that addressed contemporary public matters. These included an effort to demolish what he considered the ahistorical argumentations of Maritain and Charles Journet on the church's temporal power, and a critique, on the basis of the catholicity of the church, of a Maurrasian justification of renascent nationalism in France. He would continue such efforts during the Nazi occupation of France, most notably in essays on anti-semitic ideologies and on the causes of the decline of the sense of the sacred and in *The Drama of Atheistic Humanism,* which is a scarcely veiled critique of the master sources of the Nazi ideology.[25] And de Lubac would match these essays by active participation in the *Résistance.*

Certain features distinguish de Lubac's effort from Chenu's. De Lubac's favored sources are the Fathers of the church, whose "symbolic inclusions" he fiercely defended as genuine theology and which he much preferred to the "dialectical antitheses" characteristic of "scientific" medieval scholasticism. He was far less enthusiastic than Chenu about the Thomist achievement, which he not only thought was precarious but in his view had also made possible the compartmentalized anthropology of his later commentators, however much this latter contradicted Aquinas's intent, method, and position. There is much less insistence on one of Chenu's favorite themes, that of the autonomy of the created order and of its substantive and disciplinary laws, and much more stress on the supernatural finality of creation.[26] The horizontal finality of nature seems almost absorbed in the vertical supernatural finality of its destiny. There is less emphasis on economic questions and the phenomenon of the masses, and de Lubac was much more reserved about possible alliances with Marxism than was Chenu. At the Second Vatican Council their differences would typify two different approaches to theology, particularly in the preparation of *Gaudium et spes.* After the council they offered two different analyses and appreciations of the post-conciliar situation. At the risk of oversimplifying, one might say that de Lubac found his model for the Christian engagement with culture in the great patristic achievement and Chenu his in the Thomist achievement.[27]

Conclusion

What began in the 1930s was the end of the cultural isolation of Catholic theology, dramatically described by Karl Rahner when he said that it would be difficult to discern any significant differences between a textbook of theology published in 1750 and one on the same subject published in 1950 even though in the meantime "cultural and spiritual transformations have taken place which, to say the least, are comparable in depth and extent and power to mould men's lives, with those which took place between the time of Augustine and that of the golden age of scholasticism."[28] What de Lubac called separate philosophy and separate theology, Chenu described as theology in exile serving a "Christianity of émigrés." What de Lubac proposed as an understanding of all reality in the light of faith, Chenu pursued as a theological reflection on the experienced life of the church laboring toward a new incarnation in the dynamics of history. If de Lubac's main contribution was the recovery of the broad and deep Catholic tradition that had been narrowed down and only superficially represented in a modern system that was mistaken in thinking itself traditional, Chenu's contribution, apart from his important technical work on medieval theology, was to insist that theology found the object of its critical reflection not only in the scriptures and in the monuments of the tradition but in the life and experience of the church. In both cases theology became an expression of the church's engagement with society, culture, and history and thereby regained the genuinely catholic, integral character it had lost during the time when it was considered to be mainly for domestic consumption within an alienated church.

Notes

[1] "C'est de là que tout est parti." Jacques Duqesne, *Jacques Duqesne interroge le Père Chenu. "Un théologien en liberté"* (Paris: Centurion, 1975), 85. The words quoted end a chapter entitled "La germination des années trente" (64-85).

[2] See Georgio Campanini, "Il pensiero politico cristiano e la crisi degli anni trenta," in *Cristianesimo e democrazia: Studi sul pensiero politico cattolico del '900* (Brescia: Morcelliano, 1980), 19-40.

[3] See Joseph A. Komonchak, "Modernity and the Construction of Roman Catholicism," *Cristianesimo nella Storia* 18 (1997), 353-85.

[4] See Daniele Menozzi, "Liturgia e politica: l'introduzione della festa di Cristo Re," in *Cristianesimo nella Storia: Saggi in onore di Giuseppe Alberigo*, ed. A. Melloni et al. (Bologna: Il Mulino, 1996), 607-56.

[5] Jacques Julliard and Daniel Lindenberg, "L'histoire des intellectuels catholiques: Interview de René Rémond," *Mil neuf cent: Revue d'histoire intellectuelle (Cahiers Georges Sorel)* 13 (1995), 18. Rémond's other golden age was the decade after the Second World War. Yves-Marie Hilaire also speaks of the 1930s as "a golden age of Christian thought and letters" (*Histoire religieuse de la France contemporaine*, vol. 3, *1930/1988,* ed. Gérard Cholvy and Yves-Marie Hilaire [Toulouse: Privat, 1988], 24-29).

[6] Bruno de Solages, "La crise moderniste et les études ecclésiastiques," *Revue apologétique* 51 (July 1930), 5-30.

[7] Marie-Dominique Chenu, "Le sens et les leçons d'une crise religieuse," *La vie intellectuelle* 13 (December 1931), 357-80.

[8] Jacques Maritain, *Une opinion sur Charles Maurras et le devoir des Catholiques*, in Jacques et Raïssa Maritain, *Oeuvres complètes* (Fribourg: Ed. Universitaires, 1984), 3:739-80; "De l'obeissance au Pape," *La vie spirituelle* 90 (March 1927), 755-57; *Primauté du spirituel*, in *Oeuvres complètes*, 3:783-988; *The Things That Are Not Caesar's* (New York: Scribner's, 1930); "Le sens de la condamnation," in *Pourquoi Rome a parlé, Oeuvres complètes*, 3:1223-67.

[9] Jacques Maritain, *Religion et culture*, in *Oeuvres complètes*, 4:193-255; "Religion and Culture," in *Essays in Order*, ed. Christopher Dawson (New York: Macmillan, 1931), 1-61; Jacques Maritain, *Du régime temporel et de la liberté*, in *Oeuvres complètes* (Fribourg: Ed. Universitaires, 1982), 5:319-515; *Freedom in the Modern World* (New York: Scribner's, 1936); *Integral Humanism: Temporal and Spiritual Problems of a New Christendom* (Notre Dame, Ind.: University of Notre Dame Press, 1973).

[10] For the power and persistence of the theme, see Giovanni Miccoli, *Fra mito della cristianità e secolarizzazione* (Casale Monferrato: Marietti, 1985), 23-92; Daniele Menozzi, *La Chiesa cattolica e la secolarizzazione* (Torino: Einaudi, 1993), 15-71.

[11] See Giuseppe Alberigo et al., eds., *La chrétienté en débat: Histoire, formes et problènes actuels* (Paris: Cerf, 1984).

[12] Recalling the debate of the 1930s, and the ambiguity of the word, Chenu later remarked: "What does 'Christendom' mean? It means the Church insofar as it has found its setting (*assiette*) in the world. . . . But if the temporal is autonomous, then the Church no longer is temporal. That, of course, is idealism: the Church will always imply a Christendom. I have always opposed those who dream of a pure Church, with a pure faith, with no temporal engagement. I admit that there will always be a Christendom, but I relativize, I say that it will change. In the year 2000 there will be the same Church but Christendom will be quite different. And if one day there exists a strong Chinese Church, as there now is in India, it will be quite different. In other words, there is a plurality of Christendoms in the one Church" (Duqesne, *Un théologien en liberté*, 84).

[13] M.-D. Chenu, "Dimension nouvelle de la Chrétienté," *La vie intellectuelle* 53 (1937), 325-51.

[14] "The proper task of a Christian critique of Marxism," Chenu, echoing Maritain, wrote, "is to free this insight from the materialistic metaphysics in which it was conceptualized" ("Dimension nouvelle de la chrétienté," 341; see also 348-49). In the 1930s Chenu introduced a course on Marx into the program of studies at Le Saulchoir.

[15] For this theme in Chenu, see Christophe Potworowski, "Dechristianization, Socialization and Incarnation in Marie-Dominique Chenu," *Science et Esprit* 43 (1991), 17-54. For a differently grounded but parallel analysis of the new collective consciousness, see Pierre Teilhard de Chardin, "La crise présente: Réflexions d'un naturaliste," *Études* 222 (1937), 145-65: "We now have to recognize that humanity is entering what is probably the greatest period of transformation that it has ever known. . . . Something is happening in the general structure of human consciousness. Another species of life is beginning" (145).

[16] A parallel essay made a similar point: "I think with sadness of that narrow Christendom, strictly individualistic, which has been unable to recognize, beneath its deviations, this immense fraternal aspiration. A disembodied Christendom that fears the earthly power of man and his collective destiny, which is unwilling to follow the movement of history, and makes its believers live as if nothing were happening. Absent from its time, not even knowing how to speak its language, imprisoning its theology of grace and its social morality in outdated categories, it has lost that creative sense and that permanent discovery that would enable it to take initiatives" (M.-D. Chenu, "Classes et Corps mystique du Christ," *La vie intellectuelle*, Serie de juerre 2 [January 31, 1940], 9-31, at 27).

[17] A new edition, with critical essays, appeared as Marie-Dominique Chenu, *Une école de théologie: le Saulchoir* (Paris: Cerf, 1985).

[18] Ibid., 142-43.

[19] Yves Congar, "Une Conclusion théologique à l'Enquête sur les raisons actuelles de l'incroyance," *La vie intellectuelle* 37 (1935), 214-49, at 248-49.

[20] Henri de Lubac, "Apologetics and Theology," first published in *Nouvelle Revue Théologique* in 1930, now included in Henri de Lubac, *Theological Fragments*, trans. Rebecca Howell Balinski (San Francisco: Ignatius Press, 1989), 91-104.

[21] See Joseph A. Komonchak, "Theology and Culture at Mid-century: The Example of Henri de Lubac," *Theological Studies* 51 (1990), 579-602.

[22] Henri de Lubac, *Catholicisme: Les aspects sociaux du dogme* (Paris: Cerf, 1938); idem, *Catholicism: A Study of Dogma in Relation to the Corporate Destiny of Mankind* (New York: Sheed & Ward, 1958).

[23] Henri de Lubac, *Surnaturel: Éudes historiques* (Paris: Aubier, 1946; Paris: Desclée de Brouwer, 1991).

[24] This sentence is from an essay first published in 1942, "Internal Causes of the Weakening and Disappearance of the Sense of the Sacred," in Henri de Lubac, *Theology in History* (San Francisco: Ignatius Press, 1996), 232.

[25] See the works summarized in Komonchak, "Theology and Culture at Mid-century," 596-601.

[26] In his essay on the modernist crisis, Chenu posed the issues in terms that one never finds in de Lubac: "Reason claims the right to examine and to analyze the *facts* of sacred history, to discover their linkages and causes, as once it claimed the right to examine and analyze natures, the concepts in which these natures are expressed, and the intrinsic causes of these natures. Will there be an autonomous history of humanity, in the same way and to the same degree that there is an autonomous philosophy of the world and of man?" ("Le sens et les leçons d'une crise religieuse," 364).

27 See Joseph A. Komonchak, "Vatican II and the Encounter between Catholicism and Liberalism," in *Catholicism and Liberalism: Contributions to American Public Philosophy*, ed. R. Bruce Douglass and David Hollenbach (New York: Cambridge University Press, 1994), 76-99; and idem, "Interpreting the Council: Catholic Attitudes toward Vatican II," in *Being Right: Conservative Catholics in America*, ed. Mary Jo Weaver and R. Scott Appleby (Bloomington, Ind.: Indiana University Press, 1995), 17-36.

28 Karl Rahner, "The Prospects for Dogmatic Theology," *Theological Investigations* (Baltimore: Helicon, 1961), 1:2.

5

The Great Depression

The Response of North American Theologians

DONALD SCHWEITZER

The Great Depression was a global crisis that shook free enterprise capitalism and its liberal institutions and values. This chapter will only analyze creative Christian theological responses to this that occurred in the United States and Canada. The two most striking of these responses were Reinhold Niebuhr's critique of the liberal Social Gospel and the radical theology of a Canadian group, the Fellowship for a Christian Social Order.[1] In provoking these the depression stimulated the rise of a new realism in Protestant thought, opened Protestant theologians to Marxist social analysis, moved many to the political left, and inspired an important debate over what Christians can hope for in history.

The depression is generally reckoned to have begun with the crash of the New York stock market on October 29, 1929. Partly as a result of technological developments, the process now known as globalization had created a nascent world community with an interlocked economy. The stock market crash initiated a spiral of price deflation that spread to industries and agriculture around the world, resulting in an unprecedented number of people becoming unemployed.[2] Even many with work suffered searing frustration and humiliation as they struggled for years to make do on inadequate incomes. Economic slumps were not new in the modern economy, but previously they had been brief. The depression was unique in its global reach, severity, and duration. In the United States and Canada in 1933 roughly one in four people depended on meager public relief to survive. In 1938 the figure was approximately one in five.

Pastoral responses to the depression in Canada and the United States varied. In the revival of individualistic evangelical fervor and the reactionary radio broadcasts of Father Coughlin it was interpreted as God's judgment on a lack of religious piety. Anti-semitism intensified. An awareness of the magnitude of the crisis was slow in coming. But as the depression dragged on, a ground swell of protest rose against the failure of capitalism to provide an adequate means of livelihood for a substantial portion of the population. Some Protestants and Roman Catholics supported Roosevelt's New Deal. Several church bodies called for a restructuring of the economy. Dorothy Day and Peter Maurin launched the Catholic Worker newspaper and movement, which challenged Catholics and others to live their faith against the stream of a materialistic culture. Creative theological responses occurred in Protestant circles. In the United States the most prominent of these was Reinhold Niebuhr's critique of the liberal Social Gospel.

The Influence of the Depression on Protestant Thought in the United States: Reinhold Niebuhr

Prior to the depression, Protestants in the United States and Canada had an original theology in the Social Gospel. This was a broad movement that responded to industrialization in England, the United States, and Canada by retrieving the historical dimension of Christian hope and focusing attention on the social problems of the new urban landscape. Social Gospellers took the biblical promises of peace and justice on earth and Jesus' commandment to abstain from violence seriously. Many became pacifists. Love was seen as the great Christian virtue that would overcome social ills.

The Social Gospel, as Niebuhr knew it, was "liberal" in that it shared the cultural optimism that the human condition had steadily improved and would continue to do so through the exercise of reason and good will. Traditional Christian doctrines that clashed with this belief were discarded or reinterpreted. The human spirit and the Holy Spirit were seen as closely intertwined. God was at work to realize the Kingdom of God on earth through evolution, education, and progressive social action. A cultural commitment to liberal values went hand in hand with a reforming socialism.

Niebuhr had just moved from a pastorate in Detroit to teach at Union Theological Seminary in New York when the depression hit. His pastoral experience there had already led him to question the Social Gospel's liberal assumptions and to recognize the need for a deeper analysis of power relations in society. In response to the depression Niebuhr developed two trenchant critiques of liberalism and the Social Gospel in his famous book, *Moral Man and Immoral Society*.[3] First, he interpreted the depression using Marxist analysis to refute liberal views of history as progress. Second, he exposed liberal illusions regarding the efficacy of reason and love in social relations.

In his first line of criticism Niebuhr argued that industrial applications of modern technology had led to the concentration of wealth in the hands of a few, the overproduction of goods, and the breakdown of the capitalist economy.[4] While secular liberals and Social Gospellers saw modern technology as a tool of progress that would build a peaceful world of prosperity for all, Niebuhr showed that it had instead given rise to new social conflicts and the depression.

Niebuhr did not repudiate modern technology per se. In his view the fault lay in the failure of political, moral, and religious thought to respond to the social changes brought by the industrial revolution.[5] Liberal faith in reason had helped create modern Western society but had failed through a lack of self-criticism to keep pace with its development. In secular liberal and Social Gospel views of history, Western progress in the development of modern technology was taken as indicative of an all-embracing enlightenment. This was seen as a permanent achievement. Niebuhr argued instead that technical progress did not equal moral progress. The experience of the "proletariat" in the depression was that technical developments could temper natural evils but also increased the possibility of moral evil.[6] From this perspective, the depression revealed liberal and Social Gospel views of history as progress to be an illusion.

This interpretation of the depression radicalized Niebuhr's politics. At this point Niebuhr believed that capitalism had brought American society to the edge of disaster. Liberal reforms that left economic power in the hands of the wealthy failed to address the root of the problem. The crisis could only be resolved by the socialization of industry. Niebuhr had joined the Socialist party in 1929. In 1930 he ran as a candidate. A kind of preferential option for the poor was present in his writings of the early thirties.[7] But Niebuhr's views changed again. Though in 1938 he was still criticizing Roosevelt's New Deal as not systematic and far-reaching enough, by 1940 he had begun to admire Roosevelt and support the New Deal.

This change was partly a response to the failure of socialism to become an effective political force in America and to historical events unleashed by the depression. Niebuhr's participation in the Socialist party began to decline in the mid 1930s as he realized that the transformation of American society into a socialist state was not a political possibility. At the same time, the threat of fascism and the demonic aspects of Stalinism convinced him that the defense of democracy was a higher priority than social revolution, while the successes of the New Deal suggested there were greater possibilities for achieving a limited social justice within liberal democracy than he had previously realized.[8] Feuds between competing labor organizations and the lack of concern of some labor leaders for non-unionized workers led him to abandon his notion of a preferential option for the poor.[9]

But Niebuhr's conversion from radical politics to New Deal liberalism also followed from the second line of criticism that he had developed in *Moral Man and Immoral Society*. This attacked the faith of liberalism and the Social Gospel in the power of reason and love to overcome social conflict. In the tradition of liberal thought, reason was believed to be able to rise above the particularities of race and creed. With enough good will and clear thinking, people could come together and resolve conflicts without resorting to coercion or violence. Niebuhr believed that reason could achieve a limited self-transcendence and broaden concepts of justice. But he followed Marx in arguing that human reason is always colored by class or self-interest. The liberal view that education and the improvement of virtue could solve social and international conflicts was an illusion. Such conflicts could not be solved by reason and good will alone because both were always tainted by the inordinate self-interests of class or nation that gave rise to these conflicts in the first place.

Here Niebuhr drew upon Marxist insights to reverse the tendency in liberal Western thought to separate the mind from the body and natural impulses. He insisted instead that mind and body are always ultimately united, so that reasoning is always influenced by natural impulses to give higher priority to one's own ideals and interests than a disinterested justice would grant.

Reason dictated that the crisis of the depression could only be overcome by the socialization of industry and mutual economic cooperation between nations. But the self-interest of the classes that formed and elected governments prevented this from happening voluntarily.

Religion was also limited by the inherently self-interested tendencies of human nature, so that it could "never finally eliminate the selfish, brutal and antisocial elements which express themselves in all inter-group life."[10] Consequently, reason and love could never be as efficacious in effecting social change as secular liberals and Social Gospellers believed. "The brutalities of the conflict of power"[11] could be mitigated but never finally surmounted.

Once this was recognized the strategies of the liberal Social Gospel had to be rethought and its goals reduced. Achieving greater justice between social groups would always require some degree of coercion, and one could not "draw any absolute line of demarcation between violent and nonviolent coercion."[12] The perfectionist ethics of the Sermon on the Mount presented an absolute standard by which to critique society but could not provide the basis for a responsible social ethic. Pacifism was sometimes an admirable witness but not a responsible ethical stance. A Christian realism recognizing that justice could only be established through the exercise of power in social conflicts was more responsible, and therefore ultimately more faithful, than the idealism of the liberal Social Gospel. Responsible Christian social thought should begin with a recognition of the limits of what could be achieved in history. Because all human efforts and group actions are tainted by self-interest, the best one could hope for was achieving a rough justice that required continual critique and adjustment. The kingdom of God was an absolute ideal by which to criticize society but not a goal to work toward. Christians should work instead to preserve democracy and seek an ever more tolerable justice through balancing the powers of competing interest groups. Attempting anything more was hubris and would only end up accomplishing much less.

Niebuhr's critique did not stop here. The self-interested tendencies of human reason were present in Marxists and union members as well as in the wealthy. In claiming that a restructuring of society would remove this from the human psyche, Marxists and socialists were as deluded as liberal Social Gospellers. When their delusions ran aground they were liable to become ruthless fanatics.

Thus this second line of critique led to the conclusion that the development of a social order in which social groups transcended their self-interests was impossible. The practical consequence of this was that while Niebuhr called for the socialization of industry until 1940, his support for radical politics gradually waned. Nonetheless, he remained intensely active in social struggles through many academic and practical venues as long as his health allowed, and was sufficiently to the left in American politics to be closely watched by the FBI.[13]

Niebuhr's first depression-inspired critique radicalized his politics. The second radicalized his theology. Together, they began a dramatic shift in Christian thinking in the United States and Canada away from the idealism of the liberal Social Gospel toward a more pragmatic Christian realism. As the thirties progressed Niebuhr became convinced that a realistic social praxis required the wisdom of Augustinian and Reformation insights to sustain it, and fused his Marxist insights with classical Christian themes into a powerful reconception of sin and grace.[14] Marxist analysis helped Niebuhr identify distortions, illusions, coercions, and oppressions in society, but he used classical themes of Christian theology to understand these and explain their presence. Thus the depression moved Niebuhr politically to the left but theologically to the right, or toward orthodoxy, as he broke with the liberalism of the Social Gospel and emphasized instead the transcendence of God and the presence of sin in all human activity.

The Impact of the Depression on Protestant Thought in Canada: The Fellowship for a Christian Social Order

In Canada the depression called into being the Fellowship for a Christian Social Order (FCSO). It was formed in April 1934 by a nucleus of United Church members with Methodist roots and became a national Protestant organization with local groups meeting for study and discussion.[15] In 1936 the group published a collection of essays as a theological response to the depression entitled *Towards the Christian Revolution*.[16]

In assessing the theology of the FCSO, it is important to note that its members were not trans-Atlantic intellectuals like Niebuhr. They wrote for the Canadian context and out of the religious traditions that shaped it. Several significant influences here steered their thought in a different direction from Niebuhr's.

First, liberal theology was not as influential in Canada then as in the United States. In Canada the Social Gospel had evolved more from a evangelicalism focused on individual conversion that reinvented itself at the turn of the century to embrace the liberal ideals of the Social Gospel without discarding its evangelical roots.[17] During the depression this evangelicalism intent on individual salvation came to the fore again, eclipsing the concerns of the Social Gospel. In the mid-1930s it was a much stronger presence in Canada than the liberal Social Gospel that Niebuhr critiqued. The FCSO believed that in their context it was not liberal idealism but evangelicalism's narrow vision of salvation that prevented responsible social action on the part of the church.

Second, as the failure of the Socialists to become a viable third party in American politics was leaving Niebuhr without a political option, a radical yet democratic socialist party, the Co-operative Commonwealth Federation (CCF), was taking shape in Canada.[18] Many of the FCSO authors were connected to this through the League for Social Reconstruction, which formed a "brain trust" for the new CCF party. It, in turn, gave substance to their hopes for radical social change by democratic means.

Turning to the theology of the FCSO, we find that it differed from the Social Gospel in its use of Marxist social analysis and its starting point. FCSO authors did not share the Social Gospel vision of society as an organic unity that could grow into the kingdom of God. The depression had led them to analyze society in Marxist terms, as a realm of conflict divided by class interests. They interpreted scripture as expressing a clear preferential option for the poor.[19] This entailed a break with the progressivism of the liberal Social Gospel and made their ethical outlook revolutionary rather than reformist. The kingdom of God required the radical restructuring of society.

But the FCSO authors experienced Marx most profoundly as a moral critic. Marxism challenged the church to broaden its horizons of sin and grace and to seek to realize Christian teaching in history by transforming society.[20] At this time the Soviet Union loomed as the great example that the creation of a socialist state was possible and effective medicine against the depression, while the formation of the CCF had raised hopes that socialism might become established in Canada by democratic means. Thus while Marxist analysis set the theology of the FCSO apart from the Social Gospel, Marxism also spurred its authors to restate the hope of peace and justice on earth, but without the Social Gospel optimism that this could be achieved as an extension of present social trends or ever fully attained in history. As one FCSO author noted, while the theology of the group seemed similar to the Social Gospel in the breadth of its hope, inwardly it was quite different.[21] This difference is most noticeable in the starting point of the FCSO's theology.

The depression had destroyed for the FCSO the Social Gospel's optimistic view of history and its assumption of human goodness. The theology of the FCSO began instead with a profound sense of human failure. Salvation required a "fundamental spiritual reorientation" of the individual and a re-creation of society.[22] Their theology centered on the revelation and experience of God's judgment and grace. In this they viewed themselves as close to evangelicalism, with its emphasis on the transcendence of God, the need for repentance, and its dynamic sense of God acting to save the lost.

The depression had led the FCSO toward the new realism in theology that Niebuhr and others espoused.[23] However, its authors saw the predomi-nant sin of their context to be indifference to the sufferings of others, and unlike Niebuhr, they continued to hope for radical social change. For them, this hope was grounded by a faith in the transforming power of God, shared with evangelicalism, but which they extended to the social realm. Here the FCSO revealed its Methodist heritage, which stressed the power of God's Spirit to change lives. The FCSO authors extended this hope to include society in response to the challenge of the depression and Marxism, but also in light of the corporate dimensions of the biblical witness and their own experiences. As they participated in workshops, discussions, and re-treats, they were struck by the great openness to their ideas and the spirit of solidarity and commitment to a new society they encountered.[24] This was not optimism, but rather a hope grounded in the four elements of Wesley's theological quadrilateral: scripture, tradition, experience, and reason.

In light of this hope, the FCSO authors developed a dialectical critique of the individualistic ethos of capitalism and evangelicalism's individualis-tic understanding of salvation. They argued that capitalist individualism was a falsification of the original philosophy of individualism begun by Rousseau and others. Rousseau had recognized that an individual is always embedded in a social context. He saw that individual rights and freedoms were necessary for the uniqueness of an individual to come to full expres-sion, but so were just social conditions. Thus for Rousseau a concern for individual rights and freedoms went hand in hand with concern for equal-ity among individuals.[25] The FCSO authors wished to retrieve this notion of equality and justice as necessary for a healthy personal life without subordi-nating the individual to the community. They argued that during the industrial revolution this concern for equality and justice had been replaced by the teaching of laissez-faire economics that one contributed most to the public good by simply pursuing one's self-interests. The depression was proof that this was self-defeating as a philosophy of freedom. The society built on this self-centered individualism had destroyed liberty and equality by creat-ing social conditions in which the majority of people lived in want under the economic tyranny of a few.

The fundamental error of this individualism was its lack of concreteness. It thought of people abstractly, without considering their material needs. Consequently, it failed to distinguish between the quality of life of a slave and that of a genuinely free person.[26] The FCSO authors argued that true free-dom and dignity were only possible for persons on the basis of relationships formed in a just community. Jesus proclaimed the kingdom of God as a community in which people were delivered from material and spiritual oppressions. Laissez-faire economics that presupposed and fostered an abstract individualism directly opposed this.

This charge of abstractness was also applied to the individualistic view of salvation that evangelicalism promoted in Canada during the depression. The FCSO acknowledged the truth of the evangelical stress that salvation comes only through repentance and the acceptance of God's grace.[27] But the evangelical emphasis on the salvation of one's soul apart from others was too limited and tended to diminish one's sense of social responsibility. The ethical teaching of evangelical piety stressed only virtues of honesty, sobriety, and hard work. This made it the perfect civil religion for the capitalist economy, but left it with nothing to say about the structural causes of the depression. Like Western individualism, evangelical piety overlooked "the natural unity of life"[28] by which one's spiritual health was intimately connected to the physical and social well-being of one's self and others. This oversight truncated the gospel, which called one to a spiritual community of love that was also to be actualized in the social order. Through this critique the FCSO sought to broaden evangelicalism's understanding of sin and grace in order to direct its spiritual energy toward effecting social change.

Like Niebuhr in his critique of liberalism, the FCSO reasserted the unity of mind and body as a principle of realism in social and religious thought. But they took this in a different direction. Whereas Niebuhr employed it to deflate liberal optimism and idealism, the FCSO used it to broaden and reframe Canadians' ethical concern and sense of the public good. In conjunction with this they continued to view the kingdom of God as a concrete Utopia to be worked toward in history, while recognizing that it always transcended any given social order. The retention of this hope sparked an important debate with Niebuhr.

The Debate between Niebuhr and the FCSO

In a review of the FCSO's *Towards the Christian Revolution*, Niebuhr acknowledged that the ethical concern of many Canadian Protestants needed to be broadened.[29] But after some initial appreciations, he charged the FCSO with repeating the errors of the liberal Social Gospel: equating socialism with the kingdom of God and reducing the unconditional demands of the gospel. Niebuhr did recognize some differences between the American and Canadian contexts, but he did not see these as significant. His argument repeated his second critique of the liberal Social Gospel. The FCSO's hope that democratic socialism could establish a just society failed to recognize that even in a socialist society the ideal of equal justice would be "relativized by the organic necessities of historic existence" and "corrupted by sin beyond the requirements of social existence." This "basic contradictoriness and sinfulness of human existence" could not be overcome by changes in the social order.[30] In failing to recognize this, the FCSO had let go of an essential Christian insight into the human condition.

A few years later Gregory Vlastos, one of the FCSO authors, replied to Niebuhr, arguing that Niebuhr's understanding of the human condition (on which his critique of the FCSO was based) was one-sided.[31] In positing human freedom that is inevitably tainted by self-interest as the essence of humanity, Niebuhr omitted the "power of mutuality or community."[32] An adequate anthropology must affirm both. Human freedom includes the ability to care for others, conceive a greater common good, and enter into cooperative action, as much as it does the propensity to sin.

In analyzing this debate, we can begin by noting that Niebuhr's judgment of the FCSO was in keeping with his tendency to equate meaning with the final triumph of good over evil.[33] His criticism failed to acknowledge that meaning in history had different but related levels.[34] Though redemptive achievements to develop more humane social structures are always ambiguous and never finally overcome the human tendency to sin, nonetheless they can still be meaningful within their historical context.[35] A more careful reading of the FCSO's theology would show that they only claimed a relative meaning of this type for socialism and mutuality. They believed that in light of the gospel these were preferable to the laissez-faire capitalism that had caused the depression. To use Niebuhrian terms, democratic socialism was for them ultimately only a proximate goal, a means to attaining a relatively greater justice. There were some optimistic speculations typical of the Social Gospel in some of the essays,[36] but these did not justify Niebuhr's charge that the FCSO "simply assumed that the socialist commonwealth . . . is somehow or other identical with the Kingdom of God," when elsewhere they stated otherwise.[37] On this point, Niebuhr clearly misrepresented the FCSO. In so doing he obscured the religious sanctions for a creative political option[38] and fell into the same reduction of meaning that he later criticized in Luther.

The central issue between Niebuhr and the FCSO is what can be hoped for in history. From his critique of the liberal Social Gospel on, Niebuhr was adamant that people can never overcome their propensity to sin, and thus moral evil will never be finally banished from history. But as Vlastos pointed out, human creative capacities also present possibilities of redemptive action in obedience to God's call. Empowered and summoned by God, people can create something relatively new in history, although, as Niebuhr pointed out, such achievement is never final and always requires ongoing critique.

Niebuhr's emphasis on people's tendency to self-aggrandizement points toward a kind of Hobbesian democracy in which the self-interests of different social groups keep each other in check. Vlastos's stress on love as mutuality points toward a cooperative democracy in which people unite in joint action for the common good.

Perhaps in Niebuhr's position there surfaced a residue from his Lutheran heritage, Luther's doctrine of the two kingdoms. While Niebuhr was later critical of Luther on this point, his criticism of liberals and social radicals seems to echo Luther's restrictions regarding what Christians should try to accomplish in the social order. Certainly the FCSO's theme of the human capacity for mutuality maintained a characteristically Methodist emphasis on the sanctifying work of the Holy Spirit.

This is where the theological difference between the two lies. The source of the FCSO's hope in the struggle for a better social order was ultimately not human goodness but the empowering presence of the Holy Spirit.[39] Niebuhr's theology always remained weak on this point. He never developed an understanding of the Holy Spirit to equal his reconception of original sin. Had he done so, he might have been more appreciative of the sin of failing to heed God's call to actualize one's divinely given potential[40] and remained more open to the contribution radical social movements can make to the relative overcoming of evil in history.

The Theological Legacy of the Depression in Canada and the United States

Today the depression is fading from living memory. Few of later generations realize what a turning point it was in the history of the United States and Canada, how it gave rise to the welfare state and a more encompassing notion of the public good. It had a similar impact on theology in these two countries. Niebuhr's depression-inspired criticism of the liberal Social Gospel marked a watershed in North American Christian theology. It ended any claims to innocence in social thought, taught Christians to be self-critical, and set the agenda for much of Christian social ethics that followed. The FCSO, for its part, anticipated themes of liberation and feminist theology in its critique of individualism, notion of God's partiality for the victims of capitalism, and theme of mutuality. The controversy between Niebuhr and the FCSO remains a minor classic that paralleled in social terms the debate between Zinzendorf and John Wesley over sin and sanctification in the life of an individual. It hammered out the issues concerning the extent to which Christians can hope for something new in history.

Notes

[1] This was different from the Fellowship for a Christian Social Order organized in the United States in 1921 by Sherwood Eddy and Kirby Page.

[2] The exact causes of the Great Depression remain uncertain. See John Kenneth

Galbraith, *The Great Crash: 1929* (Boston: Houghton Mifflin Company, 1954); Charles P. Kindleberger, *The World in Depression, 1929-1939* (Berkeley and Los Angeles: University of California Press, 1986).

[3] Reinhold Niebuhr, *Moral Man and Immoral Society* (New York: Charles Scribner's Sons, 1932).

[4] Ibid., 89-90, 165-66.

[5] Ibid., 49-50.

[6] Ibid., 165-66.

[7] Ibid., 161-67. See also Langdon Gilkey, "Reinhold Niebuhr as Political Theologian," in *Reinhold Niebuhr and the Issues of Our Time*, ed. Richard Harries (Grand Rapids, Mich.: Eerdmans, 1986), 158.

[8] For a detailed chronological account of this shift in Niebuhr's position, see Richard Fox, *Reinhold Niebuhr: A Biography* (New York: Pantheon Books, 1985), 146-93.

[9] William H. Becker, "Reinhold Niebuhr: From Marx to Roosevelt," *The Historian* 35 (August 1973): 549-50.

[10] Ibid., 75.

[11] Ibid., 154-55.

[12] Ibid., 172.

[13] Fox, *Reinhold Niebuhr*, 202, 207-9.

[14] The transitional nature of Niebuhr's writing during the thirties has been often noted. See Gilkey, "Reinhold Niebuhr as Political Theologian," 158, 177; Ronald Stone, *Reinhold Niebuhr: Prophet to Politicians* (Nashville, Tenn.: Abingdon Press, 1972), 10, 54.

[15] For the group's history, see Roger Hutchinson, "The Fellowship for a Christian Social Order: A Social Ethical Analysis of a Christian Socialist Movement" (Th.D. dissertation, Emmanuel College, University of Toronto, 1975).

[16] R.B.Y. Scott and Gregory Vlastos, eds., *Towards the Christian Revolution* (Kingston, Ontario: Ronald P. Frye & Co., 1989 <1936>).

[17] Phyllis D. Airhart, *Serving the Present Age* (Montreal: McGill-Queen's University Press, 1992), 65, 77-76; Nancy Christie and Michael Gauvreau, *A Full-Orbed Christianity* (Montreal: McGill-Queen's University Press, 1996), 61.

[18] For an account of the formation of the CCF, see Kenneth McNaught, *A Prophet in Politics* (Toronto: University of Toronto Press, 1959), 259-65.

[19] Scott and Vlastos, *Towards the Christian Revolution*, 72, 88.

[20] Ibid., 224.

[21] Ibid., 39.

[22] Ibid., 40.

[23] Ibid., 39-40.

[24] Michiel Horn, *The League for Social Reconstruction: Intellectual Origins of the Democratic Left in Canada: 1930-1942* (Toronto: University of Toronto Press, 1980), 62.

[25] Scott and Vlastos, *Towards the Christian Revolution*, 7.

[26] Ibid., 65-66.

[27] Ibid., 28-29, 40.

[28] Ibid., 22.

[29] Reinhold Niebuhr, review of *Towards the Christian Revolution*, *Radical Religion* 2:2 (Spring 1937): 42-44.

[30] Ibid.

[31] Gregory Vlastos, "Sin and Anxiety in Niebuhr's Religion," *The Christian Century* 58, no. 4 (October 1, 1941): 1202-4.

[32] Ibid., 1204.

[33] Daniel D. Williams, "Niebuhr and Liberalism," in *Reinhold Niebuhr: His Religious, Social, and Political Thought,* ed. C. W. Kegley and R. W. Bretall (New York: Macmillan, 1961), 206-7.

[34] Langdon Gilkey, *Reaping the Whirlwind: A Christian Interpretation of History* (New York: Seabury Press, 1976), 284.

[35] Ibid., 286.

[36] For instance, the idea that "training and environmental factors" might overcome the influence of self-interest or that an increase in technical knowledge would make it possible to overcome the structural contradictions of capitalism (Scott and Vlastos, *Towards the Christian Revolution*, 23-24, 239-43).

[37] Niebuhr, review of *Towards the Christian Revolution*, 42; Scott and Vlastos, *Towards the Christian Revolution*, 77, 94.

[38] Donald B. Meyer, *The Protestant Search for Political Realism: 1919-1941* (Berkeley and Los Angeles: University of California Press, 1961), 409. See also Gary Dorrien, "Communitarianism, Christian Realism, and the Crisis of Progressive Christianity," *Cross Currents* 47, no. 3 (Fall 1997): 371ff.

[39] Scott and Vlastos, *Towards the Christian Revolution*, 188.

[40] Paul Lehman, "The Christology of Reinhold Niebuhr," in Kegley and Bretall, *Reinhold Niebuhr*, 277-80. See also Williams, "Niebuhr and Liberalism," 205-7; Abraham Heschel, "A Hebrew Evaluation of Reinhold Niebuhr," in Kegley and Bretall, *Reinhold Niebuhr*, 407-8; Daniel D. Williams, *God's Grace and Man's Hope* (New York: Harper & Row, 1949), 31-32.

6

Theologians in Nazi Germany

A. JAMES REIMER

The scope of this chapter is exclusively the reaction of German theologians to Hitler's National Socialism. Also of great importance, though not treated here, are the different responses of the churches and their institutions to the so-called German Revolution. These responses form part of the background for understanding the theoretical approach taken by some of the theologians discussed in the following pages. Among these ecclesiastical responses, the Barmen Declaration of the Confessing Church holds a special place. The great achievement of German church historian Klaus Scholder's treatment of the historical, political, and institutional aspects of the German churches' reaction to the Nazi movement is the interpretation of the work of the theologians in the context of the concrete conditions of their respective churches.[1] In this essay I examine the thought of the theologians under two headings: (1) the political theologies of the right, and (2) the protest theologies of different orientations.

Political Theologies of the Right

We turn first to a consideration of a few representative thinkers who in their thought illustrate the kind of arguments that were used to support the Nazi regime and ideology. Since the 1960s the term *political theology* has come to be associated with a theology of the left, the theology of Johann-Baptist Metz, for example, who, influenced by the Neo-Marxist thinkers of the Frankfurt School of Critical Theory, argued vigorously against a privatized, apolitical, and politically nonresponsible type of theology. What is frequently forgotten is that there have been forms of political theology of quite a different kind, from the time of Eusebius in the fourth-century Constantinian court to the 1920s and 1930s in Germany.[2] In the 1920s a distinctive type of conservative, right-wing theology emerged in Germany identified with Catholic thinkers like Carl Schmitt and Protestant theologians such as Emanuel

Hirsch, Wilhelm Stapel, and Paul Althaus. This type of theology took *Volk* (nationality, peoplehood) as the foundation for theological work. In contrast to the universalism of the Roman Catholic tradition, Protestants in the nineteenth century (including Schleiermacher and Hegel) put great emphasis on nationhood. According to Scholder, this Protestant nationalism took a decisive turn in the 1920s. A new type of political theology arose that systematically interpreted nationalism in terms of God and *Volk*. Three theologians associated with this new theology were Paul Althaus, Emanuel Hirsch, and Wilhelm Stapel. In Scholder's opinion this new form of theology made political ethics the key to theological thinking, rather than defining politics in terms of theology as Barth did (Scholder, 130-33, 539, 545-46). In the following pages I examine the basic arguments of two representatives of this new political theology, the Roman Catholic Carl Schmitt, and the Protestant Emanuel Hirsch.

Carl Schmitt

Until 1933 Catholics had not, like the Protestants in the 1920s, developed a comparable political theology. But in 1933-34 articles were written and positions taken that in many ways were indistinguishable from the Protestant political theologians Althaus, Hirsch, and Stapel.

Whereas earlier the *völkisch* ideology of National Socialism has been severely denounced, now *Konkordat* politics and the lifting of the ban against voting NSDAP opened the floodgates. Shortly after Hitler came to power a periodical series called *Reich und Kirche* began to be published in Münster, dedicated to "the building of the Third Reich from the united forces of the National Socialist State and Catholic Christianity."[3] Noted Catholic thinkers who contributed to the periodical series included Reformation historian Josef Lortz, Münster theologian Michael Schmaus, philosopher and ethicist Josef Pieper, and Hitler's vice-chancellor, Franz von Papen. A common tone pervades most of the articles. Schmaus observes that the similarities between National Socialism and Catholicism are so striking that the latter can be considered most useful in helping National Socialism realize its ideals.[4] Lortz talks in glowing terms of how Hitler can save Europe from the "chaos of Bolshevism and the destruction of Christian Europe."[5] He points out that Hitler is a Catholic and his early rejection by the church was false. After the completion of the Concordat, German Catholicism and the National Socialist state can become one, because National Socialism is not a system of thought but a primal life force. In a different periodical Karl Adam, theologian at the University of Tübingen (1919-49) speaks glowingly of the National Socialist revolution as connecting Germans to their "primal power, which created and formed our nationalistic consciousness: blood and spirit, blood and religion, German blood and Christianity." Speaking about Hitler in soteriological imagery, Adam declares: "And he came, Adolf Hitler. From the south he came, but we knew him not." He sees the

National Socialist action against the Jews, in the light of their increasing influence in German economics, art, scholarship, and literature, as painfully necessary for German survival.[6]

The main difference between the Catholic and Protestant political theology is the way it is justified theologically. Unlike Protestants, who had to deal with the two-kingdoms teaching of Luther and did so in ingenious ways to accommodate their religious "sanctification" of the earthly order, Catholics could draw on the Thomistic natural-law tradition to argue that divine grace did not contradict the natural orders (including the primal life force of the German *Volk*) but infused them and lifted them up to a higher level (Scholder, 541-43).

Of all the above Catholic thinkers who supported National Socialism, it is Carl Schmitt who is without a doubt the most significant. In the European and North American neo-conservative turn of recent years there has been an astonishing revival of interest in Schmitt's conservative political thought. Some even claim that he has been elevated to classical political thinker status comparable to Hobbes and Machiavelli.[7] This is both remarkable and alarming, considering the central role Schmitt played in the formulation of Nazi juridical policy in their early years in power, when they were seeking legitimation from distinguished thinkers like Schmitt. His whole political project was a sustained critique of the liberal constitutionalism of the Weimar Republic, of democracy and of socialism in favor of a strong state, with a strengthened role for the *Reichspräsident* and weakened parliament, combined with strong civil society based on a free economy. His initial dismay at the Nazi rise to power quickly changed into full support after January 1933. The day after the infamous Enabling Act of March 24, giving the Nazi government emergency powers and formalizing Hitler's dictatorship, Schmitt published a supporting commentary on the legislation, seeing it as having formally superseded the Weimar constitution and the German Revolution of 1918. Schmitt received his reward. Scarcely two months after Hitler's coming to power, on April 1, he was appointed the regime's *Kronjurist*, rapidly gaining other prominent positions in the government. He also opportunistically adopted the despicable anti-semitic ideology of the new rulers. By 1936, however, he had fallen out of favor and lost some of his key posts, because the Nazis were more concerned with power for the party than for the state, as envisioned by Schmitt. He was not, however, expelled from the party, nor did he have to forfeit his chair at the University of Berlin, where he was able to continue his academic work until the end of the war. In the spring of 1947, after extensive interrogation, he was set free by the Nuremberg Tribunal without charge. He died on April 7, 1985.

What is of particular relevance for us in this context is the philosophical and theological underpinnings of Schmitt's thought. According to Renate Cristi, Schmitt in the 1920s did not want to abolish parliamentarianism but to reform it by distinguishing between democracy and liberalism. What he rejected in liberalism was its individualism and pluralism, which had the effect of undermining the unity of the state (Cristi, 16). His theory presupposed a meta-legal, metaphysical standpoint, outlined in his *Die Diktatur* (1921) and *Political Theology* (1922, significantly republished in 1933), in which he used the nineteenth-century counterrevolutionary thought of Catholic traditionalists (like de Maistre and Donoso Cortes) to support his own political theories of the state. In the words of Renate Cristi, "Schmitt's conservative thought, nurtured by the substantive disposition of traditional metaphysics, emphasized the issue of legitimacy and relativized legality" (Cristi, 21).

In his *Political Theology* Schmitt argues that the foundations of a solid legal order have a transcendent basis. The sovereignty of the state, that which gives it the power to make decisions, is grounded metaphysically. In contrast, a liberal view of the state presupposes no such transcendent norm, thereby negating the very notion of sovereignty. Liberals are the "discussing class," caught between traditional political theists, on the one side, and democratic political atheists, on the other. They represent the liberal bourgeoisie, oscillating from the one to the other, but finally turning to the right, to the powerful monarch to protect their property rights. The essence of the political, the role of the government is to make [existentialist-like] decisions and lead authoritatively without delay. The content of those decisions is less important than the fact of decision-making. Herein lies the nature of Schmitt's revolutionary conservatism, based not on Enlightenment reason and discussion but on sovereign action (Cristi, 72-73).

Schmitt was critical of the modern reduction of the political to the economic, conceived of in scientific, technical terms, and the leveling of all traditional hierarchies to industrial, technological sameness. In this process, God is reconceived from the traditional ruler of the world to an impersonal engine driving the cosmic machine. Only the church still has the resources for a non-economic, juridical understanding of authority. It is the bearer of the truly political that is opposed to Enlightenment economic and technological rationality. For Schmitt, political theology is a theology in which sovereignty rests in the belief that God is the architect of the universe and the basis for all human authority. Only after the seventeenth century, with Rousseau's identification of sovereignty with the will of the people, was this historic understanding lost, undermining the very notion of sovereignty and the capacity to make hard decisions. In the words of Cristi, "The 'political metaphysics' of democracy could not claim political theological status. In a democratic setting 'the theistic and the deistic idea of God is unintelligible'" (Cristi, 112). Political theology is inconceivable in a democratic context. While Schmitt may not be duly representative, he did draw upon conservative elements in the Catholic tradition to defend antidemocratic, authoritarian political thought and applied them opportunistically in the first years of the Nazi regime to support brutally repressive legislation. Furthermore, he was and continues to be a highly influential thinker.

Emanuel Hirsch

In some ways Hirsch is the Protestant counterpart to the Catholic Schmitt. Hirsch was a theologian, while Schmitt was a jurist. Hirsch became enmeshed in Protestant church politics, Schmitt in Nazi party politics. But both developed a political theology for the right. Hirsch is a complicated figure in the history of theology's encounter with National Socialism and, unlike Schmitt, has not experienced a revival in contemporary theology. He was highly regarded, however, even by his opponents for his brilliant mind and comprehensive knowledge of the history of theology, especially modern Christian thought from the Reformation onward. He wrote prolifically on a wide range of topics including Luther research, German idealism, political and economic theory, systematic theology, devotional themes, and historical-critical biblical studies. He was the definitive Kierkegaard scholar outside of Denmark, translating and producing a critical edition of his work in German. He wrote at least eleven novels in the years after World War II, when he was already completely blind. It was my own fascination with the question of how it was that this accomplished thinker, pious Christian, cleric, and distinguished university professor could join the ranks of the pro-Hitler German Christians that propelled me to spend a good fifteen years of my life studying Hirsch and his relation to Paul Tillich, a friend of his from childhood.[8]

As with others who were drawn to the new authoritarianism of National Socialism, Hirsch was impressed by the crisis of modernity—the fragmentation of society and loss of a sense of shared communal values brought about by technology, democratization, and the end of Enlightenment rationalism.[9] There was a wide-ranging consensus among German intellectuals about the nature of the crisis; where they differed was in how to respond to the crisis. The followers of Karl Barth and his Word of God theology, those drawn to Paul Tillich's Religious Socialist theology, and the political theologians of Hirsch's ilk agreed that the previous age of Protestant theology, based on Enlightenment pillars of knowledge and certainty, had come to an end. They differed on the task of theology in the face of that crisis. Hirsch turned for certainty to a Kierkegaardian inward subjectivity, on the one hand, and for a new social cohesiveness to an outward political authoritarianism, on the other. He saw his own intellectual and political solution not as a reactionary retreat back to a previous pre-Enlightenment age, but as a new mediating synthesis of the modern and that which is to follow. The key to his political theory was the concept of the "hidden sovereign," a notion he developed in an article published in 1933.[10] The hidden sovereign is not the king, as in the traditional monarchy, nor the people, as in a modern democracy, but nationality (*Volk*)—the invisible boundary no one can cross with impunity. It is the hidden sovereign to which everyone in society, including those who lead as well as those who are led, are equally subject. He considers this to be a genuine, innovative supersession of previous political theories, offering a form of political life that is beyond conservative, democratic, and socialist.

For Hirsch, National Socialism as a movement, and Hitler as its head, is an authentic attempt to find meaning in a post-Enlightenment secular world in which the old attempts at finding community and cohesion no longer work. He is highly critical of those theologians (like Barth) who want to retreat into the safety of Bible, catechesis, and confession and not risk identifying with the "holy storm" of national renewal sweeping over Germany. In a 1937 article, "Weltanschauung, Glaube und Heimat,"[11] he asserts the futility of all such biblically and confessionally based projects of renewal. He calls on the church rather to contribute wholeheartedly to the National Socialist renewal movement now underway, with its new fusion of morality and order based on a life-preserving respect for nationality.

His disdain for Barth and the Confessing Church are premised on these assumptions. In a 1933 article, "Das kirchliche Wollen der deutschen Christen,"[12] Hirsch defends himself and the German Christians against the charge of heresy (as Barth had expressed it in his famous essay *Theologische Existenz heute*). Barth's Word of God theology, he says, is ahistorical, and his view of God's revelation too narrowly christological. It is true that Jesus Christ and the scriptures are the primary bearers of God's word to us, but God also is self-revealing in the mundane aspects of everyday life. Distinguishing between soteriology and ecclesiology, Hirsch maintains that Barth, as a Swiss Reformed theologian, has never understood the Lutheran freedom to shape its church polity in accordance with the demands of the hour, which in this case means making leadership conditional upon Aryan descent, despite its unfortunate ramifications for individuals.

In an essay written on October 7, 1933—and expanded and published in *Deutsche Theologie* in May 1934—Hirsch gives his personal view on the Aryan clause, as accepted by the Evangelical Church of the Old Prussian Union in Berlin, September 5-6, 1933.[13] His argument goes like this: The Jews and the Germans are two distinct peoples. Assimilation, with a few exceptions, is not possible; and were it possible, it would ruin German racially based nationality and lead to the de-Christianizing of the German national order. The new National Socialist state has rightly recognized this danger, and it is trying to correct the domination of Weimar Germany by a foreign nationality by giving Jews "guest status" in Germany. Christians should, however, not extend this into the metaphysical realm [before Christ all are equal], and ought not to categorize Jews as inferior, unworthy, or depraved, as many present-day Germans are prone to do. Here we see how an intellectual like Hirsch could justify anti-semitic policies on one level, thereby giving support to racial segregation and underlying social discrimination (even against Jewish converts), while at the same time holding to a spiritualized unity in Christ between Jewish and Germanic Christians, on the other.

Protest Theologies

Unlike Hirsch, who remained steadfast in his support of the National Socialist cause, refusing to leave the sinking ship, most of the significant theologians who in the spring and summer of 1933 had flirted with the German Christian cause were leaving in droves, a scene that earned the scorn of Karl Barth.[14] There are some surprises to this story. Friedrich Gogarten, one of the 1920s founders of dialectical theology together with Karl Barth, in the summer of 1933 publicly announced his identification with the German Christian cause. His rejection of Enlightenment rationalism and individualism drew him in the 1930s to the authoritarian state. Before the end of the year, however, he had publicly withdrawn his support of the German Christians. Paul Althaus, on the other hand, who had in the 1920s, together with his friend Emanuel Hirsch, so strongly supported the new *Volk*-oriented political theology, refused to identify himself with the German Christians; instead, he supported the Young Lutheran Movement and its candidate Bodelschwingh for *Reichsbischof*. He did this while defending his previous theological views and severely criticizing the Barthian theology of Barmen. By late November 1933 virtually all university professors who had supported the German Christians and Bishop Ludwig Müller's church administration had protested and withdrawn their support. Only Hirsch refused to do so, and in a November 27 letter to Bishop Müller he resolved: "I do not leave a banner at the moment when there is a strong fire" (Scholder, 719). He never publicly changed his mind on those years.

On the Catholic side, Hitler's skillful elimination of the Centre Party and treaty with the Vatican had reduced opposition within Catholicism to isolated acts of protest: individual voices such as Jesuit Friedrich Muckermann, Walter Dirks, Frankfurt Pastor Georg W. Rudolphi,[15] and many others. In his Easter messages of 1933 Cardinal Faulhaber of Munich defended the Old Testament and expressed in strong language that "we can never forget: We are not redeemed by German blood. We are redeemed through the costly blood of our crucified Lord" (Scholder, 661). In pastoral letters of Easter 1934 a significant number of German bishops warned against the neo-paganism of the times. Graf von Galen, bishop of Münster, was specially outspoken in itemizing the points at which Christian truth and the neo-pagan myths contradict each other.[16] There is the moving example of Dr. Erich Klausener, an active Catholic lay leader of the Catholic Action in Berlin, someone who had occupied key positions in church and state, who was shot for his aggressive call to Roman Catholics to remain steadfast in the faith.[17]

Religious Socialism: Paul Tillich

We turn now to three theological voices that stand out from others in their prescient and steadfast critique of National Socialist ideology in all its forms: Paul Tillich, Karl Barth, and Dietrich Bonhoeffer. Here too we can only be selective. They are not the only such voices, but they illustrate more dramatically than others the types of protest available to Christian theology at the time. What makes the German Protestant theological landscape of the 1920s and 1930s so fascinating a case study is that the leading figures knew each other and either debated with each other directly or at least shaped their own positions with the others in mind. Take, for instance, Emanuel Hirsch, Karl Barth, and Paul Tillich. Hirsch and Barth knew each other from the University of Göttingen, where they both received a faculty position in 1921, and where they engaged in vigorous debate about the nature and task of theology. Karl Barth and Paul Tillich came to know each other in the early days of the new movement, variously known as dialectical theology, crisis theology, Word of God theology, or Neo-orthodoxy. Tillich thought of himself as an early follower of Barth's theology but gradually distanced himself from it. In their later work they frequently and respect-fully refer to each other's work, although parting company on essential points.[18]

Hirsch and Tillich knew each other from 1907, when they studied to-gether in Berlin. They continued their friendship through the 1910s and 1920s, developing theological-political differences along the way that erupted into a full-scale debate and rupture in a public exchange in 1934-35.[19] Hirsch turned into a passionate religious nationalist during and following World War I, and a distinguished Luther and Kierkegaard scholar subsequently. Soon after the First World War Tillich became a Religious Socialist and a theologian of culture. He agreed with Hirsch that theology demanded political engagement but was critical of Hirsch's ideological/theological use of Luther's two-kingdoms teaching to sanctify German na-tionality and nation. When in 1933/34 Hirsch wrote a book in which he used categories that Tillich perceived to be virtually the same as his own, earlier Religious Socialist categories, distorting them to legitimate his sup-port of the German Christians and the National Socialist state, Tillich wrote a scathing attack from Union Theological Seminary in New York City.

Klaus Scholder and Gunda Schneider-Flume have argued that in the 1920s the political theologians of the right (religious nationalists like Hirsch) and the political theologians of the left (Religious Socialists like Tillich) had formal similarities in their thinking. Each made political categories the key to his theology. For Hirsch, it was *Volk* (as the hidden sovereign); for Tillich, it was class (the international Proletariat as the prototype for the new humanity).[20] It was for this reason that the Religious Socialists were relatively impotent against their opponents; they were in effect struggling against each other on the same turf and with similar intellectual weapons. It was Barth who understood this most clearly and engaged in the struggle on completely different terms. For him, theology dare not define itself in political terms; its sole foundation must be a confessional one. Only after theology is clear about itself on its own terms can it draw out political-ethical implications.

In my own book on Tillich and Hirsch, I relied considerably on Scholder's insight to illuminate the heated debate between the two theologians and suggest that Barth's theology was more adequate to the situation. Having said that, I was quick to point out (and do so even more strongly today) that Tillich was one of the earliest voices of protest against the Nazis, especially their anti-semitism. Speaking in retrospect, Tillich recalls that long before 1933 his lectures at Frankfurt and across Germany put him in conflict with the growing Nazi movement.[21] His helping to found and sitting on the board of *Neue Blätter für den Sozialismus* was a political act that was later held against him by the Nazis. In April 1932 he and a friend wrote a letter to the Berlin Wingolf student fraternity, of which he was member, denouncing it for its discrimination against left-wing students and Christian students with Jewish background. They expressed their solidarity with socialists and Jews and threatened to resign, which they subsequently did. On one occasion, in July 1932, fighting broke out among Frankfurt university students, with Nazi students and Storm Troopers beating up Jews and left-wing students. Tillich, as dean of the faculty of philosophy, courageously defended the socialist and Jewish students and called for the expulsion of the Nazi students.[22] Probably Tillich's most important theoretical-political act was the writing of his book *The Socialist Decision*, which appeared toward the end of 1932, was banned as soon as Hitler came to power, and found its way onto a number of book burning sites. In this remarkable work Tillich outlines his own distinctive political theory that gives priority to "the myth of demand" (the call for justice) implicit in liberal and socialist theory while at the same time retrieving "the myth of origin" implicit in conservative and political romanticism. Tillich identifies himself clearly with nondoctrinaire socialism (a tradition he interprets in light of the Hebrew prophets' call for social justice) but makes room in his socialist thought for elements of the myth of origin (like nationality).[23]

On March 18 and 25 articles appeared in the *Frankfurter Zeitung* attacking the Johann Wolfgang Goethe University, especially its Jewish faculty (which would have included members of the Frankfurt School, like Max Horkheimer, whom Tillich had assisted in gaining a faculty position). Tillich's favorable writings about Jews were criticized in these articles. On April 13 long lists appeared in newspapers with names of undesirable persons. Tillich's name, along with many of his Jewish friends, appeared among those suspended from their university positions. On September 9 Tillich was granted a one-year leave to teach abroad. He and his family arrived in New York on November 3, 1933. On December 10 his hopes of returning to Germany to teach were dashed when he received a letter from the Prussian minister of culture advising him that because of his belonging to the Social

Democratic Party and his socialist writings he was considered untrustworthy and could not occupy a civil position in Germany.[24] It is in his attitude to the Jews that Tillich went beyond Barth and the Confessing Church. Because Tillich's theology was more universal and less ecclesiastically restricted, he sooner than Barth was able to identify with the plight of those outside the church. Dietrich Bonhoeffer was also able to move beyond the confines of the Christian community in his solidarity with the Jews, and yet he did so with a much stronger confessional-communal allegiance than did Tillich, and he gave his life in the process.

Confessional Protest: Barth and Bonhoeffer

In this study we encounter three distinctly different visions of how a new sense of community might emerge after the collapse of modernity. (1) There is the *völkisch* community of the National Socialists, German Christians, and others on the fringes of this movement. Here the dynamic-living powers of origin (nature, soil, blood, family, tribe, and nation) are revered as the source of new shared values and cohesion. Hirsch is an example of this dream of a national earthly community, but he combines this with a respect for Luther's two kingdoms, which sees the spiritualized kingdom of God in universal terms. (2) There is the international working-class community, the prototype of the new humanity of the doctrinaire socialists. Tillich has one foot in this camp but after the 1920s becomes increasingly critical of dogmatic Marxism for its total disregard of the powers of the origin. Unlike Barth, however, he remains much more universalistic in his theological thinking and distinguishes his dogmatics from church dogmatics, and thus makes his community more inclusive than either Hirsch's or Barth's. (3) Barth and Bonhoeffer envision a new community in quite a different way; it is the community of the confessing church whose confession is the one Word of Jesus Christ as attested to in scripture. It is a theology of the church that works itself out in dramatic ways in the German church struggle and has had a lasting impact on twentieth-century theology.

Our comments on Barth's theological position will have to be limited. Barth distanced himself from all of the German church-political factions in the summer and fall of 1933: the official church administration under Ludwig Müller, the German Christians, the Young Lutheran (or Reformation) Movement, and even the Niemöller-led Pastors' Emergency League. For him, they were all playing church politics, engaged in a "family feud" that had lost its confessional moorings ever since the beginning of the eighteenth century. "Because the doctrine and attitude of the German-Christians is nothing but a particular vigorous result of the entire neo-protestant development since 1700, our protest is directed against a spreading and existent corruption of the whole evangelical Church," he writes in one 1933 essay.[25] The root problem is that the German Christians see nationhood as a second source of revelation, thereby believing in "another God," a problem that is not unique to them. Barth turned down an offer to sit on a theological

committee of the state-church government because any kind of cooperation with heresy was out of the question. He thought of the whole church as
having been affected by this heresy. What was needed was a conversion, not
a "Deuteronomic reform of the Temple."[26] On Easter Day, April 1, 1934, he
clarifies what such a conversion would mean: a return to the "Christian
center, which is the theoretical and outward basis of the church, and the
object of theology—the Word of God, or Jesus Christ, crucified and risen,
standing as Lord, Creator, Reconciler and Redeemer over and above the
confused separation and integration of Germanism and personal Christianity, with which alone their view [Hirsch's and that of the German
Christians] is concerned."[27] Barth saw a direct line leading from the Enlightenment anthropocentric turn, through Schleiermacher's theology of
consciousness, the Ritschlian school's *Kulturprotestantismus* (including von
Harnack and Troeltsch) right up to the theological liberalism of the German Christians—a reading of liberal theology that has come under serious
scrutiny recently.[28]

Bonhoeffer followed in Barth's footsteps, but in a number of respects
went further than his mentor (whom he visited for two weeks in July of
1931) in exploring the concrete ethical and political ramifications of such
a confessional church theology. Bonhoeffer is said to have been the first
pastor and theologian of the Evangelical church to attack the anti-semitic
law of the Aryan clause decreed on April 7, 1933, and later accepted by the
Synod of the Prussian Union on September 5-6, 1933.[29] In the same month
of April, Bonhoeffer gave a lecture entitled "The Church and the Jewish
Question," in which he attacked that law especially in relation to baptized
Jews. In the view of close friend and biographer Eberhardt Bethge, it was
the protest against the Nazi treatment of the Jews inside and outside the
church that was the primary reason for his joining the conspiracy that ended
in the unsuccessful attempt on Hitler's life in July 1944, and ultimately to
Bonhoeffer's execution at Flossenberg on April 9, 1945.

What explains Bonhoeffer's early sensitivity to the persecution of the
Jews? Partly, it was due to family circumstances. His family was regularly in
contact with Jews. His psychiatrist father had Jewish assistants; his close friend
was Franz Hildebrandt, who had a Jewish mother; and his twin sister, Sabine,
was married to the baptized Jew, Gert Leibholtz, in 1926. Bonhoeffer's own
ninety-one-year-old mother in solidarity with the Jews walked through an
SA cordon to shop at a local Jewish shop on the day of the boycott, for
which Bonhoeffer praised her at her January 1936 funeral. On the other
hand, Bonhoeffer declined to officiate at the funeral of Leibholtz's unbap-
tized father on April 11, 1933, four days after the Aryan legislation, an act
for which he later apologized in a letter to the family.[30]

More important, however, are the theological reasons that inspired
Bonhoeffer's life. Already in his two doctoral theses, the 1927 *Sanctorum
Communio* and the 1930 *Act and Being*,[31] he had developed an ecclesiology
in which the church is seen as a visible, Christlike community of believers,

a theological understanding of the church somewhat atypical for a Lutheran at the time. For Bonhoeffer, the church is the body of Christ in a visible, sociological, concrete sense. He goes even further, describing this community as Christ existing on earth. In his later 1932 address "A Theological Basis for the World Alliance," he says: "The church is the presence of Christ on earth, the church is the *Christus praesens*."[32] It is this concept of the church as Christ existing in the world for others that leads Bonhoeffer into the Confessing Church (on July 23, the day of the church elections, Bonhoeffer preaches a sermon in Berlin calling for a Confessing Church), that motivates him to accept the call to direct the Confessing preachers' seminary at Finkenwalde from 1935-37 (when the Gestapo closed it), that draws him into the conspiracy, that preserves him in prison from 1943 to 1945, that is the deep meaning of his musings on a "religionless Christianity" and "Christianity come of age" found in his prison letters, and that sustains him, in death. For him the Christian confession is intrinsically linked to a Christian community in the world, demanding the "costly grace" of the Sermon on the Mount, as he spells out in his *The Cost of Discipleship* and the posthumously published *Ethics*.[33]

Bonhoeffer freed himself from old theological ways of thinking only through a hard and painful struggle. His courageous essay on the church and the Jews is still primarily concerned with not excluding baptized Jews from the Christian community. There are in it residues of the "teaching of contempt" (Jews bear the curse of nailing Christ to the cross) and Luther's two-kingdoms teaching (the church should not dictate to the state what it should do on the Jewish issue). The teaching that Jews were responsible for Christ's death is a theme that resurfaces in the August 1933 Bethel Confession, a forerunner to the Barmen Declaration, and one that Bonhoeffer helped to write. It is only gradually that we see a shift in Bonhoeffer's thinking, evident in the resolution of the September 1933 World YMCA conference in Sofia, Bulgaria, where Bonhoeffer influenced the following resolution: "We especially deplore the fact that the State measures against the Jews in Germany have had such an effect on public opinion that in some circles the Jewish race is considered a race of inferior status."[34] After the *Kristalnacht* pogrom of November 9, 1938, Bonhoeffer vigorously rejects any suggestion by his students that the suffering caused by the pogrom has anything to do with Jewish responsibility for Jesus' death. It is sheer violence.[35] There is other evidence, especially in his growing disillusionment with the compromises and inaction of the Confessing Church and his association with those outside of the church in the resistance, that he underwent a profound development (and even shift) in his thinking of the church's responsibility for the persecution of all Jews and other victims of the Nazi terror. It is a lesson that Christian theology and the church in general might well learn as we enter a new millennium.

The debate over the roots of modern anti-semitism, racism in general, and the role Christianity has played in such racism is far from over. As in the 1930s, so in contemporary theology, the debate continues as to how Christian theology should respond: Should it rethink itself in response to present challenges or go back to its confessional beginnings?[36] What is clear is that Christian theology cannot escape serious and critical self-reflection concerning the historic compromises it has made with forces of oppression.

Notes

[1] Klaus Scholder, *Die Kirchen und das Dritte Reich*, Vol. 1, *Vorgeschichte und Zeit der Illusion 1918-1934* (Frankfurt/M: Verlag Ullstein GmbH, 1977). The second volume was completed by students of the late Scholder, and both volumes were subsequently translated into English as *The Churches and the Third Reich*, Vol. 1: *1918-1934* and *The Churches and the Third Reich*, Vol. 2: *The Year of Disillusionment 1934: Barmen and Rome* (Philadelphia: Fortress Press, 1988). My own references are to the original German first volume and will hereafter be cited in the body of the text as such. Another overview of the subject, although less exhaustive, which also includes both Protestant and Catholic responses, is Ernst Christian Helmreich, *The German Churches under Hitler: Background, Struggle, and Epilogue* (Detroit, Mich.: Wayne State University Press, 1979).

[2] For a passionately critical treatment of all right-wing political theologies throughout history, see Rudolf J. Siebert, "From Conservative to Critical Political Theology," in *The Influence of the Frankfurt School on Contemporary Theology*, ed. A. James Reimer (Lewiston, N.Y.: E. Mellen Press, 1992).

[3] Cited in Gary Lease, *"Odd Fellows" in the Politics of Religion: Modernism, National Socialism, and German Judaism* (Berlin and New York: Mouton de Gruyter, 1995), 145.

[4] Michael Schmaus, "Begegnung zwischen Katholischem Christentum und National-Sozialistischer Weltanschauung," *Reich und Kirche: Eine Schriftrreihe* (Münster: Aschendorff, 1934), 30-31. Cited in Lease, *"Odd Fellows" in the Politics of Religion*, 146.

[5] Josef Lortz, "Katholisches Zugang zum National-Socialismus," *Reich und Kirche: Eine Schriftreihe*, 2d ed. (Münster: Aschendorff, 1934), 4. Cited in Lease, *"Odd Fellows" in the Politics of Religion*, 146ff.

[6] Karl Adam, "Deutsches Volkstum und Katholisches Christentum," in *Theologische Quartalschrift* 114 (1933), 40, 41-42, 62. Cited in Lease, *"Odd Fellows" in the Politics of Religion*, 149-50.

[7] See Renate Cristi, *Carl Schmitt and Authoritarian Liberalism: Strong State, Free Economy* (Cardiff: University of Wales Press, 1998), 1. For my subsequent discussion of Schmitt I draw heavily on the work of Cristi, and hereafter citations will be in the body of the text. See also David Nichols, *Deity and Domination: Images of God and the State in the Nineteenth and Twentieth Centuries* (London and New York: Routledge Publishers, 1994), esp. 99-106.

[8] The result was my study *The Emanuel Hirsch and Paul Tillich Debate* (Lewiston, N.Y.: E. Mellen Press, 1989).

[9] Robert P. Ericksen, in *Theologians under Hitler: Gerhard Kittel, Paul Althaus and Emanuel Hirsch* (New Haven, Conn.: Yale University Press, 1985), identifies the industrial-technological revolution, the democratic revolution, and the intellectual revolution as the three modern revolutions that Kittel, Althaus, and Hirsch saw as contributing to the crisis of modernity (1-27). For my critical review of Ericksen see *Grail: An Ecumenical Journal* 3, no. 3 (September 1987), 103-7.

[10] Hirsch, "Vom verborgenen Suverän," *Glaube und Volk* 2 (1933), 4-13.

[11] Hirsch, "Weltanschauung, Glaube und Heimat," *Zweifel und Glaube* (Frankfurt a.M.: Verlag Moritz Diesterweg, 1937), 52-64.

[12] "Das kirchliche Wollen der deutschen Christen: Zur Beurteilung des Angriffs von Karl Barth," *Das kirchliche Wollen der deutschen Christen* (Berlin-Steglitz: Evangelischer Pressverband für Deutschland, 1933).

[13] Hirsch, "Theologisches Gutachten in der Nichtarierfrage," *Deutsche Theologie: Monatschrift für die deutsche evangelische Kirche* 1 (May 1934).

[14] For a helpful treatment in English of the story of some of these individuals who had ambivalent attitudes toward the German Christians and the National Socialists, see Ericksen, *Theologians under Hitler*; Jack Forstman, *Christian Faith in Dark Times: Theological Conflicts in the Shadow of Hitler* (Louisville, Ky: Westminster/John Knox Press, 1992).

[15] For a highly personal account of Rudolf J. Siebert's own participation in the Catholic underground in Germany, among other things, see "The Gospel according to Rudy Siebert," *Encore: Magazine of the Arts* [University of Western Michigan, Kalamazoo] (March 1984), 5-15. Siebert has also published an account of the life and thought of his friend and pastor Georg Rudolphi: *Recht, Macht und Liebe: Georg W. Rudolphi's Prophetische Politische Theologie* (Frankfurt am Main: Haag und Herchen, 1993).

[16] Scholder, *The Churches and the Third Reich,* 2:104.

[17] Ibid., 2:189ff.

[18] It is interesting (and relevant for the positions they took in 1933) that in 1925 Barth and Tillich each lectured on dogmatics, Barth in Göttingen and Tillich in Marburg. What they had in common was their rehabilitation of the term *dogmatics,* following its demise in nineteenth-century liberal theology. Troeltsch, in contrast, had earlier for his lectures deliberately chosen the word *Glaubenslehre* over *dogmatics* to avoid the ontological, metaphysical, and heteronomous tone of the latter. Tillich and Barth differed, however, in how they viewed dogmatics. For Barth, it was strictly a churchly enterprise; for Tillich, it was a larger philosophical-theological and "foundationalist" discipline. See A. James Reimer, "Truth and Revelation in Tillich's 1925 Dogmatics," *Truth and History—A Dialogue with Paul Tillich/Wahrheit und Geschichte—Ein Dialog mit Paul Tillich* (Berlin: Walter de Gruyter, 1998), 227-38.

[19] For an analysis of the relationship between these two thinkers and their theological-political debates, see the following works by A. James Reimer: *The Emanuel Hirsch and Paul Tillich Debate*; "Theological Method and Political Ethics: The Paul Tillich-Emanuel Hirsch Debate," *Journal of the American Academy of Religion* 47, Supplement (March 1979), 171-82; "Theological Stringency and Political Engagement," *Studies in Religion/ Sciences Religieuses* 16, no. 3 (1987), 331-45; "The Kingdom of God in the Thought of Emanuel Hirsch and Paul Tillich," *New Creation or Eternal Now/Neue Schöpfung oder ewiges Jetzt,* ed. Gert Hunnel (Berlin: Walter de Gruyter, 1991), 44-56; "Tillich, Hirsch and Barth; Three Different Paradigms of Theology and Its Relations to the Sciences," *Natural Theology versus Theology of Nature?/Natürliche Theologie versus Theologie der Natur?* (Berlin: Walter de Gruyter, 1994), 101-24.

[20] See Scholder, 175; Gunda Schneider-Flume, "Kritische Theologie contra theologisch-politischen Offenbarungslauben: Eine Strukturanalyse der politischen Theologie Paul Tillichs, Emanuel Hirsch und Richard Shaulls," *Evangelische Theologie* 33, no. 2 (March-April 1973), 114-37.

[21] "Autobiographical Reflections," *The Theology of Paul Tillich*, ed. Charles W. Kegely and Robert W. Bretall (New York: Macmillan, 1964), 14.

²² For biographical details of these and other events leading up to Tillich's departure to America, see Marion and Wilhelm Pauck, *Paul Tillich: His Life and Thought,* vol. 1 (New York: Harper & Row, 1976); and Hannah Tillich, *From Time to Time* (New York: Stein and Day Publishers, 1974).

²³ For a thorough treatment of Tillich's retrieval of the myth of origin into his socialist thinking, see A. James Reimer, "Nation and the Myth of Origin in Paul Tillich's Radical Social Thought," *Consensus: A Canadian Lutheran Journal of Theology* 14, no. 2 (1988), 35-48.

²⁴ Pauck, *Paul Tillich,* 135-38.

²⁵ Reprinted in *The German Church Conflict by Karl Barth,* ed. A. M. Allchin, Martin E. Marty, T. H. L. Parker (London: Lutterworth Press, 1965), 16.

²⁶ Allchin et al., *The German Church Conflict,* 25.

²⁷ Ibid., 31-32.

²⁸ See Friedrich Wilhelm Graf, "Kulturprotestantismus: Zur Begriffsgeschichte einer theologiepolitischen Chiffre," in *Kulturprotestantismus,* ed. Hans Martin Müller (Gütersloher Verlagshaus Gerd Mohn, 1992), 21-77.

²⁹ See *Dietrich Bonhoeffer: Witness to Jesus Christ,* ed. John de Gruchy (Minneapolis, Minn.: Fortress Press, 1991), 124.

³⁰ For some of the details of Bonhoeffer's life and views in relation to the Jews, and particularly on the shift that took place in his thinking in this regard, I am indebted to an unpublished paper of a graduate student of mine: Catherine L. Snider, "Dietrich Bonhoeffer and the Jews: An Historical/Theological Investigation in Search of His Meaning and Relevance for the Contemporary Jewish-Christian Dialogue" (a paper submitted for my course, "The German Church's Response to Fascism," Toronto School of Theology, Fall 1995).

³¹ Selections of each can be found in de Gruchy, *Dietrich Bonhoeffer,* 43-72, 72-97, respectively.

³² This was a speech he gave at the ecumenical Youth Conference in Czechoslovakia on July 26, 1932 (de Gruchy, *Dietrich Bonhoeffer,* 101).

³³ See de Gruchy, *Dietrich Bonhoeffer,* 156-77, 221-55, respectively.

³⁴ Snider, "Dietrich Bonhoeffer and the Jews," 15.

³⁵ Ibid., 26.

³⁶ An article written from an evangelical perspective, "Adjusting Theology in the Shadow of Auschwitz: Does the Holocaust Change the Context for Christian Evangelization of the Jews?" by Kenneth A. Myers, illustrates the wide range of conflicting views on the subject (*Christianity Today* [October 8, 1990], 41-43).

7

The Holocaust

Theological and Ethical Reflections

ROSEMARY RADFORD RUETHER

In the midst of the Second World War, Adolf Hitler, leader of the German people, conducted a systematic campaign to exterminate European Jewry. This genocidal campaign was directed at all Jews, on the basis of what was presumed to be a shared racial nature. It did not matter if the Jew was male or female, infant or elderly, culturally assimilated or set apart by traditional Jewish way of life, secular or religious. Even if the Jew was a convert to Christianity did not finally matter. For Nazi ideology, a Jew was a Jew. All belonged to one racial nature, which Nazism regarded as inimical to the national "purity" of the Aryan race.

This crusade of redemption through genocide almost succeeded. Six million Jews were annihilated. This meant not only more than one-third of the Jews of the world at that time, but also 90 percent of the rabbis and religious scholars of Eastern and Western European Judaism. The Holocaust pulled up an entire culture by the roots. The Nazi Holocaust was more than the killing of a large number of individuals. It was ethnocide, the effort to destroy a people as a cultural entity.

This enormity happened in the "heartland" of Western Christian Europe: the land of Goethe, Beethoven, and Mozart; of Kant, Hegel, and Schelling; of the founders of modern Christian theology, Schleiermacher, Ritschl, and Troeltsch. Germany was the center of the Christian Enlightenment, from which flowed the classics of modern European literature and music, philosophy, theology, and biblical studies. It happened with the passive acquiescence or active collaboration of most European Christians, and with no decisive protest from church leadership, Catholic or Protestant.

Individual Christians sought to save their Jewish neighbors at the risk of their own lives, but official church leadership did not mobilize in united protest. Even the Confessing Church in Germany, under the intrepid

leadership of theologians like Karl Barth and Dietrich Bonhoeffer, primarily protested against a Nazi "cultural Christianity" and failed to focus on
Nazi anti-semitism as an issue.[1]

For both Jews and Christians in the postwar period, the Holocaust throws
the viability of their religious traditions into question, but in quite different
ways. Yet it took more than two decades for theological reflection on the
Holocaust to begin to be articulated, for Jews and some Christians to recognize that theological business as usual could not continue after this fissure
had opened up in the world.

Perhaps before there could be Holocaust theology, the Holocaust had to
be articulated as story. Meaningless chaos must be shaped as meaning, even
if only as the meaning of meaninglessness, the speaking about the unspeak-
able. Translating the Holocaust into story was founded by Elie Wiesel, whose
first book, *Night*, was published in Yiddish in 1956 and became available in
French in 1958 and in English in 1960.

The first Jewish religious thinker to name the Holocaust as a crisis for
traditional Jewish theology was Richard Rubenstein in the mid-1960s.
Rubenstein, a non-establishment Jewish religious scholar, published his foundational book, *After Auschwitz: Radical Theology and Contemporary Judaism*, in
1966. In this volume Rubenstein questioned the very possibility of faith in
God after the Holocaust.

Emil Fackenheim, a German Jew transplanted to Canada courtesy of
British internment camps for German refugees, had been writing primarily
on Hegel and religious philosophy, with no reference to the Holocaust. As
he himself admits in an article in the *Christian Century* in May 1970, before
1967 he was "at work on a theology that sought to show that nothing unprecedented could call into question the Jewish faith—that it is essentially
immune to all secular events between Sinai and the Messianic days."[2]
Fackenheim took up Rubenstein's challenge and began to write about the
possibility of religious faith after the Holocaust.

Rubenstein, in a reply to this article by Fackenheim, also published in
the *Christian Century*, said that Fackenheim was the first Jewish theologian
to "agree with me concerning the unique and decisive character of
Auschwitz for Jewish religious life." Rubenstein said "at the time I wrote
After Auschwitz, one could search through almost everything written by
contemporary establishment (Jewish) theologians without finding the slight-
est hint that they were living in the same century as Auschwitz or the rebirth of Israel."[3]

By the early 1970s the Holocaust had become a key theme of theological
reflection for Jewish and Christian theologians. In 1974 a major conference, held at St. John the Divine Cathedral in New York City, brought together the leading Jewish and Christian thinkers who had made the Holocaust a central lens for revisioning their religious traditions.[4] For Jews,
particularly for American Reform Jews, the Holocaust would become the
new normative theology, central to modern Jewish identity.

The Holocaust challenged traditional Jewish and Christian religious self-understandings in quite different ways. For Jews, the central question posed by the Holocaust was theodicy. If the God who elected Israel as his people is in charge of the world, how could such an event take place? Is faith in the God of Jewish election still possible after Auschwitz? If not, what is the nature of Jewish collective identity?

For Christianity, the issue was not the existence or goodness of God, but the redemptive value of Christianity. If Christianity played a major role in fomenting the Holocaust, how can Christians continue to affirm its redemptive nature? This culpability rested not only with individual Christians, but with key Christian doctrines. Christology was thrown into question. If faith in Jesus as Christ, the Messiah of Israel, had become a major ideological factor in promoting anti-Judaism in Christian cultures and societies, is such a belief still tenable?

Irving Greenberg, writing in the mid-1970s, sought to assess the challenges to both traditional Jewish theology and traditional Christian theology by the Holocaust. Both Judaism and Christianity are religions of redemption. Both hope that the evils of human history will be finally overcome by divine redemptive action. Both base their hopes that life will win over death, good over evil, on foundational paradigms of redemption in the past that shape subsequent ways of life and self-understanding.

For the Jews, the foundational paradigmatic event is the exodus from slavery in Egypt and the giving of the covenant on Sinai. For Christians, it is Easter, the revelation of the resurrection of the Crucified One. In the light of Easter, the crucifixion is remembered, not as meaningless evil, but as an act of divine atonement for human sin. Both religions insulate themselves from further crises of meaning or revelations of God by living between this foundational paradigm and the expected fulfillment of messianic deliverance at the end of history.

The Holocaust challenges both of these Jewish and Christian strategies of insulation from history. For Jews, the Holocaust threatens the basic faith in a God who has entered into a covenant with the Jewish people. There can be no covenant, if there is no covenant people. There can be no God of the covenant if that God could will or allow the people of the covenant to be exterminated.

But the Holocaust offers an even more devastating challenge to Christianity, for Christians have not been innocent victims but collaborators with the Holocaust. Christianity was the major source of the "teaching of contempt" for Jews and Judaism that was translated into secular terms by Nazi racial anti-semitism.

Christianity did not only hope for a future deliverance from evil, but believed that it had already received the down payment on the messianic advent in Jesus's death and resurrection. But if Christianity can use its faith in Christ to foment hatred against Jews, leading to pogroms and to Nazi-attempted genocide, its claims to possess the beginnings of redemption through this same Christ have lost credibility. Belief in Jesus as the Christ has become a font of evil, not the beginning of redemption.[5]

Greenberg also perceives in the Holocaust a challenge to modern secular messianisms as well, the redemptive claims of the Enlightenment, of scientific rationalism and liberal universalism. These secular gods of modern civilization failed in the death camps. The claims of progress through science and technology were turned into a means for racist destruction. Science provided the tools for mass murder.

The failure of human projects of redemption, religious and secular, is experienced as an absence of the divine presence in the modern world. We live in the time of the silence of God. For Greenberg, this divine absence and silence does not justify a denial of God's existence. We have entered into a time of profound silence that no longer knows how to speak adequately about God. The test of adequate language about God has become the burning children of the crematoria. Today any statement about God or about religious truth must be tested by the light of the burning children. Any religious statement that cannot be uttered in the presence of these innocent victims cannot be uttered at all.

For Greenberg, the Holocaust has shattered all certainties about how God is acting in history. Today we can only have "moment faiths" that spring from the tentative human acts of redemptive concern. New ways of speaking about God must grow experimentally from such concrete human redemptive acts. Greenberg wishes to speak cautiously of what such acts are. Humans have to demonstrate by real actions on behalf of life that faith in human goodness is still possible. Through building up signs of commitment to life, one can begin to posit that there is a divine life and goodness that is stronger than evil and violence.

Greenberg sought to balance concern for the state of Israel with concern for Jews in the diaspora, concerns for Jews with concerns for humanity as a whole. Both religious and secular cultures have to seek to overcome the denigrating stereotypes that denied full and equal human dignity to one another. "This," Greenberg says, "is the overriding command and essential criterion of religious existence today," not to create another matrix of intergroup hostility that could lead to another genocide. Only by joining together in the work of rehabilitation of the image of God in the face of other human beings can we also rehabilitate the presence of God in our midst in history.[6]

Other less traditional Jewish religious thinkers who had come out of the antiwar movement of the 1960s, such as civil rights activist turned religious thinker Arthur Waskow, sought to make connections between the Holocaust and the threat of nuclear war. Waskow seeks to restate the moral and mystical connection between Jewish particularity and universal humanity by seeing the Jewish people as a paradigmatic people who have gone ahead of the rest of humanity and tested the threat of annihilation that now looms over all humanity in nuclear war. The Jewish victims call all people into solidarity to avoid the "fire next time" that will destroy us all.[7]

On the Christian side, church bodies, both Catholic and Protestant, have felt the need to respond collectively to the Holocaust. During the Second Vatican Council, in the early 1960s, there was a major discussion of how the Holocaust must impel Catholic Christianity to take a critical look at its heritage of anti-Judaism. In the document on the relation of the Catholic church to other religions, the section on relations to the Jewish people specifically repudiated the ancient Christian charge of deicide. The death of Jesus was the particular responsibility of certain Jews and Gentiles in the first century. It is also a paradigm of all humanity's apostasy from God. But there can be no inference from the death of Jesus of any special or inheritable guilt of all Jews.[8]

Protestant responses to the Holocaust have focused on the question of mission to the Jews. This was central to the statement of the German Evangelical Church issued in 1975.[9] This statement confessed the historical complicity of Christianity with anti-semitism. It also made a link between anti-semitism and anti-Zionism. Not only must Christians oppose anti-semitism in their own nations, but they must also support the independence and security of the state of Israel.

Such support for the state of Israel is not simply a recognition of a human need of the Jewish people, like all people, for a secure homeland, but it is an event in the salvation history of the people of God. The return of the Jews to their national homeland is a fulfillment of prophecy and the beginning of redemption.[10] Yet this German Christian statement did not reject mission to the Jews but remained committed to the idea that full salvation for the Jews awaits their conversion to Christ.

A number of Christian denominations have developed statements on Jewish-Christian relations that seek to repudiate anti-semitism and have revised educational programs and liturgical and catechetical materials to purge their teachings of negativity to Jews and Judaism.[11] Yet such purges of anti-semitism in Christian thought have generally not seen the Christian view of God present in Christ as deeply shaken by such revisions.

For those Christian theologians who have taken the Holocaust and the critique of Christian anti-Judaism as central themes of their thought, the issue of Christology has been the critical problem. Is it possible to continue to believe that Jesus is the Christ, the fulfillment of the Jewish hopes for the Messiah, and yet purge Christianity of anti-semitism?

In the book I published in 1974, *Faith and Fratricide: The Theological Roots of Anti-Semitism,* the question of Christology was central.[12] Is it possible to affirm that Jesus is the Christ without at the same time teaching a negated and supersessionary relation to Judaism, as an incomplete faith that has failed to accept its own "fulfillment" in Christ? In that book I defined anti-semitism as the "left hand" of Christology. The negation of Judaism is the shadow side of the affirmation that Jesus is the Christ. This relation goes back to the earliest roots of Christian faith. The two are interwoven already in the New Testament.[13]

Christian symbolism constructed a series of negations of Jews and Judaism: Judaism as the "old" covenant, superseded by the church as the new covenant; Judaism as an ethnic particularistic religion, superseded by Christianity as a universal, inclusive religion; Judaism as outward letter, as external conformity to law, in contrast to Christianity as spirit, as obedience to God informed by inward spiritual power or "grace." In each of these theological dualisms Christian self-affirmation of its superior and higher spiritual status is built on a corresponding negation of Judaism as its incomplete or even antithetical "other."

Christian purgation of anti-semitism must grapple with these patterns of thought. Christology in particular must be rethought. Faith in Jesus' messianic identity must be defined as proleptic and contextually limited, not as absolute, universal, final, and fulfilled. We can affirm the truth of the hope of that prophetic announcer of God's coming redemption. But fulfillment, overcoming of violence and injustice, are as much ahead of us today as they were ahead of that Jewish teacher two thousand years ago. Christians as much as Jews struggle with an unresolved history, holding on to our past paradigmatic experience as the basis of our hope that evil will not have the last word and God will win in the end.

But it is not enough simply to admit that salvation is incomplete. Christians must also accept the contextually limited relevance of their theological symbols and the historical experiences on which they are based. Remembering Jesus, his life and death, are the paradigms drawn from our interpreted experience that mediate hope in the midst of adversity to us. But this does not mean that they are the only paradigms that may do this. Other people with other collective memories continue their struggle for redemption on other grounds, namely Jews, for whom Jesus' life, death, and anticipated coming again did not become the normative paradigm and who continue to found themselves efficaciously on the Exodus and the Torah as their memory and their Way.

Several other Christian writers have made the revision of Christology, in the light of the Holocaust, central to their writings. One example of this rethinking is the writings of Roy and Alice Eckardt, in books such as *Long Night's Journey into Day: Life and Faith after the Holocaust* and *Jews and Christians: The Contemporary Meeting*.[14] For the Eckardts, a full and adequate Christian response to the Holocaust necessitates fundamental revisions in the interpretation of Christian teachings. All notions that Judaism has either an inferior understanding of ethics or an incomplete capacity to redeem vis-à-vis Christianity must be decisively rejected.

The Eckardts believe that Christianity must rethink the basic understanding of Jesus' resurrection and the claim that Jesus is the Messiah of Israel. Jesus cannot be said to have fulfilled Israel's messianic hope because the world is still unredeemed.[15] The Eckardts take seriously the Jewish view that the coming of the Messiah does not refer simply to a changed spiritual relation to God, but to a decisive shift in human relations that begins the conquest of historical evil. Since this obviously has not happened, it is impossible and indeed meaningless to say that the Messiah has already come.

Jewish rejection of Jesus as Messiah is not unfaithfulness, but faithfulness to the God and to the understanding of the messianic advent of their tradition. Jews have remained faithful both to the one covenant that God made with them and also to a realistic and holistic understanding of redemption. This understanding of redemption does not split the spiritual from the physical, the personal from the political, as Christianity has generally done. This is a central insight that Christianity needs to learn from its Jewish "elder brother." It is key to understanding the importance of the state of Israel for contemporary Jewish identity, both religious and secular.

The Eckardts do not make absolutist claims for a relationship of Jewish peoplehood to a divinely given land in Palestine. All human claims to land are partial and relative. While seeking to avoid "territorial fundamentalism," the Eckardts typically characterize any criticism of the policies of the state of Israel, whether from Palestinians or other Arabs, or from Christian peace activists, such as Quakers, as motivated by anti-semitism. They see all criticism of Israel as springing from a hostility to Jewish empowerment and self-determination.[16]

A somewhat different view of the state of Israel is taken by Franklin Littell, whose long commitment to struggle against Christian anti-semitism is expressed in his book *The Crucifixion of the Jews*.[17] Littell's theology springs from the Anabaptist free church tradition of radical rejection of church-state amalgamation.[18] The church is a community set apart from the state to witness to an alternative, redemptive lifestyle of God's messianic age. This kingdom lifestyle is characterized by pacifism, egalitarianism, and communal sharing.

Littell uses this Anabaptist critique of Christendom in his battle against Christian anti-semitism. He was influenced in this particularly by the Barthian theological attack on German Christianity as "culture Christianity." However, these free church principles come out oddly in Littell's thought when he turns to the necessity for Christians to give absolute support for Israel as a Jewish state. He sees such a state as an essential component of Jewish identity.

Like the Eckardts, Littell sees Jewish peoplehood as a holistic social and political community, not just a spiritual people divorced from political expression. Littell identifies this communal nature of Judaism with the necessity of a state. Moreover, the right of the Jews to a state is not simply a particular expression of a universal right of all people to a state. Rather, the Jewish people have a unique right to a state on this particular land. God has chosen the Jewish people as a unique community and promised them this particular land. The Jews are set apart from all other people as the only people whose ethnic identity has been mandated by God and who have been given a land in which to express their national identity.[19]

Littell scores any criticism of Israel, whether from Arabs or from Quakers, as anti-semitism. Opposition to a Jewish state is a lingering expression of an ideology that decrees powerlessness and misery for Jews as divine punishment and sees Jewish empowerment as a threat to this ideology.[20] Littell also condemns Islam as an extreme example of a false sacral political order that fuses religion, culture, and state. He claims that Israel as a Jewish state challenges the idea of an Islamic state.[21] It is hard to know what Littell means at this point, if Israel is itself a divinely mandated theocratic state. Islamic states and a Jewish Torah-state would seem more to be rivals in the Middle East, with similar ideas of religious law and theocratic politics.

One of the most systematic efforts to rethink Christian theological claims in the light of a sorry history of Christian anti-semitism has come from Episcopal theologian Paul van Buren. Van Buren has developed a three-volume magnum opus entitled *A Theology of the Jewish-Christian Reality.*[22] Van Buren's theology is deeply shaped by Protestant Neo-orthodox rejection of the liberal universalism of nineteenth-century Enlightenment theologians. Neo-orthodoxy takes the doctrine of original sin with radical seriousness. All human beings are fallen and have lost any natural connection with God. Christological exclusivism is demanded by this human condition. Only through Christ is there authentic revelation of God and redeeming relation to God.[23]

Van Buren transfers this exclusivist view of revelation and redemption to God's covenant with Israel. God has made himself known in only one way, as the God who chose the people Israel as his people.[24] The covenant of God with Israel at Sinai is God's foundational and normative work at the center of the redemption of creation. All other work of God in history flows exclusively from this one elect center where the true God is revealed and creation is being healed from its brokenness. The Gentile, lacking any natural relation to God, is by nature sunk in darkness, both spiritually and morally. Gentiles are the "natural" humans or "pagans."[25]

God is not only the God of Israel, but the creator and redeemer of all nations. God has chosen to reach out to the Gentiles through his covenant with Israel. Israel is called to be God's unique people, walking in the Way of Life that God has given them in the Torah. But Israel is also called to be the light to the nations, to communicate its revelation of God and the healing of the nations to the Gentiles.

The Christian church is this extension of the covenant of God with Israel to the nations. The Christian church is not a "new covenant" of God that supersedes the covenant of God with Israel. That covenant is eternal and unchangeable. Salvation to the Gentiles is a new work of God in history, but in a strictly auxiliary and dependent relation to the sole covenant of God with Israel.[26]

Van Buren rejects the title of Christ for Jesus. Jesus was not the Messiah of Israel.[27] The appropriation of this title for Jesus is an error that manifests how deeply Christianity misinterpreted its own mandate. Jesus is central for Christianity—not as Messiah of Israel or as the basis of a new covenant superseding that of Israel, but as the paradigmatic expression of the extension of the covenant of God with Israel to the Gentiles. Jesus is where Israel is summed up in one person and given to the Gentiles. The Gentiles plug into the covenant of God with Israel through their relation to Jesus as Israel-for-us. While Jesus is central to the salvation of Christians, he is unnecessary for the salvation of Jews, who are the primary possessors of this covenant.[28]

By seeing itself as a "new covenant," superseding the covenant of God with Israel, Christianity cut itself off from its Jewish roots and therefore lost the source of the authentic interpretation of its mission. Christianity responded with hostility when Jews refused to accept this false concept of Jesus as the Messiah and the church as the New Israel, superseding the Jewish people. Such a gospel of Christ could only be rejected by the Jews with a resounding no. This rejection expresses the faithfulness of the Jewish people to its God.

The culmination of Christian self-deception, expressed in hostility to Jews, was the Holocaust, the effort to destroy the Jewish people entirely so that all memory of their negation of a secularized Christian triumphalism could be erased. Van Buren parallels the crucifixion of Christ and the Holocaust, Golgotha and Auschwitz. Both represent the power of Satan, or the evil impulse that resists God's love. But they are also the places where God himself entered into history and was present in the suffering of the faithful man of Israel, Jesus, and in the sufferings of the people of Israel.[29]

The state of Israel is a resurrection sign, the sign that God's faithfulness to life against death perseveres. By aligning itself in solidarity with Jewish remembrance of the six million and in support for the state of Israel, the church participates in this saving hope against the horror of human resistance to God and is recalled to its true identity. God's covenant with Israel includes the Promised Land. The land has been given by God to Israel in perpetuity, whether or not God's people are actually present in it.

No other people, however long they have lived there, have any true right to this land. Jewish presence in the land must take the form of a Jewish state. Such a Jewish state cannot be like other states. It is called to a higher destiny, not only to be an exemplar to all other nations, but also to be the place where creation itself is being healed. The Jewish state is the beginning of the redemption of creation, the overcoming of fallen creation's resistance to God manifest in Golgotha and Auschwitz.

The Jewish state must realize its redemptive nature by becoming a Torah state. This is why Israel cannot be governed by a secular constitution. It is called to take on the full yoke of the Torah as its law in order to fulfill its redemptive task, both for itself and for the healing of creation.[30] By implication this also means encouraging the state of Israel to become fully a theocratic state, where the commandments of Torah are enforced as state law.[31]

The true Jew is the Torah-observant Jew. The non-observant Jew is not only apostate from God's commands but threatens the redemption of creation that flows from Torah observance. Thus it is for the sake, not only of Jews, but of all creation, to encourage Jews to become Torah-observant. Van Buren's ideas of becoming Torah-observant center on things like food and sabbath laws. There is no acknowledgment at all that there is any injustice involved in the relation of the state of Israel to the Palestinians, whom van Buren calls "the strangers in the land."[32]

Christianity should render service to the people Israel, in atonement for its past sins of anti-semitism and also as an expression of its authentic subsidiary relation to Israel, by combating anti-semitism among Gentiles. Christians should also raise money for the defense of the state of Israel and defend Israel against all anti-Zionist criticism.

Although Holocaust theology began to be articulated less than twenty-five years ago, by the end of the 1980s it was heading into an impasse. Its credibility as a fruitful avenue of theological and ethical thought was in jeopardy. It had become too uncritically a tool of Jewish empowerment in the state of Israel and in the United States, discarding any moral critique of the possible misuse of such power.

Christian Holocaust theologians particularly have tended to compensate for anti-semitism by a hyperbolic philo-semitism that is unwilling to admit that Jews in power can be like anyone else in power, namely, abusers of power. Such compensatory philo-semitism betrays an unwillingness on both sides, Jewish and Christian, to accept that Jews are normal human beings, capable, like any other people, of taking power in a dominating way and using it to make victims of other people.

The imagery of former powerlessness and victimization is constantly rehearsed to claim that such use of power is necessary for "survival" and that, without more weapons and more land, "another Holocaust" is around the corner. Anyone who suggests that the time has come to concede human rights and some areas of national self-determination to the Palestinians who remain in the present occupied territories is accused of desiring this future Holocaust and being opposed to the rights of Jews to defend themselves from annihilation.

With the fourth largest army in the world, including nuclear armaments, and fifty years of economic and cultural assault on an unarmed Palestinian people, this rhetoric of survival has lost its credibility. It is time to say *Yesh G'vul*, "there is a limit," the slogan of the Israeli army reservists who refuse to serve in the occupied territories. Jews have had a tragic history of powerlessness and victimization, but this history does not justify the victimization of another people, the Palestinians, a people who have had little to do with that past history of Jewish oppression, but who have become the main victims of Jewish power in Israel.

A Jewish theologian who has sought to find a way forward from this denouement of Holocaust theology is Marc Ellis. In his books Ellis seeks to rescue Holocaust theology from its misuse as a tool of abusive power, particularly in relation to the Palestinian people.[33] Ellis affirms the original insights of Jewish and Christian Holocaust theology. Reflection on the Holocaust led theologians, like Greenberg, to probe the questions of divine power and presence in history and seek ways of affirming life and hope for all threatened human life in universal solidarity.

But, increasingly in the 1980s, Greenberg's thought became focused on the justification of Jewish empowerment as an end in itself, impervious to the possibility of serious ethical failing.[34] Ellis affirms Jewish empowerment as good and necessary to rescue Jews from abject vulnerability. But he asks the Jewish community to take ethical responsibility for the use and abuse of this power, to stop using the rhetoric of past powerlessness to cover up present power and to refuse to face the possibility that they too, like any other people, can become abusers of power.

Ellis sees a parallel between Christian abuse of its theological and political empowerment by victimizing the Jews, and the current Israeli victimization of Palestinians. Just as Christians after Auschwitz can reclaim the moral content of their tradition only through solidarity with the Jewish people, so Jews, both in Israel and in the diaspora, can reclaim the moral basis of their tradition only by reaching out in solidarity with the human and national rights of the Palestinian people. Ellis quotes Catholic theologian Johann-Baptist Metz's statement:

> We Christians can never go back behind Auschwitz. To go beyond Auschwitz, if we see clearly, is impossible for us by ourselves. It is possible only together with the victims of Auschwitz.[35]

Ellis paraphrases this statement for Jews today:

> We Jews can never go back behind empowerment. To go beyond empowerment, if we see clearly, is impossible for us by ourselves. It is possible only with the victims of our empowerment.[36]

Ellis calls for a new framework for Jewish theology capable of a positive future. Holocaust theology, emerging from reflection on the death camps, represents the Jewish people only as they were then, helpless and suffering. But it does not and cannot speak to the people the Jews have become—powerful and often oppressive.

Holocaust theology, Ellis says, spoke radically about the question of God in the midst of a threatened annihilation and argued rightly for Jewish empowerment. But it lacks the framework to face the costs of that empowerment. It has no ethical guidelines for a Jewish state with nuclear weapons, supplying military arms to authoritarian states, such as Guatemala, unjustly expropriating the land and houses of Palestinian peasants, and torturing resisters to the occupation.[37]

The new framework for theology that Ellis delineates is a theology of solidarity with the Palestinian people. This is not simply a generic call for solidarity with all victims. Rather, it demands that people in power take responsibility for the particular victims of their particular power. Jews are not simply to flee back again into general humanitarianism that pays no attention to who they are in particular. Rather, by taking responsibility for who they are as a particular people at this time in history, they also have to take responsibility for that people whom their power has victimized most specifically, namely, the Palestinian people.

This theology of solidarity means a "de-absolutization" of the state of Israel. This is not a disregard or abandonment of the state of Israel by diaspora Jews. Rather, there must be a more mature relationship to it. Israel should be seen as one Jewish community among others. As Jews in the diaspora needed Christians to "de-absolutize" Christian states to make room for their own equal rights as citizens, so in Israel they need to "de-absolutize" the redemptive claims of the Jewish state in order to make room for Palestinian civil rights within Israel and Palestinian national rights alongside Israel's national rights.

As Ellis was defining a post-Holocaust theology of solidarity with the Palestinians, a parallel theology was being developed by Palestinian Christian theologian Naim Ateek. In *Justice and Only Justice: A Palestinian Theology of Liberation,* Ateek showed how militant Zionist use of the Bible as the basis for expropriating Palestinian land has thrown the validity of the Hebrew scripture and its God into question for Palestinian Christians. Palestinians experience themselves as the victims of this God of Israel and can no longer acknowledge this God as their God.[38]

Ateek distinguishes between the ethnocentric and the universalist directions of scripture. He sees the latter as the authentic direction, not only for Christians, but also for the prophetic tradition of Judaism as well. This maturation toward a God of all people, not of one people only, does not lead to generic universalism or Christian triumphalism. Rather, we are called into concrete solidarity between neighbors, each of whom must affirm the other as God's people at the same time that they affirm their own relation to God.

Ateek calls for a sympathetic understanding of the Holocaust among Palestinians. Although the Holocaust does not justify the oppression of Palestinians, nevertheless Palestinians must understand the trauma of this experience for Jews. They must see themselves as needing to make room to share their land with Jews as recompense for this horror, even though Palestinians were not the perpetrators of it. At the same time, Israeli Jews must acknowledge that they have deeply wronged the Palestinian people by expelling them from their land and homes in 1948-49 and, since 1967, by mounting an oppressive occupation over the remaining Palestinian people living in their lands.

Like Ellis, Ateek believes that neither people can go forward by itself. Neither can have the whole of the land or absolutize its claims at the expense of the other. Each has to concede space to live to the other and to be able to forgive each other's past misdeeds. Each has to learn to enter into the perspective of the other. Israelis claim they need security, and Palestinians say they seek justice, but neither security nor justice is possible for one without the other. Israelis need to acknowledge that security for them is possible only through justice to the Palestinians. Palestinians need to realize that justice will be possible for them only through acknowledging Israeli fears and insecurity, even if these fears appear irrational to a disarmed, landless, and stateless people, suffering under Israeli military might.

A post-Holocaust theology, in effect, must critically examine the shadow side of all monistic theologies of liberation and redemption. We must ask, Who is going to be the victim of our liberation? Who is to be enslaved by our redemption? A theology of solidarity beyond the victim-victimizer relation must free itself from the shadow side of its redemptive claims. Whenever the Messiah of one people triumphs only by cursing another people; whenever our promised land is claimed by expropriating the land of an earlier people, whether ancient Canaanites, modern Palestinians, Indians in America, or blacks in South Africa, not only is redemption incomplete, but the seeds have been planted for new evils, new Holocausts.

Christians and Jews, Israelis and Palestinians, must recognize that power construed as domination over others always creates violence, injustice, and hatred. Christians have been amply guilty of this in the past, both toward Jews and toward other peoples whom they have conquered and colonized, and toward each other. The very possibility of power, much less oppressive power, is new to Jews. It is difficult for them to realize that they, too, cannot only gain power but use it unjustly.

Dialogue and solidarity between Christians and Jews today cannot be based solely on the innocent victim–guilty victimizer relation of the remembered pogroms and death camps. It must be a mutually self-critical collaboration of peoples, each of whom knows it is capable of abuse of power. Each is seeking to regain its prophetic voice toward injustice, both in its own society and in relation to the other.

This means that Jews and Christians must overcome their antagonism to Arabs and to Muslim people. They must extend their dialogue to the Muslim world and the Arab people as well, without in any way being blind to the parallel tendencies to violence and competitive domination in that culture.

All such relations must seek a conversion that shifts from an ethic of competitive power, in which the victory of one is possible only through the defeat and humiliation of the other. We must seek a theology and ethic of co-humanity that fosters a quest for mutual justice between neighbors who must learn to live together in one land and on one earth. This quest must curb the tendencies of all three monotheistic faiths to foster triumphalistic self-affirmation through hatred and negation of the others. It must call forth and develop the best of all three religious traditions, Judaism, Christianity and Islam, of compassion, forgiveness, and mutual regard for the neighbor as oneself.

Notes

[1] Arthur C. Cochrane, *The Church's Confession under Hitler* (Philadelphia: Westminster Press, 1962), 206-8.

[2] Emil L. Fackenheim, "The People Israel Lives," *The Christian Century* (May 6, 1970), 563.

[3] Reader's response: Richard Rubenstein, *The Christian Century* (July 29, 1970), 919-21. There was an unconscious irony that this exchange appeared in *The Christian Century*, a magazine named for the idea that the twentieth century would see the universal triumph of Christianity throughout the world.

[4] The Jewish speakers at this conference were Irving Greenberg, Alfred Kazin, Yosef Yerushalmi, Emil Fackenheim, Seymour Siegel, Shlomo Avineri, Paul Jacobs, Milton Himmelfarb, Arthur Waskow, Edith Wyschogrod, Lionel Rubinoff, Paul Ritterband, Charles Silberman, and Elie Wiesel. The Christians were Alan Davies, Rosemary Ruether, Walter Burghardt, Gregory Baum, Johannes Hoekendijk, Aarne Siirala, John Pawlikowski, Claire Huchet-Bishop, Thomas Hopko, Eva Fleischner, Michael Ryan, and Charles Long. Gabriel Habib of the Middle East Council of Churches sent a statement. The talks are printed in *Auschwitz: Beginning of a New Era*, ed. Eva Fleischner (New York: KTAV, 1977).

[5] Irving Greenberg, "Cloud of Smoke, Pillar of Fire: Judaism, Christianity and Modernity after the Holocaust," ibid., 44.

[6] Ibid.

[7] Arthur Waskow, "Between the Fires," *Tikkun* 2, no. 2, 84-86.

[8] "Declaration on the Relationship of the Church to Non-Christian Religions," in *Documents of Vatican II*, ed. Walter Abbott (New York: America Press, 1966), 663-66.

[9] "Rat der Evangelischen Kirche in Deutschland," in *Christen und Juden: Eine Studie des Rates der Evangelischen Kirche in Deutschland* (Gutersloh: Gutersloher Verlagshaus Gerd Mohn, 1975).

[10] For the history and ideology of Christian Zionism, see Regina Sharif, *Non-Jewish Zionism: Its Roots in Western History* (London: Zed Press, 1983). Also Rosemary Ruether and Herman Ruether, *The Wrath of Jonah: The Crisis of Religious Nationalism in the Israeli-Palestinian Conflict* (San Francisco: Harper & Row, 1989), 74-91.

[11] For Christian documents on Jewish-Christian relations published between 1963 and 1976, see *Stepping Stones to Further Jewish-Christian Relations: An Unabridged Collection of Christian Documents*, ed. Helga Croner (London: Stimulus Press, 1977).

[12] Rosemary Radford Ruether, *Faith and Fratricide: The Theological Roots of Anti-Semitism* (New York: Seabury, 1974).

[13] Ibid., 64-66.

[14] Roy and Alice Eckardt, *Long Night's Journey into Day* (Detroit, Mich.: Wayne State University Press, 1982), and *Jews and Christians* (Bloomington, Ind.: Indiana University Press, 1986).

[15] Eckardt, *Long Night's Journey*, 125-33.

[16] Eckardt, *Jews and Christians*, 79-81.

[17] Franklin Littell, *The Crucifixion of the Jews* (New York: Harper & Row, 1975).

[18] Franklin Littell, *The Anabaptist Concept of the Church* (Hartford, Conn.: American Society of Church History, 1952).

[19] Littell, *The Crucifixion of the Jews*, 95-96.

20 Ibid., 88.

21 Ibid., 83-84.

22 Paul van Buren, *A Theology of the Jewish-Christian Reality*, vol. 1, *Discerning the Way* (1980); vol. 2, *A Christian Theology of the People Israel* (1983); vol. 3, *Christ in Context* (1988). All three volumes published by Harper & Row.

23 Karl Barth, *Christ and Adam: Man and Humanity in Romans 5* (New York: Macmillan, 1956).

24 Van Buren, *A Christian Theology of the People Israel*, 70-76, 116-28.

25 Ibid., 350.

26 Ibid., 268-94.

27 Ibid., 33-37.

28 Ibid., 161-62, 195-97.

29 Van Buren, *Christ in Context*, 176-83.

30 Van Buren, *A Christian Theology of the People Israel*, 127-28, 312-13.

31 Most Israeli Jews are secular and fiercely opposed to having a Torah state imposed on them, but this reality doesn't deter van Buren's view.

32 Ibid., 338-41.

33 Marc Ellis's books include *Toward a Jewish Theology of Liberation* (Maryknoll, N.Y.: Orbis Books, 1987; new edition with "Postscript on the Palestinian Uprising and the Future of the Jewish People," 1989); *Beyond Innocence and Redemption: Confronting the Holocaust and Israeli Power* (San Francisco, Calif.; Harper & Row, 1990); *Ending Auschwitz: The Future of Jewish and Christian Life* (Louisville, Ky.: Westminster/John Knox Press, 1994); *An Unholy Alliance: Religion and Atrocity in Our Time* (Minneapolis, Minn.: Fortress Press, 1997).

34 Irving Greenberg, "On the Third Era of Jewish History: Power and Politics," in *Perspectives* (New York: National Jewish Resource Center, 1980); and "The Third Great Cycle of Jewish History," in *Perspectives* (New York: National Jewish Resource Center, 1981). Ellis's critique of Greenberg's more recent views are in his book *Toward a Jewish Theology of Liberation*, 26-36.

35 Johann Baptist Metz, *The Emergent Church: The Future of Christianity in a Postbourgeois World* (New York: Crossroad, 1981), 19; quoted in Ellis, *Toward a Jewish Theology of Liberation*, 24, 123-24.

36 Ellis, *Toward a Jewish Theology of Liberation*, 124.

37 Ibid., 132-36.

38 Naim Ateek, *Justice and Only Justice: A Palestinian Theology of Liberation* (Maryknoll, N.Y.: Orbis Books, 1989).

8

The Golden Years of Welfare Capitalism

The Twilight of the Giants

GARY DORRIEN

The giant figures of twentieth-century Protestant theology were products of the generation that lived through two world wars and the Great Depression. Most of their writings reflected the prevailing mood of crisis and threat under which the bulk of their careers took place. In pointed opposition to the rhetoric of cultural progress and moral optimism that they inherited from their liberal Protestant teachers, theologians such as Karl Barth, Emil Brunner, Friedrich Gogarten, Rudolf Bultmann, Paul Tillich, Dietrich Bonhoeffer, Reinhold Niebuhr, and H. Richard Niebuhr reclaimed the biblical language of sin, redemption, and transcendence for modern theology. The first name that the Barthian or dialectical theology movement acquired in the early 1920s was crisis theology. Barth insisted from the outset that the Great War was merely a symptom, and not the cause, of a pervasive spiritual crisis that liberal theology was too weak and compromised to address.[1] For the next quarter-century the dominant currents of modern Protestant theology resounded with images of collapsing civilizations and tragic dilemmas. Theologians as different as Barth and Tillich spoke of God as transcendent holy mystery or as hidden "wholly other" source of revelation.

In their politics, with significant exceptions, the leading thinkers of the dialectical theology generation were generally democratic socialists committed to realist views of human nature and history. They opposed capitalism and liberal idealism with nearly equal fervor. Tillich forged his early reputation as a theorist of Neo-Marxist religious socialism; Barth joined the Swiss and German Social Democratic parties, respectively, in 1915 and 1931; Brunner grew up in the Swiss Religious Socialist movement, and, even after leaving the movement, continued to condemn capitalism as debased, irresponsible, and anti-Christian; throughout the 1930s, Reinhold Niebuhr railed against the "illusions" of Franklin Roosevelt and the New Deal, claiming that there was no third way between socialist revolution and capitalist barbarism. History will either move forward to a new socialist order or backward to an even more predatory capitalist order, Niebuhr insisted.[2]

By 1941 it appeared that history was moving in the direction of a fascist totalitarianism that was even more backward and barbaric than Niebuhr's depression-era warnings had envisioned. Niebuhr implored pacifist-leaning Protestant church leaders and an isolationist American Congress to face up to the necessity of stopping Hitler from conquering Europe.[3] While insisting that liberal democratic civilization was worth killing and dying for, he lectured that the liberal "children of light" who governed the Western democracies needed to become more realistic about the power of self-interest and the pervasive reality of evil in all social groups. As children of Enlightenment liberalism, he argued, the democratic "children of light" were virtuous in paying respect to moral law, but they tended to be stupid about human evil. By contrast, the fascist and Stalinist "children of darkness" were evil in their disregard of moral law, but they were wise in their understanding of the human will-to-power. This dialectic of idealism and realism yielded Niebuhr's most famous epigram: "Man's capacity for justice makes democracy possible; but man's inclination to injustice makes democracy necessary."[4]

Niebuhr explained that the primary value of democracy is not the idealistic value that democratic leaders routinely invoked. Liberal democracy is worth fighting for not because it fulfills an ideal that people deserve on account of their moral worth. It is worth fighting for because it is the most effective and just way to restrain human evil and will-to-power. From *Moral Man and Immoral Society,* written at the depth of the Great Depression, to *The Children of Light and the Children of Darkness,* written near the end of World War II, Niebuhr pressed this argument as a case for democratic socialism. Just as democracy is needed in the political sphere as a brake on political tyranny, he argued, democracy is needed in the economic sphere as a brake on the overweening will-to-domination of the capitalist class. As late as 1944, Niebuhr could still write that "since economic power, as every other form of social power, is a defensive force when possessed in moderation and a temptation to injustice when it is great enough to give the agent power over others, it would seem that its widest and most equitable distribution would make for the highest degree of justice."[5]

"It would seem" was a signal, however. By the mid-1940s, like many of his theologian friends, Niebuhr was holding onto democratic socialism more from desire than conviction. He still regarded economic democracy as essential to social justice, but he was no longer certain that the social democratic vision of a democratized economic order was attainable. Having ridiculed Roosevelt's "whirligig reformism" as a mere palliative throughout Roosevelt's presidency, in the late 1940s he edged steadily closer to the mainstream New Deal verdict that the highest attainable degree of social justice was attainable only through a liberal welfare-state politics. Having identified socialist economics with a "commanding heights" nationalization strategy, he stopped calling himself a socialist. In 1947 his primary social Christian organization, the Fellowship of Socialist Christians, changed its name to Frontier Fellowship. The same year he folded his chief political organization, the Union for Democratic Action, into a new organization dominated by establishment liberals, the Americans for Democratic Action. Niebuhr and his "Christian realist" comrades entered the mainstream of U.S. politics and devoted themselves to the question of how a triumphant American democracy should exercise its international and domestic power in a morally responsible way. In 1949 Niebuhr remarked that there was "a bare possibility that the kind of pragmatic political program which has been elaborated under the 'New Deal' and the 'Fair Deal' may prove to be a better answer to the problems of justice in a technical age than its critics of either right or left had assumed."[6]

This "possibility" became Niebuhr's guiding political truism in the 1950s. His somewhat reluctant endorsement of welfare-state capitalism tamed his passion for economic justice and his rhetoric about it. Following his lead, Frontier Fellowship changed its name in 1951 to Christian Action and reduced its economic plank to a vague political exhortation "to maintain a high and stable level of economic activity, avoiding inflation and depression."[7] This prescription was compatible with any conceivable Democratic or even Republican economic policy. The following year Niebuhr explained that he no longer thought in terms of general positions regarding capitalism and socialism.[8] He had become a good liberal Democrat. He embraced not only the militant anticommunism of his party's "vital center," but also its pragmatic managerialism with regard to economic power. The right-wing and left-wing enemies of the New Deal continued to think of economic justice in ideological terms, he observed, but the New Dealers established a basically just social order in the United States by thinking and acting pragmatically.

"We have equilibrated power," Niebuhr enthused in 1952. "We have attained a certain equilibrium in economic society by setting organized power against organized power."[9] Against the grain of its still-reigning hyper-capitalist creed, he explained, the United States had created a basically just social order by building up a threefold structure of countervailing labor, capitalist, and governmental power. Welfare-state capitalism was attaining as much of the democratic socialist ideal of social justice as appeared to be attainable. It was creating a just society not by appealing to good will or to moral ideals, but primarily by restraining human egotism through a democratic balance-of-power politics. Niebuhr allowed that his country was still far from being a just society in one area. America's racial situation was still an abysmal failure and disgrace, he conceded. But even here, he believed that postwar New Deal America was on the verge of fulfilling its creedal commitment to maximal freedom and equality. The United States had already achieved degrees of liberty and equality that were "beyond the dreams of any European nation," Niebuhr claimed in 1957. In light of the Supreme Court's 1954 decision barring racial discrimination in public schools and its subsequent recognition of equality as a criterion of justice, he judged that the U.S.'s dilemma over race was "on the way of being resolved." Having prevented the triumph of an intolerable fascist tyranny and having steeled itself for a long struggle of containment warfare against Soviet Communism, postwar America appeared to Niebuhr to be turning "the seeming sentimentality" of its Jeffersonian creed into political reality without exception.[10]

Niebuhr's acute sense of irony, sin, and tragedy saved him from becoming a conventional 1950s "American Celebrant." His writings in the late 1940s and early 1950s were enormously influential in formulating the case for an aggressive anticommunist consensus in U.S. foreign policy, but he also warned unfailingly that every struggle for justice and every fight against tyranny is inevitably corrupted by collective self-interest and the sinful human desire to dominate others. In the later 1950s he also began to regret some of the effect of his work in mythologizing America's Cold War against the Soviet Union. Against the presumed implications of his early Cold War thinking, Niebuhr insisted that Soviet communism was not an immutable monolith, an overpowering enemy, a world-threatening conspiracy, or an enemy with which the United States could not learn to coexist.[11] A decade later he was forced by his country's debacle in Vietnam to further rethink the foreign policy implications of his containment-strategy opposition to communism.

But it was Niebuhr who epitomized the shift in mood and perspective in modern theology that flowed from the outcome of the Great Depression and World War II. In the 1930s, following his lead, a host of Christian theologians and ethicists repudiated Social Gospel idealism, vowing with Augustine that the peace of the world is gained only by strife. John Bennett declared in 1935 that capitalism was plainly not working and that some form of democratic socialism would better serve the common good. "It is the present system which has turned out to be impractical," he urged.[12] A decade later, no major Christian theologian still spoke this way about the crisis of capitalist civilization or the need for a democratic socialist alternative. Nearly the entire U. S. Christian realist movement, including Bennett, followed Niebuhr into the "vital center" Democratic Party establishment. Tillich remained a religious socialist in theory, but he stopped writing about sociopolitical issues. His attention turned to depth psychology, and later to the writing of his massive *Systematic Theology*. Brunner concentrated on dogmatic theology and confined his statements on political economics to vague endorsements of the welfare state.[13] Unlike most North American and West European theologians, Barth refused to provide a Christian endorsement for the West's Cold War against communism; but for the same reason he also gave little attention to political issues in general and none at all to problems in political economy.

The defining political crisis of the "dialectical theology" generation had passed. The losers of World War II and most of the victors worked together to build a new capitalist world order and a host of new international institutions devoted to economic development and security. Any prophetic inklings that West European or North American theologians may have felt during this period were stifled by the mood of the times and the sense of threat engendered by an expansionist Soviet enemy. The threatening character of the Cold War deterred religious thinkers from pressing strong critiques of Western capitalist inequality or imperialism. Postwar debates about how Christian theology should relate to sociopolitical issues were pervaded by the politics of the Cold War. Perhaps the most significant debates of this kind took place between Barth and Niebuhr.

In 1948 Barth gave the opening address at the inaugural assembly of the World Council of Churches in Amsterdam. The theme of the conference was "The Disorder of the World and God's Design," but Barth protested immediately that this order was backward. He urged the newfound World Council of Churches not to begin by speaking of the world's disorder, nor by speaking of whatever social or even religious measures that it hoped would solve the world's problems. The place from which Christian speech about the world must begin is God's kingdom, he countered, "which has already come, is already victorious, and is already set up in all its majesty." The world's churches needed to begin "with our Lord Jesus Christ, who has already robbed sin and death, the devil and hell of their power."[14]

Much of the WCC's preconference literature was secular and politicized by comparison. Barth reported that these documents gave him "the same strange impression as garments of deep mourning." He called the World Council of Churches to come out of its mourning. Christians are called to be God's witnesses, he urged; they are not called to be God's lawyers or managers or engineers. The conference literature was long on Christian plans to rebuild and reform the postwar world, but Barth countered that "God's design" is not "something like a Christian Marshall Plan." It is not the business of the church to straighten out the world, he exhorted. The churches are called to confess and remain mindful that the world belongs to God. Put differently, Barth admonished, the church is not the world's caretaker. The church is rather the body of God's children that is called to trust in God and proclaim God's victory over sin and live according to God's way.[15]

To Barth's disappointment and surprise, Niebuhr took strong exception to this prescription. In the United States it was commonplace to link Barth and Niebuhr together as proponents of a theologically "Neo-orthodox" and ethically realist alternative to liberal idealism. Though Barth recognized that he and Niebuhr were far apart theologically, he presumed that they shared essentially the same critique of the moralistic reformism that informed much of the WCC's preparatory literature.[16] For all of his scorn for liberal Christian pacifism and moralism, however, Niebuhr was still essentially a product of the North American Social Gospel tradition. He still believed that the church is called to use its power and persuasive force to promote world order, freedom, and social justice. His Christian realism rejected the moralistic idealism that most Social Gospelers took for granted, but he took for granted the Social Gospel assumption that the church is called to help bring about the right ordering of the world.[17]

Niebuhr was therefore appalled by Barth's assertion that Christians have no business accommodating the gospel faith to the axioms of modern secular thought. He protested that Barth's otherworldly evangelicalism negated the church's capacity to defend Christian belief from its modern critics. He added that it also made Barth's ethical thinking seriously deficient. Niebuhr did not dispute that Barth's vigorous opposition to pro-Nazi German Christianity during the German crisis of the 1930s had given "a very powerful witness to Christ." The problem was that Barth's theology seemed to provide no moral guidance for Christian statespeople in normal times. "It can fight the devil if he shows both horns and both cloven feet," Niebuhr explained. "But it refuses to make discriminating judgments about good and evil if the devil shows only one horn or the half of a cloven foot." To Barth it was axiomatic that the church has no business seeking to fulfill or accommodate any of the promises of the modern cultural enterprise, but to Niebuhr it was axiomatic that "the Christian must explore every promise and every limit of the cultural enterprise."[18]

This debate had a Cold War subtext. By 1948 Barth had made it clear that he did not endorse the West's Cold War against communism in the name of Christianity.[19] In pointed opposition to Brunner, who urged that Christian churches were obliged in principle to oppose communist totalitarianism with the same militant fervor that they had aroused against Nazi totalitarianism, Barth insisted that the two cases were dissimilar from a Christian standpoint. From the standpoint of a *Christian* ethic, he argued, it was not pertinent whether communist "totalitarianism" was structurally similar to fascist "totalitarianism." There is no such thing as a Christian political system, he explained. The church does not rightly sacralize or condemn political systems as such. It does not properly concern itself with ideologies, and therefore it does not speak "on principle" about the legitimacy or illegitimacy of political systems as such. In Barth's view, the church had no business anathematizing the Communist political system as such because it had no business making "principled" judgments that identified Christ with or that excluded Christ from any political ideology.[20]

Brunner objected that Barth passionately condemned the Hitler regime in the name of Christ and called for its overthrow, but Barth replied that it was not on the basis of any political principle that he had done so. As much as he despised National Socialism, he explained, what made Nazism different was its power to overwhelm and corrupt Christian souls. Nazism was an evil religion that subverted the soul of the German church. Niebuhr later claimed that Soviet communism was also, in effect, an evil religion, but Barth sharply dissented from the judgment that communism was religiously corrupting.[21] The German church nearly lost its soul to Nazism, he reasoned, but where was the spiritual threat that communism posed to North American or West European churches? That is, in the countries where church leaders were calling for "Christian" crusades against communism, where was the spiritual threat to the church that the truth of an anticommunist crusade might extinguish? "Are they not already sure enough of the justice of their cause against Russia without this truth and our Christian support?" Barth asked. He left the implication between the lines. In light of the overwhelming economic and military power of the United States, the existence of a militantly "Christian anticommunism" was not a spiritually healthy phenomenon.[22]

On various occasions afterward Barth spelled out the implication, sometimes infuriating Christian anticommunists like Niebuhr and Brunner. In 1958 he declared, "I regard anticommunism as a matter of principle an evil even greater than communism itself."[23] The following year, after an East German pastor asked Barth if he should pray for the abolition of the Communist government in East Germany, Barth cautioned the pastor to beware that such a prayer "might be awfully answered, so that some morning you would wake up among those 'Egyptian fleshpots,' as one obligated to the 'American way of life.'" He advised the pastor that it would be better for him to pray for the East German government than against it. He cautioned that from a Christian standpoint, the ascendance of a dreadful Communist government in East Germany had to be regarded in some sense as the rod of divine punishment. Barth's various writings on this subject always emphasized that historically, communism was an unwelcome but natural product of Western developments. He believed that the Western nations had only begun to pay the full price for Western imperialism and war.[24]

This was never the heart of the matter for Barth, however. For him the crucial issue was always the question of who sits in the seat of judgment. Barth urged that the only judge who should be taken seriously is the gracious and merciful God who wills that all people—"Christians and the whole of mankind"—should be saved. Because God is surely above all things, he urged, God was certainly above "the legalistic totalitarianism of your state." As a system of political rule, he judged, communism was limited precisely by its godlessness and inhumanity. Barth predicted that "one day its officeholders will halt at those limits, or else they will be destroyed." In either case, he reasoned, communism was not sustainable and not worth the spiritual price of committing the church to anticommunism. The church is not called to support or to force anyone to accept any particular political system:

"She can only follow Jesus; that is, she cannot but keep her sights constantly fixed on the merciful God and on man who is to receive God's mercy and be set free."[25]

Niebuhr took Barth's "Egyptian fleshpot" crack about the American way of life as a sneering cheap shot. He took Barth's Christian neutralism as a provocation. He shot back that the East Germans surely had been no more sinful than their West German kin. If the East Germans were suffering for their sins, how was one to account for the immunity of West Germany? Niebuhr allowed that for the most part Barth did adhere to "the strategy of approximating divine impartiality" to which he aspired. He recalled that in the days of the Nazis, Barth dared to make "hazardous detailed judgments" on a regular basis, but now it was only on a rare occasion that Barth's "robust humanity" so betrayed him. Now Barth desperately aspired to be impartial, like God. "The price of this desperation is of course moral irrelevance," Niebuhr declared. Barth's pursuit of prophetic purity was necessarily a pursuit of moral irrelevance. Niebuhr did not grant, however, that Barth had actually attained pure impartiality in his moral judgments. He judged that Barth's writings were still loaded with "merely human political" sentiments, such as, most notably, his animus against the United States. He also believed that Barth overestimated his prophetic stature. These points built up to a vintage Niebuhr verdict: "Barth is a man of talent to the point of genius. But even a genius cannot escape the dilemma that the price of absolute purity is irrelevance and that the price of relevance is the possible betrayal of capricious human loves and hates even in the heart of a man of God."[26]

Protestant theology in the late 1950s lived off the massive achievements of the Barth and Niebuhr generation. A younger generation of theologians assumed that it was their generational task to update and refine the monumental theological legacies of Barth, Niebuhr, Tillich, Brunner, Bultmann, and Bonhoeffer. Young Jürgen Moltmann judged that Barth had already said nearly everything worth saying. Theologians such as Thomas F. Torrance and Helmut Gollwitzer also pursued their work along Barthian lines. Schubert Ogden and John Macquarrie made cases for Bultmannian demythologizing and existential interpretation. Various young theologians sought to mediate the differences between major figures. Langdon Gilkey proposed to synthesize the work of Niebuhr and Tillich. Hermann Diem and James D. Smart looked for a third way between Barth and Bultmann, while Heinrich Ott sought a way station between Barth and Bonhoeffer. William Hordern defended a North American–style Neo-orthodoxy that drew from Barth, Brunner, Niebuhr, and Tillich. A dominant school of Christian realists proposed to carry on Niebuhr's style of theological ethics. Against the "early Heidegger" existentialist emphasis of the Bultmann school, Gerhard Ebeling and Ernst Fuchs advanced a post-Bultmannian "new hermeneutics" that drew heavily upon Heidegger's language-oriented later thinking.[27] Gilkey later spoke for many of these thinkers in describing their generational self-understanding: "We saw ourselves a generation of 'scholastics' whose function would be to work out in greater detail the firm theological principles already forged for us," he explained in 1965. "We knew from our teachers what theology was, what its principles and starting point were, how to go about it."[28] Theology in the last third of the twentieth century would presumably synthesize and refine the Barth-to-Niebuhr theologies.

But this is not what happened. In the mid-1960s, mainline Protestant theologians in North America and much of Western Europe still thought of themselves as theoreticians of a dominant religious establishment, or at least as representatives of an academic elite within it. Creative new works by Moltmann and Wolfhart Pannenberg gave the appearance that the next generation of Protestant theologians was prepared to sustain the field-dominating influence and public standing of its teachers. The material basis of this self-understanding began to seriously erode in North America during the mid-1960s, however, just as it had already eroded in the European democracies. Sharp declines in church membership and participation rates began to diminish the cultural authority and public visibility of mainline North American churches. With the erosion of Protestant institutions that began during the mid-1960s, mainline Protestant theology lost its presumed centrality and much of its public audience. The emblematic works of this period, most notably John A. T. Robinson's *Honest to God* and Harvey Cox's *The Secular City,* tried to put a positive spin on the apparently deepening secularization of West European and North American societies.

At the same time, the Roman Catholic Church dramatically opened its doors to the modern world and, shortly afterward, a host of new liberationist movements proclaimed that all of the dominant Neo-orthodox and liberal theologies of the past generation were implicated in the very structures of oppression that needed to be overthrown.

The regnant Neo-orthodox establishment that Gilkey had taken for granted in his early career was brushed aside by an explosion of liberationist, feminist, and other politically radicalized theologies that took little instruction from the dominant theologies of the previous generation. The modernization of Roman Catholicism and the rise of liberation theology movements disabused mainline Protestant theologians of the presumption that such terms as *critical* and *modern* applied only to their tradition. Mainline Protestantism continued to produce highly significant work—especially by Moltmann, Gilkey, and Pannenberg—but the public impact of Protestant theology in any form, even at its best, began to compare poorly to the level of public attention that the writings of Gilkey's teachers (Tillich and Niebuhr) had routinely received. Among the generation of Protestant theologians who began their careers in the 1960s, only Moltmann attained a comparable international prominence. The successors of Barth, Tillich, and Niebuhr no longer spoke for a presumed religious establishment or even an academic elite within it.

Theology in the liberationist era became too pluralized to exalt or privilege the works of system-building Protestant synthesizers. Schubert Ogden's 1959 monograph on Bultmann, *Christ without Myth*, was a seminal work in its time, but when Ogden introduced a new edition of the book nearly twenty years later, he acknowledged that it belonged to a bygone era of theological reflection. Modern theology was no longer preoccupied with the modernist problem of myth interpretation, he explained. Liberation theology was much more concerned with the fact that most people in the world "still do not share in the benefits of modernity." This was still a modernist way of framing the issue, but Ogden's reflection at least signaled his recognition that a profound change in religious consciousness was occurring. He acknowledged that the argument of his book was not only dated but severely limited by the global way in which it made pronouncements about "modern man" and "the theological situation."[29] This concession implicitly identified the key to the rhetorical power of the liberationist and feminist movements. Liberation theology movements outstripped the liberal and Neo-orthodox Protestant traditions in the later 1960s because they gave voice to the concerns and experiences of previously silenced religious communities. In its liberationist modes, Christian theology not only privileged the question of social justice but also insisted that theology must speak in a plurality of voices.

The latter was a novel theme for modern Protestant and Catholic theology. Mainline Protestantism prized its liberal spirit during its hegemonic era, but it did not view pluralism as a positive value or a desirable condition. In the late 1940s, an anxious U.S. Protestant establishment viewed a rising U.S. Catholic population with considerable foreboding. The boundaries of mainline Protestant tolerance extended, often grudgingly, beyond mainline Protestantism, but the boundaries of its ecumenism did not. Few ecumenical Protestant theologians placed the Roman Catholic Church within their ecumenical purview. In 1948, the founder and longtime editor of the *Christian Century*, Charles Clayton Morrison, warned against the "illusion" that genuine ecumenism had anything to do with Protestant-Catholic dialogue or cooperation. "Protestantism cannot cooperate ecclesiastically with a dictatorship," he insisted. "It must make a clear-cut decision to accept its task of winning America to Christ without any illusion that it has a collaborator in Roman Catholicism." For Morrison, realism began with the recognition that a great struggle for America's soul was being waged by competing Protestant, Catholic, and secularizing social forces, and that each of these forces was incompatible with the other two.[30]

Many mainline Protestant leaders routinely said the same thing with nicer words. And some used even harsher words. At the founding convention of the World Council of Churches, Anglican archbishop Michael Ramsey reflected that it was perhaps a good thing that the Catholic church was not represented at Amsterdam, because the absence of Rome reminded the ecumenical World Councilers "that we are merely fragments and not the true church." This was a nice way of holding out hope for better ecumenical relations between Rome and the Protestant churches, but Barth sharply rejected Ramsey's underlying sentiment. Despite his numerous friendships with Catholic scholars and church leaders, Barth claimed to feel no regrets at all that the Vatican had spurned ecumenical relations with the Protestant churches. He pronounced at Amsterdam, "I am also glad that Rome is not here because it is a pseudo-church which worships itself."[31]

Like many Protestant theologians and church leaders of his generation, Barth's adversarial posture toward Catholicism softened after Vatican Council II reformulated church teaching on a host of divisive issues. Especially significant among these statements were the historic *Decree on Ecumenism (Unitatis redintegratio)* in 1964, which recognized Protestant churches as "separated brethren"; the *Declaration on the Relation of the Church to Non-Christian Religions (Nostra aetate)* in 1965, which acknowledged the existence of grace and truth in other world religions; the *Dogmatic Constitution on Divine Revelation (Dei verbum)* in 1965, which emphasized the divine and human (historically conditioned) character of the scriptural witness; the *Declaration on Religious Liberty (Dignitatis humanae)* in 1965, which proclaimed the church's support for religious freedom; and the *Pastoral Constitution on the Church in the Modern World (Gaudium et spes)* in 1965, which inaugurated a major shift in the church's relation to the struggles of oppressed people in third-world countries. Reform movements set into motion by Vatican II significantly influenced the development of liberation theology and inspired the formation of diocesan peace-and-justice commissions throughout the Catholic world. Though the decision to convene Vatican II was made entirely by Pope John XXIII, the extraordinary achievements of this council were made possible by a generation of Catholic religious thinkers whose work laid the theoretical foundations for the council's rethinking of official Catholic teaching pertaining to biblical criticism, the doctrine of revelation, liturgical reform, Christian ecumenism, world religious pluralism, relations between church and state, and the social meaning of the gospel.

The Vatican Council was prepared, accompanied, and further explored by a series of open-minded, ecumenically oriented Catholic theologians in dialogue with modern thought, such as Yves Congar, Jean Danielou, Marie-Dominique Chenu, Henri de Lubac, Karl Rahner, Bernard Lonergan, Hans Urs von Balthasar, Edward Schillebeeckx, and John Courtney Murray. These theologians effected a renaissance in modern Catholic thinking during the period that mainline Protestant theology lost much of its creative edge.

Notes

[1] Karl Barth, *The Epistle to the Romans*, 6th ed., trans. Edwyn C. Hoskyns (London: Oxford University Press, 1975 <1933>), 28.

[2] See Paul Tillich, "Basic Principles of Religious Socialism" (1923), and "Religious Socialism" (1930), reprinted in Tillich, *Political Expectation*, trans. James Luther Adams and Victor Nuovo (New York: Harper & Row, 1971), 40-57, 58-88; Tillich, *The Socialist*

Decision, (1932), trans. Franklin Sherman (New York: Harper & Row, 1977); Emil Brunner, *The Divine Imperative* (1932), trans. Olive Wyon (Philadelphia: Westminster Press, 1947), 423; Reinhold Niebuhr, *Reflections on the End of an Era* (New York: Scribner's, 1934); Niebuhr,"The Blindness of Liberalism," *Radical Religion* 1 (Autumn 1936), 4; Niebuhr, "Roosevelt's Merry-Go-Round," *Radical Religion* 3 (Spring 1938), 4; Niebuhr, "New Deal Medicine," *Radical Religion* 4 (Spring 1939), 1-2.

[3] See Reinhold Niebuhr, *Christianity and Power Politics* (New York: Scribner's, 1940; reprinted by Archon Books, 1969); Niebuhr, "Christian Moralism in America," *Radical Religion* 5 (1940), 16-19; Niebuhr, "An Open Letter," *Christianity and Society* 5 (Summer 1940), 30-33; Niebuhr, "To Prevent the Triumph of an Intolerable Tyranny," *The Christian Century* 57 (December 18, 1940), 1580-81.

[4] Reinhold Niebuhr, *The Children of Light and the Children of Darkness: A Vindication of Democracy and a Critique of Its Traditional Defense* (New York: Scribner's, 1944), xi.

[5] Ibid., 113-14. See Reinhold Niebuhr, *Moral Man and Immoral Society: A Study in Ethics and Politics* (New York: Scribner's, 1932); Niebuhr, "The Creed of Modern Christian Socialists," *Radical Religion* 3 (Spring 1938), 16.

[6] Reinhold Niebuhr, "Plutocracy and World Responsibilities," *Christianity and Society* 14 (Autumn 1949), 7-8. See Reinhold Niebuhr, "Frontier Fellowship," *Christianity and Society* 13 (Autumn 1948), 4. For his account of the formation and politics of Americans for Democratic Action, see Reinhold Niebuhr, "The Organization of the Liberal Movement," *Christianity and Society* 12 (Spring 1947), 8-10.

[7] Reinhold Niebuhr and others, "Christian Action Statement of Purpose," *Christianity and Crisis* 11 (October 1, 1951), 126.

[8] Reinhold Niebuhr, "The Anomaly of European Socialism," *Yale Review* 42 (December 1952), 166-67.

[9] Reinhold Niebuhr, *The Irony of American History* (New York: Scribner's, 1952), 101.

[10] Reinhold Niebuhr, *Pious and Secular America* (New York: Scribner's, 1958), 76.

[11] Reinhold Niebuhr, "Uneasy Peace or Catastrophe," *Christianity and Crisis* 18 (April 28, 1958), 54-55. See Niebuhr, *The Structure of Nations and Empires: A Study of Recurring Patterns and Problems of the Political Order in Relation to the Unique Problems of the Nuclear Age* (New York: Scribner's, 1959), 282-83. For his early Cold War thinking, see Niebuhr, *Christian Realism and Political Problems* (New York: Scribner's, 1953), 33-42; Niebuhr, "Communism and the Protestant Clergy," *Look* 17 (November 17, 1953), 37-38; Niebuhr, "The Peril of Complacency in Our Nation," *Christianity and Crisis* 14 (February 8, 1954), 1.

[12] John C. Bennett, *Social Salvation: A Religious Approach to the Problems of Social Change* (New York: Scribner's, 1935), 133.

[13] See John C. Bennett, *Christian Realism* (New York: Scribner's, 1952); Emil Brunner, *Justice and the Social Order,* trans. Mary Hottinger (New York: Harper & Brothers, 1945), 175-183. On postwar "vital center" liberalism, see Arthur M. Schlesinger Jr., *The Vital Center: The Politics of Freedom* (Boston: Houghton Mifflin, 1949).

[14] Karl Barth, "Amsterdamer Fragen und Antworten," *Theologische Existenz heute* 15 (1949), 3-4. An edited version of this speech featuring a somewhat problematic translation by the World Council of Churches staff was published under the title, "No Christian Marshall Plan," in *The Christian Century* 65 (December 8, 1948), 1331.

[15] Ibid., 4-7.

[16] See Karl Barth, "Continental *vs.* Anglo-Saxon Theology: A Preliminary Reply to Reinhold Niebuhr," *The Christian Century* 66 (February 16, 1949), 201.

[17] For extensive discussions of these themes, see Gary Dorrien, *Soul in Society: The Making and Renewal of Social Christianity* (Minneapolis, Minn.: Fortress Press, 1995), 84-161, 308-10, 343-50.

[18] Reinhold Niebuhr, "We Are Men and Not God," *The Christian Century* 65 (October 27, 1948), 1138-40.

[19] See Karl Barth, "The Christian Community in the Midst of Political Change," trans. Stanley Godman and E. M. Delacour (1948), reprinted in Barth, *Against the Stream: Shorter Post-War Writings, 1946-52* (London: SCM Press, 1954), 51-105.

[20] See Karl Barth, "Karl Barth's Reply," reprinted in Barth, *Against the Stream,* 114-15. See Emil Brunner, "An Open Letter to Karl Barth," reprinted in ibid., 106-13; Reinhold Niebuhr, "An Answer to Karl Barth," *The Christian Century* 66 (February 23, 1949), 234.

[21] See Niebuhr, *Christian Realism and Political Problems,* 37-42; Niebuhr, *The Irony of American History,* 128-29.

[22] Barth, "Karl Barth's Reply," 116-118.

[23] Karl Barth, "How My Mind Has Changed" (1958), reprinted in Barth, *How I Changed My Mind* (Richmond, Va.: John Knox Press, 1966), 66. See Barth, "The Church between East and West" (1949), reprinted in Barth, *Against the Stream,* 127-46.

[24] Karl Barth, "Karl Barth's Own Words: Excerpts from the Swiss Theologian's Letter to an East German Pastor," *The Christian Century* 76 (March 25, 1959), trans. RoseMarie Oswald Barth, 353-55. On Barth's theme regarding communism as a product of modern Western history, see also "How My Mind Has Changed" (1958), 63-65.

[25] Barth, "Karl Barth's Own Words," 354-55.

[26] Reinhold Niebuhr, "Barth's East German Letter," *The Christian Century* 76 (February 11, 1959), 167-68.

[27] See Moltmann's interview with Teofilo Cabestrero in Teofilo Cabestrero, ed., *Faith: Conversations with Contemporary Theologians* (Maryknoll, N.Y.: Orbis Books, 1980), 121-22; and Moltmann's exchange of letters with Barth reprinted in Jürgen Fangmeier and Hinrich Stoevesandt, eds., *Karl Barth Letters, 1961-1968,* trans. Geoffrey W. Bromiley (Grand Rapids, Mich.: Eerdmans, 1981), 348-49.

[28] Langdon Gilkey, "Dissolution and Reconstruction in Theology," *The Christian Century* 82 (February 3, 1965), 135.

[29] Schubert Ogden, "Afterward—1978," *Christ without Myth: A Study Based on the Theology of Rudolf Bultmann* (Dallas, Tex.: SMU Press, 1979), 184.

[30] Charles Clayton Morrison, *Can Protestantism Win America?* (New York: Harper & Brothers, 1948), 1, 85-87.

[31] Barth, quoted in Reinhold Niebuhr's letter to Ursula Niebuhr, August 22, 1948, reprinted in Ursula M. Niebuhr, ed., *Remembering Reinhold Niebuhr: Letters of Reinhold and Ursula M. Niebuhr* (San Francisco: HarperSanFrancisco, 1991), 260.

9

Emergence of a World Church
and the Irruption of the Poor

VIRGILIO ELIZONDO

Many factors coalesced providentially to mark the emergence of a world church. The most important actor to be mentioned in the Catholic church is, in my opinion, Pope John XXIII. He asked the missionary bishops to Asia and Africa to resign in favor of having native Christians named as bishops, as pastors of their local communities, thus initiating the end of a European–North American Catholicism claiming global status, domination, and control. This policy had, unfortunately, no effect in Latin America, since the local bishops born on that continent were the descendants of the white European colonizers, so that the notion of "native" did not include the original natives or the Africans who had been imported as slaves.

When John XXIII convoked Vatican Council II, it became evident to the casual observer that this was truly a world assembly. It was the first such assembly of the Catholic church. It was not perfect; it was still dominated by European and North American Christian thought. I know of no native American bishop or theologian who participated. Nor were there bishops or theologians from the Native American, Latino, or African minorities of the United States. Yet the council was the beginning of the breakthrough

Several issues of the review *Concilium* are dedicated to this topic. The main ones are *Theologies of the Third World: Convergences and Differences*, no. 5 (1988); *Tensions between the Churches of the First World and the Third World*, no. 4 (1981); *Different Theologies, Common Responsibility*, no. 1 (1984); *Christianity and Cultures*, no. 2 (1994); *World Catechism: Unity and Diversity in the Churches*, no. 4 (1989); *Transgression of Borders and New Identities* (1999). *Dictionary of Mission*, ed. Karl Müller (Maryknoll, N.Y.: Orbis Books, 1997) deals with the present topic in such articles as "African Theology," "Chinese Theology," "Colonialism," "Ecumenical Association of Third World Theologians," "Filipino Theology," "Globalization," "Inculturation," "Japanese Theology," "Korean Theology," "Latin American Theology," and "Liberation Theology."

from a European–North American church to a pluri-cultural and pluri-centered world church.

Vatican Council II, in its participants, deliberations, documents, and spirit, set the stage for the emergence of a world church. It was the starting point for a new Pentecost, a holy spark that released a set of movements toward the creation of a truly global community of believers.

At the time of Vatican II, the Catholic church of North America was at its high point of development. It had emerged out of the immigrant experience, out of the migration of the millions of poor Catholics of Europe who had come to America with their priests and nuns, with their national parishes and Catholic schools, to share in the great American Dream. Vocations were at an all-time high, and the church appeared to be doing well in every respect. John Kennedy had been elected the first Catholic president of the United States, and nothing seemed to be wrong, nothing seemed to need fixing. Some of the U.S. bishops thought the council would be completed in a few weeks!

It was not quite so with the rest of the world. John XXIII wanted the council fathers to speak openly about the pains and expectations of modern society. It was to be a pastoral council concerned with the spiritual and social problems people experienced in their lives. Most participants came to the council with a deep awareness of the failures of historical and contemporary Christianity, but also with great expectations for the present and the future, provided the church was willing to renew itself in radical and refreshing ways. It should come as no surprise that the preparatory documents prepared by the Roman Curia were rejected by the pastor-bishops of the world as inadequate to the need for authentic renewal.

The European council fathers came with the painful and shameful consciousness of how Christians had killed each other in the two world wars of the twentieth century. Never had the world known such horror and cruelty, and it came out of the heart of Christendom. Even deeper was the pain of the Holocaust—how Christians throughout Europe had remained silent as millions of Jews, Gypsies, homosexuals, and handicapped people were systematically killed. It was a Christian land, the United States, that had first exploded the atomic bomb, killing thousands of innocent lives in an instant. How did all this fit in with the Christian mandate to "love one another"? Old Christian Europe was giving way to communism, secularism, atheism, or simply total religious indifference. There were great Christian theological faculties throughout Europe with the best of scholars, but what difference had they made in the greatest madness the world had ever known?

But this was not the only failure of Western Christianity. This point was made strongly by Christian voices from the other continents. Colonial missionary Christianity had accompanied the conquering, colonizing, and dominating powers of Europe in the great European expansion that had started in 1492. It had sanctioned the conquest of peoples and lands, destroyed great civilizations, and participated in the massive African slave trade.

Europe and its Christian religion became a world-dominating power, much more than the liberating good news of Jesus Christ. Christian Europe set itself up as the norm for all humanity, all races, all civilizations, all religions. Western Christianity absolutized itself as the one and only form of authentic Christianity. This is not to say that it ceased to contain elements of evangelical truth, but this truth had become so encased in Western forms and categories that it hid and even distorted the true universality of the gospel. The particularity of Western Christianity was thus declared and imposed as universal civilization and religion.

Europe had been sending missionaries to Latin America, Africa, Asia, and Oceania. By 1775, two-thirds of the world population was under European colonial domination![1] By the time of the Second Vatican Council, some burning questions began to be raised: Were the missionaries true messengers of the gospel, or had they acted more as agents of cultural and political colonization and domination? Had they in effect legitimized and even sacralized the colonial enterprise of Europe while thinking they were leading people to Christ? Had they enslaved and crushed bodies in favor of saving souls? Had they destroyed rather than liberated ancient cultures and traditions? In spite of their often heroic and sincere efforts, had they in effect been agents of the deepest type of violence—the destruction of the spiritual soul of a people? Missionaries had been among the greatest representatives of the Christian world, but to what had they really converted people—to the Jesus of the gospels or the religion and culture of the West?

In spite of the limitations and negative aspects of the great missionary expansion into the various continents of the world, the gospel came through. Regardless of how it is handed on, the gospel has a life-giving power of its own. People throughout these lands accepted the gospel freely and often at great personal cost,[2] and the seeds of evangelical new life started to take root in the various continents. It would take a few centuries for the gospel to flourish in the new soil and for the native local churches to achieve maturity, acquire their own ecclesial identity, and provide their own theological reflection. It is never easy to break away from the tutelage of the parents and begin one's own life, to move from complete dependence to a new interdependence. But it is a necessary part of the process of maturation. Today, the churches of the South are beginning their new adventure as mature churches. With the migrations from the South to the nations of the North, these churches are also bringing new faith expressions to the old churches. The parent churches are often uncomfortable with this new relationship and, like any parent, find it difficult to appreciate that their children have come of age and are now forging their own life, not abandoning the parents, but relating to them in a new way. This new way that the local churches in the South are relating to the old church is creating a pluri-centered church. This process is just beginning, yet it is already exciting.

The Irruption of the Poor

The Catholic church could brag about the incredible miracle of the evangelization of Latin America—an entire continent has been evangelized by zealous missionaries and now calls itself Christian. Christianity has indeed penetrated the collective and individual soul of Latin America. At the same time, this success is also a great scandal: the great sin of a Christian continent, the great sin of the Catholic church, the great sin of Catholic education, the great sin of Christian leaders. On the continent that considers itself Catholic, the dehumanizing and death-bearing structures of poverty, oppression, and deprivation established by Christian Europe and continued by its descendants in the New World, are truly colossal. In general, the Catholic church has been known for its prestige Catholic schools for the elites of society and for its absence from the masses of the poor. The preaching and teaching of the church legitimized and maintained the status quo. Because the rich were not given a sense of social responsibility in Latin American Catholicism, there are today extremely rich people on this continent with no sense of philanthropy whatsoever. The great majority of priests and religious could be found among the rich, while a minority, usually foreign missionaries, were thinly scattered among the poor. Yes, there were beautiful colonial churches, magnificent cathedrals, original religious expressions of the people, and a rich and deep spirituality, but the hunger and misery of the masses cried to heaven for rectification.

Even deeper was the scandal that the Afro Latin Americans, Amerindians, mulattos, and dark-skinned mestizos throughout North, Central, and South America were excluded systematically from the ranks of the clergy, religious, and academics. They had no voice in the life and ministry of the church: their customs, rituals, and symbols had no place in the official worship of the God of Western religion.

Responding to the council's mandate that churches be attentive to the dreams and aspirations of their people and become of service in the development of humanity, the Latin American bishops convoked the now famous Medellín Conference of 1968. It came in the wake of Vatican II, but more important still, it came at the end of the 1960s, a period of profound social and economic upheaval bringing to light the massive and ever-escalating levels of poverty and violent repression. This was a human and Christian scandal! Young bishops like Dom Hélder Câmara of Brazil, Manuel Larrain of Chile, Sergio Mendez Arceo of Mexico, along with young theologians and social scientists who had just returned from advanced studies with the avant-garde of European thinkers were starting to speak of the unjust and sinful roots of this systemic poverty. For the first time in the church's history, the question of poverty, the structural causes of poverty, and more important still, the poor themselves as subjects of their history became the central focus of a major church assembly of bishops, religious, theologians, and pastors.

I dare to say that the transformative impact of the Medellín Conference on the church's pastoral practice and theology was far greater than that exercised by any other council of the church. No dogmas or confessions of faith were questioned or challenged—Protestant or Catholic. Instead, the whole edifice of Constantinian Christian thought, imagery, and symbolism was radically challenged in the name of Christianity itself. What was initiated was not a new academic or philosophical theology, but rather the transformation of the very structures and methods of doing theology. To be faithful and authentic, Christian theology will have to emerge out of the spiritual experience of the believing community grappling with its history and responding to its contemporary situation. In the learned theologies of the West, the poor and unschooled were left out: their task was to listen and to learn. In the new Latin American context, the poor and unschooled were becoming the privileged subjects of the theological process. The people wrestling with their daily challenges now began to reflect critically on the meaning of their faith. An evangelical instinct grounded in faith enables people to know whether the gospel preached to them serves love and justice or is drained of its salvific power.

In fidelity to the spirit of Vatican II, the church of Latin America challenged itself and the entire church. For the first time, the poor became the central focus and primary subject of theological reflection. At issue here was not voluntary poverty, but the scandalous reality of misery, filth, disease, abuse, exploitation, malnutrition, abandonment of children and elderly, and other dreadful consequences of the massive death-bearing poverty of Latin America.

How can Christians preach salvation and fellowship in a world subjected to material damnation by Christians ruling society? As Dom Hélder Câmara, the great prophet of Latin America, has stated: The Europeans and their descendants have "institutionalized the violence" that continues to reign over Latin America. Sin is not just personal; it has become an intimate and integral dimension of all the structures of society, including those of the churches. The descendants of the white European colonizers have continued to escalate the structures of oppression and widen the gap between rich and poor. While the churches of Europe and North America anguish about secularism, modernity, and the relation between faith and reason, the churches in Latin America anguish about the dehumanization of the masses. How can anyone talk about God when millions of human beings are treated as non-persons by economic exploitation, political repression, and exclusion from full participation in the church's life?

Gustavo Gutiérrez speaks of the masses of the poor of Latin America as those who die long before their time because of hunger, disease, fatigue, oppression, and massacre. Enrique Dussel speaks of them as those absent from history: no history book makes mention of their misery and suffering, and when they are hunted and killed, nobody takes notice. Ignacio Ellacuría and Jon Sobrino spoke of them as the crucified peoples of the world. The cries of the poor are the deepest expression of a humanity in search of the God of life. Who but those deprived of the most basic conditions of human life can better know the God who alone sustains them in life—abandoned as they are by everyone else. Since God alone guards them and keeps them alive, they have deep insights into the God of life that are hidden and unsuspected by those who trust other resources and who therefore leave God on the periphery of their lives.

The Second Vatican Council reaffirmed the biblical teaching that the church is the people of God, a priestly people of all baptized believers and not just the academically educated. All share in the task of theological reflection. All must scrutinize the signs of the times in the light of scripture and tradition to discover God's holy will for the present. The poor may not be excluded from this task. Since they see better than others the prison from which humanity is to be freed, and hence have a better grasp of God's redemptive will and power, they are in a privileged position for hearing God's word. Since the biblical books record the faith experiences of the poor, the oppressed, and the landless, who better than today's *apiru*, today's nameless and homeless, can gain a deeper understanding of the message of salvation? "God has chosen what is foolish in the world to shame the wise, God has chosen the weak in the world to shame the strong, God has chosen what is low and despised in the world . . . to bring to nothing things that are" (1 Cor 1:27-28).

The greatest achievement of Medellín was the initiation into this new pastoral and theological process. It opened the way for the masses of the poor (especially through the Christian Base Communities and the popular expressions of the faith) to become actively involved in the life and ministry of the church, the development of new art and music, and especially the process of theological reflection. Gustavo Gutiérrez often said that theology is too important to leave to theologians alone. I would add that ritual is also too important to leave to the discretion of liturgists alone. Theological reflection and liturgical celebration belong to the people of God. Experts should help but not dominate or impose. The people, especially the poor, are no longer just to sit and listen; they are to think, explore, judge, and act. This has led to a simple but profound way of doing theology, revealing the power of the Bible to transform the existing order. Academic theology published in books and articles is but a weak echo of the exciting and life-giving theologizing process that is going on among grass-roots communities. Gustavo Gutiérrez often mentions that the professional theologians of Latin America are but scratching the surface of what faith reflection is bringing forth among the people.

The process of theological reflection begins when the assembled people examine their life situation with its burdens and unrealized possibilities. From the perspective of this concrete reality, they read and discuss the biblical text. Enlightened by the divine word, they then reread their life situation and opt for the course of pastoral action to be followed. Out of their praxis they have reflected on the biblical text, and out of this reflection they now commit themselves to a renewed praxis. A professional theologian accompanying the people must never dominate but simply clarify and amplify the ideas proposed. Here is a true community of teachers and learners created by the Spirit, each one listening carefully to the other as they gradually approach a common understanding. Through the professional, the group is linked to the wider church, and through the assembled group the professional becomes rooted in a living community of faith. We have here a mutually enriching relationship.

The theological voices of the poor and marginalized are still largely ignored by professional theologians at the great centers of learning. At best, they consider these ideas useful reflection for local communities in the hinterland. European and North American theologians tend to look at Latin American theology as regional, while they consider their own as universal. But the specific, scandalous truth of the poor of Chiapas, the Amazon, the *favellas* of Brazil and the altiplano of Bolivia has a universal message addressed to all Christians. The local truth calls upon the whole world to recognize a people in its particular identity and struggle. Theological reflection of this kind is as particular and universal as that of a Hans Küng of Tübingen, a David Tracy of Chicago, or a professor at the Pontifical Gregorian University in Rome.

The Decolonization of the Church

If Medellín and Latin America have become known for the preferential option for the poor, Asia and Africa are becoming known for a preferential option for the poor linked with a preferential option for the heritage and spirituality of the ancestors. Voices from Asia and Africa are saying that geography, culture, and spirituality can be enriched by the gospel, but that they must never be annihilated by its Western messengers. Christians in the former colonies want to be Christians, but they do not want Western religion to be imposed upon them. By being Christian, they do not want to become aliens among their own people. Nor do they want to abandon the ways in which God had spoken to their people for thousands of years in favor of a religion brought by Western imperialism.[3]

The first great movement for independence from colonial domination took place throughout Latin America between 1810 and 1830. Yet since it was the children of the European colonizers who claimed independence from their mother countries, Spain and Portugal, there was no attempt at racial, cultural, and religious decolonization. White superiority continued to be imposed throughout Latin America, even to the present times. The first stages of Latin American liberation theology were concerned exclusively with political and economic liberation, without paying attention to the ethnic subjugation of Amerindians, Afro-Latin Americans, mulattos, and dark-skinned mestizos. Nor were they concerned with issues emerging from gender and culture. Now women in Latin America have raised their voices offering theological reflection on liberation from the patriarchal structures of church and society.[4] And as the poor are speaking out from within their own reality, the deep issues of culture and ethnicity have started to emerge. The ancient (pre-Columbian) religions and traditions of the native Amerindians and Africans in Latin America have started to emerge at the periphery of Latin American theology.

The second great movement of independence and decolonization that took place after World War II in Asia and Africa moved the focus of attention to theological questions of race and ethnicity, spirituality and culture, and the gospel's relation to the world religions. Participants from these continents came to Vatican Council II full of enthusiasm and pride in the new awareness of their communities. Practices that had previously been ridiculed by well-intended and hard-working but ignorant and self-righteous Western missionaries were now being recognized as honored traditions and sacred wisdom. The particularity of Western "universality" became unmasked as just that: a particular cultural expression, not reflecting universality, or worse, sanctioning the enslavement of non-Western peoples and the massive destruction of whole civilizations. The universalized particularity of the West had betrayed the true universality of Christianity! The time of conversion had arrived.

What Medellín was to Latin America, the All India Seminar of 1969 was to Asia, and the African General Synod on Evangelization of 1974 was to Africa. Medellín dealt with poverty, Asia with the salvific relationship to other religions, and Africa with ancestral traditions and rituals. Each continent offered new challenges and possibilities for the creation of an authentic, pluri-centered world church, a truly universal fellowship. Names like Gustavo Gutiérrez, D. S. Amalorpavadass, and Meinrad Hegba started to emerge as the new theological teachers for the Christian world. Each speaking out of his own particularity offered something to the universal fellowship, not by claiming to be universal but by acknowledging the uniqueness of his situation. These men, soon to be followed by women,[5] were pioneering movements of thought that are presently challenging and enriching the entire field of Christian worship and theological reflection.

Africa had suffered the worst, but now it would begin to resurrect with the strongest force possible. Africa had not only been pillaged more than any other continent, but thirty million of its people had been abducted and sent to the New World to be sold into slavery. Christian theologians and philosophers had elaborated the eighteenth-century "doctrine" according to which Africans were the accursed children of Ham whose punishment was to be slaves of the whites. Blackness was equated with inferiority, ugliness, and sin. Whiteness as the sign of full humanness and virtue was so interiorized by the Africans that many of them longed to become white.[6]

The 1960s were a great time for the African church. Not only were the African countries experiencing independence, but their own thought was beginning to irrupt with a great sense of pride and self-confidence. Black is beautiful, and Africa is human! African Christians were multiplying faster than anywhere else on the planet, and native African religious, priests, bishops, and theologians also were increasing at a fast rate. Africans would not be Christians of buildings, doctrines, and rules but of cheerful singing, dancing, emotion, and spontaneity. Europeans had become scared of bodily expression, while the Africans were natural in expressing the deepest spiritual experience through the totality of their body and soul. African spirituality could well liberate the imprisoned bodies of the West, paralyzed by fear of spontaneity.

The new Christian vitality in Africa was, of course, much more than song and dance. It reclaimed many ways of the ancestors that had not been respected by the missionaries. It reaffirmed a way of knowledge that privileged personal and collective stories over abstract definitions. It rediscovered the long tradition of African achievements and heroes, which had long been buried. It reevaluated in critical fashion social traditions of the West that had been imposed as Christian ethics. It retrieved the world of the Spirit, the living spirit of a tree, a flower, a river, and an animal, which the Western world had ignored or looked upon as superstition. African Christians also wanted to end the opposition between Christian priest and local healer.

As an authentic African Christianity emerged, so did Asian Christianity. Asia is the most populated continent, but it is the least Christian. Christians live there not only as a minority, but as one of the younger religious traditions alongside more ancient and more popular ones. Christians are surrounded by people practicing Hinduism, Buddhism, Confucianism, and Shintoism. Christians have discovered that Asians take these religions as seriously as Christians do their own faith and that these religions offer spiritual paths leading to good, holy, and life-giving values, often closer to the gospel than Western values. Many of the older Christians of Asia had to go through the painful experience of abandoning everything that had been sacred to their families in order to become Christians.[7] Honest and critical Asians are quick to ask Christians how the gospel relates to political domination and uncontrolled capitalism practiced by Christian nations. Asians also observe that becoming Christian often means eating flesh, drinking alcohol, and ceasing to honor one's parents. So what does Christianity have to offer the great religions of Asia, and what do they have to offer Christianity?

Asian Christians want to be Christians in freedom, but they also want to be Asian and partake of the spiritual treasures of the religions practiced by their ancestors and the majority of their contemporaries. The ancient religions are essential elements of the cultural fiber of Asian countries. One cannot totally abandon them, even if one wanted to, and remain Asian. Hence the important issue raised in Asia is the role of Christianity among the other great world religions. This poses difficult questions to a religion that has previously claimed exclusive possession of truth and salvation and imposed this claim upon others through conquest and colonization more than through witness and the practice of love. Can Christianity stand on its own merits, or does it need material power, political or financial, to impose and defend it? The history of recent centuries suggests that the Christian religion of the West can spread and flourish only if sustained by material force. This is an issue that touches the essence of Christian faith and demands reappraisal of what is meant by the universality of Christian salvation.

For Asians, the spirituality of Christianity is more important than dogmas defined and explained in Western rational categories. Christianity must be seen and experienced as a spiritual force. Asian Christian theologians argue that alongside the great religions of their continent, Christianity cannot continue to claim to be the one and only true religion. It is definitely a true religion, but God is ever greater and God's presence has revealed itself through other spiritual traditions. Reflection on the story of Noah and God's covenant made with humanity (Gn 9:1-17) suggests that the growth and development of diverse cultures with their own religious traditions correspond to the great blessing pronounced by God after the flood. Because of God's universal will to save (1 Tm 2:4), it is unthinkable that God would exclude entire continents from divine love and care. Vatican II has acknowledged that "God did not abandon humans after the Fall, but ceaselessly offered them helps of salvation."[8] God gifted each people with a specific wisdom and revelation. As the Christian scriptures are a source of divine revelation, so too in their way are the scriptures of the world religions.

Asian theologians wrestle with the question of what the universality of salvation in Christ means in view of this new recognition. They are convinced that the Incarnation, God becoming human, did not intend to eliminate what makes people concretely human, namely, their particular cultural and religious identity. They hold, therefore, that the gospel of salvation does not invalidate the great religious traditions but aims at purifying and enriching them, as it intends to purify and enrich the Christian religion of the Western world.

This bold theological interpretation does not deny that Jesus is the universal savior of the world. The very particularity of the Jesus event is seen as the manifestation of infinite love introducing a new kind of universality, one that does not destroy particularities but enriches them. The new commandment that we are to love one another as God has loved us summons forth this new universality in practical terms. Not by dogmas or confessions of faith do we do justice to Jesus of Nazareth, but by unconditional love extended to others, to all others, beyond the inherited divisions created by gender, race, class, culture, and religion.[9] In Jesus Christ the walls that divide humanity are torn down. The old understanding of universality—the universality of a particular religion—is giving way to new understanding— the universality of divine love acknowledging the worth, beauty, and dignity of every human being and every human culture. Christian witness does not call upon people to convert to the ways of the church but to believe that a new and truly universal love is possible, is available as a great gift, and is a joyful and exciting experience. This love, Christians believe, has been brought by Christ.

Prayerful, critical, and creative dialogue with the great religions of Asia has led Asian Christian thinkers to new theological insights into the mystery of God and God's revelation. Out of the continent where Christians are a minority, new light is emerging capable of enriching, liberating, and expanding the deepest notions of Western Christianity, on the condition that this Christianity is willing to abandon its theological arrogance, take on the mind and heart of Jesus Christ, and empty itself of its quasi-divine status so as to become one among others. No longer the dominating and controlling parent, but the loving sister and brother willing to struggle for love and wisdom together with the rest of the human family.

Human beings have in common that they are religious and that their religion defines the deepest aspects of their personal and collective identity. Must this fact create a radical opposition among humans, making them blood enemies of one another? This is what happened in the past and, in some parts of the world, continues to happen now. There is nothing bloodier than religious wars. Today's task and challenge of salvation is to begin the construction of the living mosaic of world religions, each one in its particularity enriching the others. This is a new way of understanding difference. As Christians try to renew their religious practice by returning to the essential message of their faith, so do the members of other religions seek greater fidelity to the deepest inspiration of their own traditions. At this time no religion is as faithful as it wants to be. Moving beyond the search for what religions hold in common, we now want to recognize and appreciate the differences between them, their struggle to renew themselves, and their particular path as a source of our own enrichment.

A great difference among Latin America and Asia and Africa became evident during the recent Roman synods. The synod on the Americas was characterized for the total absence of any cultural expression save the Roman. Except for the ever-present Virgen de Guadalupe, one would have concluded that America—North or Latin—had no cultural expression of its own. By contrast, the synods on Asia and Africa were full of cultural expressions accompanied by the call for an appropriate decentralization of the Catholic church. Will this church become truly global, truly Asian, truly African, truly American? While the Curia continued to defend uniformity for the sake of central control, the Asian and African bishops at the synods demanded respect for local autonomy and diversity for the sake of a deeper Christian unity. No one wanted division or separation. Both the Curia and the continental churches want unity, but unity in totally different ways. Unity in diversity is the glorious sign announcing the presence of the Holy Spirit.

Globalization and Resistance to Uniformity

Christianity, I have argued, is no longer centered only in Europe and North America; there also exist Asian, African, and Latin American Christianity, each with its own style and identity. These new centers do not wish to act alone or to become separated from the unifying center in Rome, but they wish to assume the responsibility for the development of their own form of Christianity in keeping with the values and challenges of their surrounding cultures. While the entry into the pluri-centrality of the church may not be smooth, it is, in my opinion, the most important challenge of the day and the one that can render the greatest service to human well-being.[10] The age-old tension between the uniformity desired by the center and the diversity demanded by the outlying regions has become greater than ever. On the one hand, modern means of communication and transportation make the control from the center faster and more effective. On the other hand, the inner thrust for local and regional identities is also getting stronger. At the grassroots and among the younger generation, the issues dear to the center are not perceived as issues at all. Many young Christians today no longer understand why ecumenism needs a special effort or why inculturation is not the normal way of Christian faith. For them, ecumenism and inculturation are spontaneous developments. At present, the power of the Roman center seems to be indifferent to the aspirations of the regional churches.

The strength of the early church was a unity of faith that allowed a multiplicity of local customs and theological interpretations. There existed several cultural centers that practiced and celebrated the common faith in diverse ways in keeping with their cultural heritage.[11] This produced the church's dynamic catholicity.[12] Yet after the great schism between Eastern and Western Christianity and, even more so, after the Reformation, the ancient tradition of pluriformity and pluri-centrality was gradually replaced by the practice of uniformity and Roman centralization. The Catholicism exported in the great missionary expansion that started in 1492 was highly uniform and became even more so after the Council of Trent. It was only Vatican Council II that reclaimed the original pluralism of Catholic Christianity and opened the door for a decentralizing dynamic within the Catholic church. Yet Rome is not the only obstacle to Catholic pluriformity. Another obstacle, I think, is Western theologians who control the major theological universities and who still see their theology as universal, while looking down upon all others as regional. The breakthrough will come when

Western theologians, liturgists, and ecclesiastics begin to recognize their own particularity and then enter into dialogical and cooperative relations with the other theological, liturgical, and ecclesiastical regions of the world.

The conflict in the church between centralizing and decentralizing forces is taking place against the background of a historically unparalleled economic, political, and cultural globalization. After the collapse of Eastern European communism and its sphere of influence, the World Bank, the International Monetary Fund, and the giant transnational corporations have forced the countries of the South to become part of a single, neo-liberal economic system, the deregulated free market economy on a global scale. Yet the economy is not the only globalizing force. At the United Nations Organization the countries of the world engage in dialogue, cooperation, common projects, and the formulation of human rights charters. Computer technology of communication and production, moreover, is bridging the great distance between the continents, distributing production to the so-called developing countries and extending the market for the same kind of consumer goods to all corners of the earth.

This multidimensional globalization is an ambiguous phenomenon. It has a positive impact on human self-understanding because it reveals the interdependence of peoples and cultures on the global scale. The new productive and medical technologies are capable of freeing people from many material burdens and many forms of suffering. At the same time, globalization draws the entire world into a single economic system that enriches the financial and industrial centers at the expense of the outlying regions. Economic globalization under neo-liberal auspices widens the gap between the rich and the poor countries, and between the rich and the poor within each country. The United Nations Organization supports greater equality in the emerging global interdependence, but its power is quite limited. Increasingly powerful, by contrast, is the U.S.-based monoculture of technology, entertainment, and rapid consumption, which is invading all parts of the world, weakening local and regional traditions and values. Some authors detect serious dangers in present-day globalization.[13] They see the world on the brink of a cultural disaster as the aims and values of Western technological materialism wipe out traditional cultures and transform all of us into identical mechanical robots. American fast foods are replacing the traditional bistros in France and the taquerías in Mexico, American jeans and sneakers are becoming the world uniform, and U.S.-produced movies and videos have replaced local entertainment groups.

The materialistic technoculture imposed upon peoples by the forces of globalization provokes among many groups the defense of traditional values and religious cultures. We are witnessing in all world religions the emergence and growth of fundamentalist movements that fight the globalization of culture by building walls of separation, fostering cultural isolation, and rejecting humanistic universal values. This unfortunate situation has been labeled Jihad versus McWorld.

If the church in the new millennium is willing to listen to the voices of the South, abandon the effort to create unity by control and domination, and allow the divine Spirit to invigorate the regional churches in their search for genuine self-expression and universal solidarity, the church—in this new way of being—will be able to render an important service to the human family threatened by the globalizing monoculture and the isolationist countercurrents. This service to humanity, I suggest, has two dimensions. The church in solidarity with the poor and marginalized will be a voice in various parts of the world that protests the growing, death-dealing inequality and supports movements that foster a more just and compassionate global interdependence. Second, as the pluri-centered church safeguards and promotes regional cultures and local heritages, it will offer opposition to the invading materialistic monoculture without creating pockets of isolation. For as the culturally and spiritually diverse churches promote ecclesial and ecumenical unity in the Spirit, they protect cultural identities not, as do the fundamentalists, by setting up barriers, but by fostering universal respect for otherness and by giving witness to a love that transcends all boundaries. An ancient antiphon acquires powerful, new meaning: *Ubi caritas et amor, ibi Deus est.*

Notes

[1] Walbert Bühlmann, *The Coming of the Third Church* (Maryknoll, N.Y.: Orbis Books, 1977), 27.

[2] See Mai Thành, "Aspects of Christianity in Vietnam," in *Any Room for Christ in Asia?*, ed. Leonardo Boff and Virgilio Elizondo, *Concilium*, no. 2 (1993).

[3] See Virginia Fabella, "Ecumenical Association of Third World Theologians (EATWOT)," in Müller, *Dictionary of Mission*, 117-20.

[4] Virginia Fabella and Mercy A. Oduyoye, eds., *With Passion and Compassion*: *Third World Women Doing Theology* (Maryknoll, N.Y.: Orbis Books, 1988).

[5] Virginia Fabella, ed., *We Dare to Dream: Doing Theology as Asian Women* (Maryknoll, N.Y.: Orbis Books, 1989).

[6] Bühlmann, *The Coming of the Third Church*, 151.

[7] See *Any Room for Christ in Asia?*, ed. Leonardo Boff and Virgilio Elizondo, *Concilium*, no. 2 (1993).

[8] *Lumen gentium*, no. 2. See also *Lumen gentium*, no. 16, *Gaudium et spes*, nos. 16, 22, and *Nostra aetate*, no. 2.

[9] Alejandro R. García-Rivera, *The Community of the Beautiful*: *A Theological Aesthetics* (Collegeville, Minn.: Liturgical Press, 1999).

[10] Roberto S. Goizueta, *Caminemos con Jesus*: *Toward a Hispanic/Latino Theology of Accompaniment* (Maryknoll, N.Y.: Orbis Books, 1995), 162-85.

[11] Gregory Riley, *One Jesus, Many Christs* (San Francisco: HarperSanFrancisco, 1998).

[12] Jean-Marie Tillard, "Theological Pluralism and the Mystery of the Church," in *Different Theologies, Common Responsibility*: *Concilium*, no. 1 (1984), 62-73.

[13] Samuel P. Huntington, "The West and the World," *Foreign Affairs* (November/December 1996).

10

Genesis of a New World

*Globalization from Above
vs. Globalization from Below*

LEE CORMIE

Contradictory Signs of the Times

At the end of the twentieth century there are signs of many new things under the sun, epochal changes and possibilities for great progress on many fronts, but also of entrenched contradictions, growing suffering, and great perils along humanity's path into the future. And it is difficult to distinguish between probabilities and inevitabilities, possibilities and impossibilities, nightmares and hopes.

This is a time of the deaths of old hopes for progressive reforms and revolutions, symbolized by the tearing down of the Berlin Wall in 1989. Many commentators point to rapidly growing gaps between rich and poor, within countries and between them, and to the stunted lives and deaths before their time of too many people. Even in rich countries, many analysts argue, the middle class is being hollowed out. "Restructuring" is tearing apart the fabric of workplaces, communities, and whole societies. "Progress" appears to be out of control. And growing choruses of voices are crying out in a deepening sense of imminent social and ecological chaos. Indeed, apocalypse is an already existing reality for many, like people in Rwanda, Bosnia, Chernobyl and its environs, and for tens of thousands of species already driven into extinction. They foresee waves of turmoil and conflict engulfing much of the world in the twenty-first century, sweeping from poor

An earlier version of this essay appeared as "Esperanza para el Nuevo Milenio," in *Globalizar la Esperanza,* ed. Néstor Da Costa et al. (Cochabamba, Bolivia: CEPROMI, 1997), 305-18.

countries to rich countries, and outward from the inner cities and devastated rural communities of the United States and other developed countries. Confusion, cynicism about politics, despair, desperation, rage are also spreading.

But this is also a time of expanding horizons, emergent global solidarities, cultural revolutions. New theories and instruments are expanding the human capacity to map previously unseen domains and dimensions of reality: from the interior of the atom to distant galaxies on the edge of the universe and back to the very beginning of time; from holes in the ozone layer high in the atmosphere to mysteries deep in the bowels of the earth; and from the distribution of genes on the human chromosome to the inner workings of the brain. New technologies and forms of organization make possible global communications and transportation, vast reorganizations of the division of labor, and worldwide collaboration in educating and mobilizing people and resources in pursuit of shared goals. In centers of power around the world choruses of influential voices have been joyfully announcing a new "golden era" for global civilization, even a new stage in the history of the cosmos.

Clearly, the discourses of possibility, despair, and hope exhibit astonishingly diverse perspectives, claims, and judgments. Typically they proceed, like ships passing in the night, on separate paths, with commentators concerning developments in one area routinely ignoring claims about other important developments, even in adjacent areas. There is no single discourse or theory encompassing all of these matters, providing terms and a framework for specifying their character and interrelationships, identifying key issues and levers of change, envisioning alternatives, articulating ways to choose among them. Different experts appeal to different kinds of authority—natural science, social science, common sense, God—singly and in often-surprising combinations. These partial theories, incomplete knowledge, and competing claims and authorities are also signs of these "postmodern" times, helping to sow seeds of confusion, relativism, and paralysis everywhere.

Yet, it is becoming possible to discern major contours and key issues in this confusing babel about the future. My goals in these pages are, first, to chart ways in which these discussions are expanding horizons of thought and action, and second, to explore the challenges and opportunities they pose for theology and ethics in the new millennium. In particular, I point to three constitutive dimensions of the debates about globalization and epochal changes: (1) substantive claims concerning changes in technologies, economy, culture and politics, ranging from claims about the globalization of the economy to claims of epochal changes and sweeping visions of a new era, and beyond to a new stage in the history of the cosmos; (2) epistemological claims (or assumptions) concerning the growing role of knowledge in shaping history, the character of science and its authority, and (for some) growing awareness of its limits; and (3) religious and philosophical claims concerning expanding human creativity and power, freedom and responsibility, and (for some) the growing historical significance—for good and ill—of hopes that transcend knowledge and the faiths which ground them.

Above all, I am concerned with the rebirth, resurrection, and reincarnation of authentic hope in history. Over years of listening to discussions in many different areas, I have tried to listen especially to the voices of poor and marginalized peoples and constituencies, like those seeking to speak on behalf of the earth and of peace, in Canada and the United States and around the world, especially friends in Latin America. I believe deeply that our seeing, our hope for the future, and the faith which grounds it, must be woven together and shared globally.

A Time of Great Changes: Perspectives

There are three distinct but overlapping discourses of the future, each more radical and comprehensive than the preceding.

Globalization of the Economy

Observers refer to globalization most often in terms of economic globalization, and one set of claims has become "common sense" in the centers of power around the world.

Developments in global communications and transportation are facilitating the emergence of global markets for goods, services, and capital. Banks, stock markets, and investment houses around the world are linked; investing and trading proceed around the clock, with more than a trillion dollars flowing daily at the touch of computer keyboards; and currency traders have made money itself a major commodity subject to global pressures and affecting the fate of nations.

International competitiveness, flexibility, and adaptability are increasingly decisive in deciding the fate of corporations—and of nations. Governments everywhere are promoting competitiveness, reducing deficits by slashing welfare and social programs, privatizing public assets, fighting inflation, reducing taxes, cutting regulations and red tape, eliminating tariffs and other barriers to trade, and promoting exports.

International financial institutions, like the World Bank, the International Monetary Fund, the World Trade Organization, and agreements, like the North American Free Trade Agreement linking Canada, the United States, and Mexico, are playing increasingly important roles in setting the rules of trade and investment and policing them.

The distinctions among First, Second, and Third worlds, which defined the post–World War II era, are disappearing as people everywhere face the inevitable challenges and opportunities of globalization.

Epochal Changes

Many see globalization as not only an extension but a fundamental transformation of the economy. Knowledge and the manipulation of data and symbols are increasingly central to the production of goods and services everywhere. Mining, forestry, agriculture, and manufacturing are increasingly automated, producing huge increases in output with fewer and fewer workers. Services like banking, insurance, advertising, catering, travel, and entertainment, are rapidly expanding. These developments signal the transformation to a new, more flexible, dynamic, cybernetically based postindustrial economy in which global research, production, marketing, sales, and service continually spur new developments.

However, most claims concerning "epochal changes" concern developments in areas not immediately related to the economy, concerning perhaps more basic matters and with uncertain implications for the production, distribution, and consumption of goods and services.

It is clear that the human capacity to see is expanding with theories, instruments, and techniques enabling us to map previously unseen realities and dimensions of reality.[1] Developments in the philosophy of management and in institutional forms are vastly expanding capacities to plan and orchestrate vast agglomerations of resources and people. Rapidly expanding tracking systems, data storage and processing capabilities, feed-back loops, and accounting systems are intensifying the process of learning through practice.

Fiber-optic cables, satellites, computers, telephones, and television are being stitched together in a global web of instantaneous communications, creating countless new "virtual" spaces, new virtual communities, maybe even a "world brain."

New technologies for mapping the brain, new drugs and forms of surgical intervention, and new technologies for shaping perception and desire are transforming human nature. Human genetic engineering and new reproductive technologies are changing the character of reproduction, the nature of parenthood, and the significance of gender. "Six hundred million years after its invention, sexual intercourse is no longer a prerequisite to reproduction."[2] Virgin birth is becoming an everyday possibility. Designer children—"virtual children"—are already realities. And, many experts claim, humanity is poised on the brink of a new evolutionary stage, with the emergence of genetically, technologically, surgically, and drug-enhanced Techno sapiens.[3]

Space is shrinking with the capacity to see and act in real time across great distances. Time is expanding, with developments enabling us to see more clearly and farther into the past and to project elaborate scenarios into the future. Matter is changing with the creation of new realities (like global links) and new dimensions of reality, "virtual" realities, which, like global financial flows, increasingly hold sway over old realities. Human reach is expanding around the world and far out into space.

Society is changing. Waves of refugees and immigrants are transforming communities, cultures, nationalities, languages. Increasing exposure to numerous "others" and increasing intermarriage are shifting the contours and dynamics of ethnicity and race. Increasing life spans and population explosions are transforming the calculus of human reproduction, the meaning of sexuality, and the relationships among generations. Walkmans, cell phones, and global TV increasingly link us to distant others while distancing us from physically present family, neighbors, and co-workers. The multiplication of "faces, languages, relationships" in ever-expanding global networks requiring continuous deconstruction and reconstruction of every self is transforming the nature of identity, friendship, and community.[4]

In the eyes of many, these changes are epochal. They signal the erosion of previously established forms of order in many domains. They point to increasing turmoil and an uncertain future. Some, though, are ready to announce a new planetary order. "The world is no longer a dream, a prophecy, a project," proclaims Gustavo Esteva. "It has become real."[5] For some, this new world marks "the end of nature,"[6] as more and more of the "natural," on earth at least, is being mediated by the "social" of global civilization. Some insist that it marks the "end of tradition" and of traditional authorities too, as people everywhere are exposed to plural standpoints undermining the taken-for-granted character of each, exposing diversity in past and present communities and their traditions, and confronting individuals everywhere with multiple perspectives, claims, and authorities. In this view, new creative capacities, actors, and realities are transforming the contours and dynamics of history and of evolution. "We are present at a new creation. . . . "[7]

New Golden Era

So far there is little agreement concerning the character and scope of these developments, their overall coherence or lack of it, their costs and benefits. There is, though, one very influential pole in these discussions. Incorporating an emphasis on free markets, this vision brings together converts from earlier expressions of liberalism and conservatism in a project appropriately labeled neo-liberal, but also sometimes referred to as neo-conservative. This vision is widely influential, inspiring technical and popular commentaries on economic developments around the world. But its spirit reaches far beyond economics, influencing perception of developments in every area, and the articulation of hope for the future. These broader claims, in turn, inspire the narrower discourse of economic progress. By the mid 1990s many influential voices insisted that this neo-liberal agenda was obviously successful; it had launched the United States into a new stage of robust world leadership; the success of the Asian tigers and Chilean miracle confirmed the openness of the system in enabling underdeveloped countries to leap quickly forward; and these examples are leading all willing to follow into a new golden era of global growth and prosperity, expanding freedom, and a future of unimaginable progress.[8]

Some even insist that a neo-biological civilization is dawning. "The realm of the *born*—all that is nature—and the realm of the *made*—all that is humanly constructed—are becoming one. Machines are becoming biological and the biological is becoming engineered."[9] This future holds possibilities for unbounded progress on every front.

At the center of this story of progress, scientists and technicians are developing the capacity, in the words of renowned physicist Stephen Hawking, to "design an improved human."[10] In the foreseeable future we will be able not only to "cure ourselves but transcend the human condition."[11]

These developments signal nothing less than the transcendence of spirit over matter in history.[12] According to these visionaries, they have implications for all of life on earth and in the heavens above. For we are also witnessing a revolution in space technology that will make real "the dream of expanding the domain of life from Earth into the universe."[13] In the words of Joel De Rosnay, director of the City of Sciences in Paris, "the curtain is going up on the fourth act [in the history of the cosmos], an act covering the next thousand years in which humanity will play the starring role."[14]

Key Issues

Given the complexity, scope, scale, and pace of change in so many areas, it is not surprising that there is so little agreement concerning the appropriate discourse for addressing them, so few efforts to paint a comprehensive picture, so many disagreements concerning specific developments. Global neo-liberalism is a special case.

Scientific Consensus or Fundamentalist Orthodoxy?

According to the architects and advocates of neo-liberalism, this discourse is natural, the reflection of scientific consensus and simple common sense around the world. The developments associated with the neo-liberal vision and project are natural. They are already far along—and gathering momentum. There are no rational or desirable alternatives. In the short term there may be some costs. But in the millennium to come these developments promise unlimited progress. They are good, for people everywhere, for other species, even for the cosmos.

All along, though, there have been other voices with other perceptions and conclusions. The global chorus of these "others" includes many more voices, and a far wider range; it is growing, and it increasingly includes "moderate" and "conservative" voices.[15] Of course, they do not speak with a single voice. But, increasingly, they converge at important points.

In different ways they reject the claims that neo-liberal globalization is altogether new, natural, inevitable, or good. They point to many contradictory facts and trends. They insist that history is open-ended, that there are many plausible future scenarios, and that fundamental choices are being made in charting the world's path into the future. They point to matters of meaning and value involved in these decisions. And they stress the political questions concerning inequalities misshaping the socially mediated processes of seeing what is and what might be, and deciding on appropriate courses of action.

In this light neo-liberal discourse is neither scientific nor common sense. Rather, it is an orthodoxy characterizing thinking in certain limited, if very powerful, circles.[16] Indeed, it has become commonplace to hear that it is a fundamentalist orthodoxy, antithetical to the spirit of both science and democracy.[17]

Neo-liberalism is infused with a spirit of blind faith in an unseen trinity of science, technology, and (allegedly) free markets, and in the capacities of elites to understand, order, and manage global changes in the interests of all people and the whole earth. It is blind to the self-interests served by these policies and their many bad fruits; it is deaf to the cries of its victims. All its claims, even its basic categories and points of reference, are suspect.

Empirical Questions

So, many critical voices question the novelty of globalization, pointing out that international linkages, colonialism, and imperialism have marked capitalism since its origins, and that greater openness to trade and global finance characterized the early years of the twentieth century more than it did the decades immediately following World War II. They question how far globalization has already developed, as if it were inevitable and an already-existing reality leaving citizens and governments with no alternatives. Indeed, they point to the increasing power of governments in constituting and managing international financial institutions and agreements.[18] And they note many parallels between key features of globalization and historic complaints about capitalism: the development and implementation of technologies to exploit and manage workers more efficiently; deepening contradictions between the expanding capacity to produce and the shrinking capacity of ordinary people to purchase goods and services; burgeoning financialization in the frantic search for higher profits through sheer speculation; increasing concentrations of wealth and power; unevenness across countries and regions; and growing gaps between rich and poor, among nations and within them.[19]

Emergent Planetary Civilization

In trying to understand the possibilities and choices it is important to recognize that the neo-liberal agenda is capitalist, perhaps contributing to a new more intensive form of global capitalism, with the tensions, contradictions, and gaps historically associated with capitalist development. But hope for a different future requires resisting the temptation to see capitalism as a structure or process naturally unfolding according to its own logic or laws. This is a claim implicit in liberalism, neo-liberalism, and ironically, many Marxisms. It also requires seeing more than what appears through the lens of economics. Such approaches obscure broad ranges of important issues, many key choices, the character of human agency, and the significance of accidents in shaping history.

In recent decades intellectuals within popular movements have insisted that social—including capitalist—order, to the degree that it exists, is continuously reproduced in more or less familiar ways in periods of stability, and in significantly novel and unanticipated ways after periods of crisis, like the Great Depression and World War II. In this process, which involves restructuring the economy in significant respects, factors associated with gender, ethnicity, race, culture, and religion, as well as class, play important roles. To some degree and in various ways, accidents make a difference, and history is open. Knowledge is limited. And hopes for justice and commitments to acting accordingly play important roles in the lives of individuals and social movements for the status quo, for reform, and for revolution.

In this light, it seems clear that capitalism is more than an economy, and that globalization is "not only, or even primarily, an economic phenomenon."[20] Indeed, there are many reasons for doubting that "it" is a single entity or process. Rather, the discourses of globalization and epochal change address diverse, complex, apparently incongruent and contradictory processes. These developments reflect many forces predating the birth of neo-liberalism. They appear to be transforming virtually every aspect of global life, including the nature of the economy. They have no apparent single logic or structural imperative. There is no single center of power or kind of power. Individuals, families, communities, institutions, and movements everywhere are caught up in decision-making with epochal implications.

Social and Ecological Apocalypse

But there are historic concentrations of intellectual, cultural, economic, political, and religious power, and connections linking them in global webs of power. Indeed, till now the single most powerful unifying dimension in the dynamics of globalization has been the broad neo-liberal "political project of restructuring."[21] In the judgment of an extraordinary range of critics, this project is skewing discernment, decision-making, and overall trajectories of development everywhere and in every sphere.

For those with eyes to see and ears to hear, the signs are everywhere. Democracy is being strangled as power is transferred from governments to the executive suites of private corporations, corporate associations, institutes, think tanks, coalitions, international financial institutions, and bond-rating agencies. More and more of life is being commercialized and subjected to the single logic of private profit. Wondrous capacities for global collaboration and the advancement of knowledge and technology are being skewed in the interests of corporate power. Even in rich countries the middle class is shrinking, and everywhere gaps between rich and poor are growing. So-called third-world debt actually means continued massive transfers of wealth *from* poor countries *to* rich countries, the equivalent from 1982 to 1990 of "six Marshall Plans for the rich."[22] Across the former Third World many lament losing the "privilege" of being exploited in a regular job.[23] And globalization in the spirit of neo-liberalism appears ever more clearly as a declaration of a global "war on the poor."[24]

Even in wealthy and well-developed countries like Canada and the United States the feeling grows that we are "on the edge of disintegration,"[25] that "we were all taking part in some kind of assisted national suicide,"[26] that civilization has entered a "twilight."[27] Across the former Third World many refer to the 1980s as the "lost decade," even as the "worst period" in their history.[28] Russia, the heart of the former Second World, is plunged into depression and disintegration infecting the whole global economy and risking shock waves of geopolitical destabilization with the erosion of the capacity to manage safely nuclear and other weapons of mass destruction. Commentators around the world speak of the "totalitarian process of globalization."[29] And growing numbers conclude that the world has entered "a period of chaos which is far from being over."[30]

Renewing Hope and Faith in History

At the end of the twentieth century, "it is increasingly clear," in the words of historian Eric Hobsbawm, "that if humanity is to have a recognizable future, it cannot be by prolonging the past or the present."[31] And authentic hope for the future requires a radically different vision and choices.

Limits of Science

At the heart of this vision is a radically different view of science. There can be little doubt that the tree of knowledge lies at the center of this story. Great advances in knowledge have fueled progress in many areas of life in the modern world, and no end is in sight. Yet the conditioned, limited, and contradictory character of science and technology is also becoming clear. As the various hermeneutics of suspicion of the popular movements of the 1960s and 1970s confirmed, knowledge and the development of technology are inevitably influenced by standpoint, perspective, and interests. Positivist notions of "neutral" science leading to "objective," universally relevant truths and the "natural" development of technology rest on blind faith in the confluence of expertise, knowledge, power, and wealth in the evolution of modern Western societies, which has so often legitimated imperial exploitation of other classes, races, nations, and nature. Even their "successes," like nuclear energy and plastics, involve unanticipated side effects, making it clear that "science and technology create as many uncertainties as they dispel—and [that] these uncertainties cannot be 'solved' in any simple way by yet further scientific advance."[32]

These lessons point to a more dynamic and reflexive understanding of the pursuit of truth, in which the character of knowledge as a social product is recognized, the standpoint and interests of knowers are acknowledged, the voices of the historically silenced and marginalized are strengthened, and openness in the knowledge-producing process is central to hope for truth.[33] They also point to epistemological humility as an essential virtue. And they open the door to rediscovering at the frontiers of the human capacity to know with certainty and to project confidently into the future the terrain of hope and faith. On the eve of the third millennium we can recognize that, perhaps more than ever, the future also depends—for good and ill—on hopes that transcend the limits of knowledge, and on the faiths that ground them.

History and Salvation

There are many reasons for anticipating renewed significance for theology and ethics in sorting out these epistemological issues, and substantive matters concerning the expanding horizons of knowledge, human agency, hopes, and faiths in history.

For example, reread with a fuller sense of history the great themes at the heart of Jewish and Christian theologies—creation, fall, liberation/redemption, salvation—have renewed relevance. As Salvadoran theologian Sobrino has argued, "The cross suggests that the reality of God may be viewed as a process that is open to the world." In Jesus (the Son) God (the Father) is actively, fully incorporated into the historical process. Through the Spirit, human beings and history are incorporated into God. And "thus human life can be described as a participation in God's process."[34]

This historicized, trinitarian image of the Divine has profound implications for interpreting the epochal changes associated with globalization and articulating hope-filled responses. In this light, creation, redemption/ liberation, and the fullness of salvation at the end of time do not refer to events on separate levels of existence (heaven/earth, sacred/ profane, body/ soul) in an essentially unchanging history, or to three separate moments in a linear story of creation from the beginning (creation), through the middle (history), and on to the end (salvation). Rather, they are three omnipresent dimensions of a single historical process of creation, liberation, and salvation, with shifting configurations in different historical contexts.

These intuitions have profound implications for our stance toward the developments associated with emergent planetary civilization. Renewed appreciation for ongoing divine creativity and the openness of history requires more attention to the human vocation to (co-)creativity. It encourages attention to the vastly expanding human capacities to create and to

transform creation. These are not options that may be rejected but requirements of participation in the life of the Divine in history.

This perspective also calls attention to the great temptations associated
with these vast new powers of creation, to false pride, power and greed, the
great costs of succumbing to them, and the misguided faith—idolatry—
that inspires them. It points as well to the humility and radical openness to
the Spirit, which more than ever are important in deciding the fate of life
on earth and in the heavens above.

Hope for a Different Kind of New Beginning: Globalization from Below

In this light, biotechnology, global institutions and structures, global
trade, and global culture are not *the* problem. Rather, the problems are the
specific forms and directions of these developments; our underdeveloped
capacities collectively to orient, monitor, and manage them; and the role of
global neo-liberalism in shrinking the circles of consultation and decision-
making, distorting these developments and multiplying their bad fruits. It
is difficult, though, to imagine a general retreat from these expanding human capacities and global links. On the contrary, it seems clear that the
capacity to address many problems depends on recent developments in
science, technology, and global networking. It is clear that hope for a different future requires expanded capacity to orient, manage, and police
some aspects of these global processes of development, with far greater
humility, openness, patience, and prudence. And it is clear that, just as
global neo-liberalism forecloses many options, this alternative path will also
involve repudiating some lines of development in science and technology,
politics and economics.

This hope is not a matter of blind faith. Partly it rests on deepening
insight into the many contributions—unacknowledged in conventional
accounting frameworks—that have made life in modern capitalist societies
possible from the beginning: slaves; colonies; women's unpaid labor in
homes and communities; the unacknowledged contributions of workers;
the exploitation of workers in so-called informal sectors, especially in developing societies; and all the contributions of nature in providing raw
materials and absorbing wastes. In the great turmoil and skewed development associated with globalization, these unacknowledged contributions
are more significant than ever.

All along, the organizations of everyday life in communities of ordinary
people have been infused with different sensibilities and priorities. Without being naively romantic, they reflect many strands of wisdom. In various
ways they have infused the thinking of popular movements struggling for
justice, peace, and the integrity of creation. Increasingly converging in confronting hazards along the path of neo-liberal globalization, they offer many
seeds of a different future.[35]

In the expanding web of faithful remnants, reincarnations, and rebirths
of popular movements around the world, and of all those in solidarity with

them, there are signs of an emergent alternative global culture coalescing around the signposts of a different path (or paths) to the future: solidarity with poor and marginalized peoples everywhere, and with the earth; support for the right of all to speak for themselves and to have a voice in the centers of power; deep respect for others, openness to other cultures and religions, and commitment to dialogue and genuine pluralism; humility in the face of the many mysteries of creation and the magnitude of human ignorance; concern for the common good and future generations, and willingness to sacrifice for them; spiritualities of austerity or sufficiency or "enough," rather than infinitely expanding desire, new "needs," and perpetually expanding consumerism.

Along this path all have a voice; fairness and equity count more than efficiency, workers and their families matter more than competitiveness; local communities, future generations, and the planetary community count more than corporate bottom-lines and markets; global solidarity means more than national self-interest. Debts are forgiven. Ethics is not relegated to "private" decisions *after* markets and other economic arrangements are institutionalized but is a constitutive dimension of the articulation of economic categories; analytic frameworks and theories; economic institutions, structures, and accounting systems; and the policies of corporate organizations both public and private.[36] Decision-making processes are open, transparent, and accountable. Faith is placed not in markets, or in the wisdom of the powerful and affluent, or in science, or in technology, but in the Divine, and in the presence of the Divine among the poor and marginalized peoples of the world.

On the eve of the third millennium since the birth of Jesus the moral of the creation story in Genesis (Gn 1-3) rings truer than ever before—in human hands increasingly rests responsibility for the whole of creation! The vocation to sisterhood and brotherhood in a single planetary community is more urgent than ever. In solidarity with those on the margins and with the earth the vocation of Christian theology and ethics, and of the whole church, to witness concretely to a different hope in history and faith in a different God is more relevant than ever. And the challenge of the third millennium is to create—more accurately to participate with the Spirit in co-creating—a new heaven and a new earth.

Notes

[1] Stephen Hall, *Mapping the Next Millennium: The Discovery of New Geographies* (New York: Random House), 1992.

[2] Lee M. Silver, *Remaking Eden: Cloning and Beyond in a Brave New World* (New York: Avon Books, 1997), 63.

[3] Murray Buechner, "Techno Sapiens," *Time* [Canadian Edition] (May 25, 1998) (*Time Digital* insert), 8-13.

[4] Alberto Melucci, "The Global Planet and the Internal Planet: New Frontiers for Col-

lective Action and Individual Transformation," in *Cultural Politics and Social Movements*, ed. Marcy Darnovsky, Barbara Epstein, and Richard Flacks (Philadelphia, Pa.: Temple University Press, 1995), 294.

[5] Gustavo Esteva, "Regenerating People's Space," in *Towards a Just World Peace: Perspectives from Social Movements*, ed. Saul Mendlovitz and R. B. J. Walker (London: Butterworths, 1987), 287.

[6] Bill McKibben, *The End of Nature* (New York: Random House, 1989).

[7] William Shawcross, "Using Old Dreams to Forge New Order out of Chaos," *Toronto Star* (October 4, 1994), A15.

[8] Mortimer Zuckerman, "A Second American Century," *Foreign Affairs* 77, no. 3 (1998), 18-31.

[9] Kevin Kelly, *Out of Control: The New Biology of Machines, Social Systems, and the Economic World* (Reading, Mass.: Addison-Wesley, 1994), 1.

[10] Stephen Hawking, quoted in "The Man with the Theory of Everything," *Toronto Star* (March 8, 1998), A5.

[11] Charles Platt, "Evolution Revolution," *Wired* (January 1997), 160.

[12] George Gilder, *Microcosm: The Quantum Revolution in Economics and Technology* (New York: Simon and Schuster, 1989), 381.

[13] Freeman Dyson, "Warm-Blooded Plants and Freeze-Dried Fish," *The Atlantic Monthly* (November 1997), 79.

[14] Hubert Reeves, Joel De Rosnay, Yves Coppens, and Dominique Simonnet, *Origins: Cosmos, Earth, and Mankind* (New York: Arcade Publishing, 1998), 194-95.

[15] Joseph E. Stiglitz, "More Instruments and Broader Goals: Moving toward the Post-Washington Consensus," http://www.wider.unu.edu/ stiglitx.htm (1998); Robert Borosage, "More Attacks on Globalization from Prominent Right-Wingers," *CCPA Monitor* (October 1998), 17.

[16] Stephen Clarkson, "Economics: The New Hemispheric Fundamentalism," in *The Political Economy of North American Free Trade*, ed. Ricardo Grinspun and Maxwell Cameron (New York: St. Martin's Press, 1993), 61-69.

[17] Jane Kelsey, *Economic Fundamentalism: The New Zealand Experiment* (East Haven, Conn.: Pluto Press, 1995); John Mihevc, *The Market Tells Them So: The World Bank and Economic Fundamentalism in Africa* (Penang, Malaysia: Third World Network, 1995); Franz Hinkelammert, "The Economic Roots of Idolatry: Entrepreneurial Metaphysics," in *The Idols of Death and the God of Life*, ed. Pablo Richard et al. (Maryknoll, N.Y.: Orbis Books, 1983), 165-93.

[18] Leo Panitch, "'The State in a Changing World': Social-Democratizing Global Capitalism?," *Monthly Review* 50, no. 5 (1998), 11-22.

[19] Ellen Meiksins Wood, "Capitalism, Globalization and Epochal Shifts: An Exchange," *Monthly Review* 49, no. 9 (1997), 21-32.

[20] Anthony Giddens, *Beyond Left and Right: The Future of Radical Politics* (Stanford, Calif.: Stanford University Press, 1994), 4.

[21] Philip McMichael, "Globalization: Myths and Realities," *Rural Sociology* 61, no. 1 (1996): 41.

[22] Susan George, *The Debt Boomerang: How Third World Debt Harms Us All* (Boulder, Colo.: Westview Press, 1992), xvi.

[23] Dom Pedro Casaldáliga, "Neo-Liberalism Is Death," *Letter to the Churches* 13, no. 291 (October 1-15, 1993): 6.

[24] "War on the Poor," *The Guardian*, http://reports.guardian.co.uk/articles/1998/8/19/17074.html (August 19, 1998).

[25] James Laxer, *False God: How the Globalization Myth Has Impoverished Canada* (Toronto: Lester Publishing Limited, 1993), 3.

[26] Thomas Walkom, "Silent Night, Holy Night, All's Not Calm, All Is Blight," *Toronto Star* (December 23, 1992), A25.

[27] Cornel West, "A Twilight Civilization," *In These Times* (March 18, 1996), 14-15.

[28] Arturo Escobar, "Culture, Economics, and Politics in Latin American Social Movements Theory and Research," in *The Making of Social Movements in Latin America*, ed. Arturo Escobar and Sonia Alvarez (Boulder, Colo.: Westview Press, 1992), 64.

[29] Pablo Richard, "Desde América Latina Hacia el Año 2000," *Pastoral Popular,* No. 254 (1996), 18.

[30] Samir Amin, "Fifty Years Is Enough!" *Monthly Review* 46, no. 11 (1995), 15.

[31] Erich Hobsbawm, *Age of Extremes: The Short Twentieth Century 1914-1991* (London: Abacus, 1995), 585.

[32] Anthony Giddens, "Risk Society: The Context of British Politics," in *The Politics of Risk Society*, ed. Jane Franklin (Cambridge: Polity Press, 1998), 28.

[33] Bonaventura de Sousa Santos, "A Discourse on the Sciences," trans. Maria Irene Ramalho, *Review* 15, no. 1 (1992), 9-47.

[34] Jon Sobrino, *Christology at the Crossroads: A Latin American Approach*, trans. John Drury (Maryknoll, N.Y.: Orbis Books, 1978), 234.

[35] Serge Latouche, *In the Wake of the Affluent Society: An Exploration of Post-Development*, trans. Martin O'Connor and Rosemary Arnoux (London: Zed Books, 1993).

[36] Clifford Cobb, Ted Halstead, and Jonathan Rowe, "Why the GDP Doesn't Show Economic Reality," *CCPA Monitor* 2, no. 7 (December-January 1995-96), 5.

Part II

Theological Evaluation of Events and Movements

11

The Myth of the Twentieth Century

The Rise and Fall of "Secularization"

HARVEY COX

History may be servitude,
History may be freedom. See, now they vanish,
The faces and places, with the self which, as it could, loved them,
To become renewed, transfigured, in another pattern.
                                        —T. S. Eliot, *Little Gidding*

One hundred years ago, as the nineteenth century ended, predictions of what the twentieth would hold were varied and often contradictory. Some prophesied the final disappearance of religion, ignorance, and superstition. Others confidently predicted a "Christian" century, and some American Protestants even christened a new magazine with that name. A hundred years later, both these forecasts appear to have been wrong. In this essay I wish to inquire into the career of one idea that became a touchstone for both the theology and the cultural criticism of the twentieth century. Indeed, it became for some the single most comprehensive explanatory myth of its era. I want to ask what became of that myth and of the reality it was supposed to illuminate. The myth, of course, is secularization.

Max Weber initiated the discussion by suggesting that although Calvinism had provided the original value foundation for modernity, the religious substance was being displaced by the very worldview it had spawned. This was a revolution that was devouring not its children but its parents. Then, throughout the twentieth century, students of large-scale social change saw religion and modernization within a kind of zero-sum equation: the more modernization, the less religion. The larger the role religion played, it was held, the less chance modernization—which was widely held to be a desirable process—had to bestow its benefits. Conversely, the more modernization—with its subversion of traditional patterns, urbanization, high mobility, and technical rationality—the more religion, including the religion that had laid the groundwork for modernity, would be undercut and marginalized. Modernization and secularization were both the offsprings and the murderers of religion. Max Weber was the clearest proponent of this view. Religion was seen to play the role of John the Baptist to modernization's Messiah: preparing the way, but then pointing its long bony finger and announcing, "I must decrease; he must increase."

Today this zero-sum construction seems entirely implausible. Religion has not only survived, it has even thrived in some of the most modernized areas of the world. There is every indication that in many places it has even continued to stimulate the modernization process. Japan, for example, is in some ways the most modern society in the world. (Few other countries can boast taxi doors that open by themselves!) By most criteria, however, modern Japan can hardly be thought of as a secular society. Both local and state Shinto are undergoing a certain revitalization, to the dismay of democrats, Buddhists, and Christians, who view this development with alarm. The so-called new religious movements continue to proliferate, in part— some observers say—precisely because they enable people to cope effectively with the dislocations of modernization. In Africa, Latin America, and Asia both Christianity, mainly in its Pentecostal form, and other new religious movements—which are often creative adaptations of traditional religions—are burgeoning. In the United States, religion, though changing in important ways, is hardly in decline. In the so-called Third World some traditional and many innovative religious movements appear to prosper. Only Europe, some claim, is an exception to this global process. But even that is not clear. Is religion, in a characteristically European way perhaps, also making a comeback there? Paradoxically, by some standards the world may be even less secular at the end of the twentieth century than it was at the beginning. How are we to explain the dramatic failure of the secularization thesis as an explanatory paradigm for religion, culture, and politics in the twentieth century? Where does that leave us as theologians of culture at the beginning of the twenty-first?

Religious revival, unlike some other large-scale cultural trends, often begins on the periphery and only subsequently works its way to the center. This has happened time and time again in the history of the several religions. The Israelites were never a major power in the ancient world. Jesus came from an outlying province. The Mecca in which Mahomet was born was not at that time a leading city. Spiritual energy, it seems, comes from "the bottom and the edges." The current Islamic resurgence began in the slums of Cairo and other Middle-Eastern cities. The base communities of South America generated the energy for liberation theology. The fastest-growing Christian groups in the world today are probably the Pentecostal/ Charismatic ones, which began in the poorer sections of cities and still grow most quickly there. Some observers forecast that by A.D. 2010, Pentecostals will account for one of every three Christians in the world. Why such phenomenal growth?

The pattern of growth tells us something important about religion and secularization. Pentecostals, though they are theologically and cultically very different from Max Weber's worldly ascetic Puritan, generate a functional equivalent to the work ethic that makes them particularly well suited to certain features of modernization. This may help explain why Pentecostalism is growing most dramatically in regions and among classes that are not yet in the mainstream. For example, there are already nearly 400,000 Pentecostals in Sicily. But in that epitome of traditional Catholic, patriarchal, southern-European culture, the Pentecostal movement is often associated (in the traditionalist mind and quite unfavorably) with women. In particular, it is associated with the women who opt out of the existing religious culture, often against the express wishes of husbands and fathers, to become healers and prophetesses. Studies have shown that Pentecostal sermons and testimonies in Sicily markedly alter existing patriarchal images of God, emphasizing God as lover and companion. It will be important to note whether the growth of this movement in other parts of the world will have an effect not just on the roles traditionally assigned to women in more conservative areas, but on the hegemonic religious symbol system itself.

In France, on the other hand, the charismatic movement (a milder form of Pentecostalism) has appeared within the educated/technical classes, a sector not usually considered marginal. Why? Perhaps in part because these people must spend so much time immersed in the flat, homogeneous language of the computer world. For them, the charismatic practice of glossolalia (speaking in tongues) provides an alternative, emotionally rich but less denotative idiom for expressing human emotion. It could be a protest against the technological reduction of language.

The vigor and expansion of new religious movements often create both collisions and fusions with "modern" societies. For example, the rapid spread of Islam in Europe through immigration is forcing people to rethink long-cherished notions about church and state and the proper place of religion in culture. The debate assumes different forms in different places. The result of the famous conflict in France about whether Muslim girls were to be allowed to wear scarves to school indicated that French officials are reluctant to allow what they see as ethnic differences to assume a religious coloration. True to a secularist tradition dating back to the Revolution, religion is supposed to be a strictly *private* affair, but schools are *public*.

Islam, unlike Pentecostalism, provides a difficult test for prevailing definitions of religious liberty in liberal societies. Pentecostals separate faith from state power even more emphatically than most traditional Protestant denominations. It would be hard to imagine an established or specially favored Pentecostal church comparable to the Anglican or Lutheran churches of the UK or Scandinavia. In Islam, though there are clear ideas about religious tolerance in the Qur'an, discussions about a Muslim equivalent to the liberal conception of separation of church and state are just beginning. But such a development will need to recognize that in Islam the faith is expected to guide the polity and inform the culture. There are other religious and ethical considerations that make the integration of Muslims into Western societies more problematical than that of previous waves of immigrants. Among these are differences in marriage laws, in beliefs about the proper age for women to marry, and whether boys and girls should be educated together. The situation is different in the UK, where some people have begun to notice the logical inconsistency of providing tax support for Protestant, Catholic, and Jewish schools but not for the country's growing Muslim population. These conflicts will soon become a matter of public debate. The result could be ironical. It could force a recognition that we are moving neither into a secular nor a Christian century but into a pluriform one. For example, if in order to prevent public funding for Islamic schools, the UK should reverse tradition and give up all public support for confessional education, then the society would have taken a long step into a kind of secularization most Britons firmly reject. On the other hand, if Muslim and then eventually other religious schools are accepted and publicly supported, it would mark a step toward a de jure as well as a de facto religiously *pluralistic* (not secularized) culture.

In many places in eastern and western Europe today, churches established for centuries either in culture or in law are now facing a much more radically pluralistic and therefore competitive situation. There is every indication that various forms of Pentecostalism and evangelical Protestantism will burgeon in some areas of the former Soviet Union. Some years ago an American religious magazine featured on its cover a picture of well-groomed young Southern Baptist missionaries handing out Russian-language bibles both to the crews of the tanks surrounding the Russian White House during the August coup and to the people picketing them. The smiles on the faces of both groups of recipients suggested that they were pleased. This response is a matter of grave concern to the Russian Orthodox hierarchy, which has pushed for laws to guarantee its hegemony if not its monopoly.

In many places in Europe today one gets the distinct impression that although the *institutional* forms of religions may be weaker than they once were, religion still plays a strong role in public culture. References and allusions appear in such widely disparate places as poetry and drama, film, political debates, and even popular music. Pope John Paul II's avowed hope for the restoration of a Christian Europe finds an echo in a vague popular nostalgia for religious roots. Indeed, hundreds of thousands of young people from France, the rest of Europe, and other parts of the world gathered two years ago for a papal visit in—of all places—Paris. This in the city of the Boulevard St. Michel and Pigalle, a metropolis closely identified with the radical secularism of the French Revolution, and more recently with atheistic existentialism and consumer hedonism. Also in allegedly post-Christian Europe journeys to the old pilgrimage sites such as Lourdes, Fatima, and Santiago de Compostella are increasing. Could Christianity in Europe be moving away from an institutionally positioned model and toward a culturally diffuse pattern, more like the religions of many Asian countries, and therefore more difficult to measure by such standard means as church attendance and baptism statistics? Again, though this would make a significant change in religion, it can hardly be thought of as secularization.

The key theological question is how we are to evaluate *both* the demise of the secularization myth as an explanatory paradigm *and* the subtle but important changes that are going on in the religious situation of the world today. Are existing techniques of cultural analysis suitable to address this question? There is a contradiction here. One of the reasons for the religious renaissance is said to be a restlessness and dissatisfaction with the values and meanings of modernity. But the very tools of modern social and cultural analysis often used to analyze this shift are themselves squarely based on modern assumptions about the nature of human life, the good society, and the meaning of freedom. All this seems to press us toward a more explicit declaration of what the underlying, often unspoken, "theologies" of secular modernity really are. How would the emergence of a genuinely postmodern culture in Europe, one presumably free of all culturally established master narratives (including secular ones), change all this? Might it alter the present anomalous situation in which a liberal/modernist critique of religion is generally presumed to be a legitimate part of public and scholarly discourse, but a religious critique of modernity is viewed as the inappropriate intrusion of a private or inaccessible argot into the public realm?

Beneath these rather large questions lurk even larger ones. Forms of discourse and modes of inquiry gain their legitimacy because they rest on worldviews that are encoded in subtle and frequently unexamined cultural patterns. The unanticipated renaissance of religion in many parts of the world today, which surprised so many cultural observers, *might* turn out to be ephemeral, a merely superficial adjustment. But it could also mark the beginning of a long and fundamental reordering of worldviews, one in which cultural patterns that have endured since the Enlightenment would be markedly altered or even replaced. But our mental equipment for understanding a sea change on such a scale seems woefully lacking. How then are we to talk about it intelligently?

This is an especially urgent question for those theologians—including myself—who once accepted the secularization view of modern history in whole or in part. My own work on this topic has led me to the tentative conclusion that what we are witnessing is *neither* secularization *nor* its opposite ("resacralization"). Rather, it is a fascinating *transformation of religion*, a creative series of self-adaptations by religions to the new conditions created by the modernity some of them helped to spawn. Viewed in this light, I can see more continuity than discontinuity between my earlier work on the theology of secularization, especially as it was voiced in *The Secular City* (first published in 1965) and my current work on the theological significance of new religious movements.

The thesis of that earlier book was that God, despite the fears of many religious people, is also present in the "secular," in those spheres of life that are not usually thought of as "religious." But current religious movements have vigorously reclaimed many of these "secular" spheres as places where the holy is present within the profane. My early book was also, at points, a severe criticism of the traditional churches for ignoring the poor and marginalized populations of the world. Now, many of the new religious movements appeal to millions of people the traditional religious institutions have consistently failed to reach. I also argued in *The Secular City* that there was a kernel of truth in the overblown claims of the so-called (and now largely forgotten) death-of-God theologians. They saw, in a somewhat sensational way, that the abstract God of Western theologies and theistic philosophical systems had come to the end of his run. Their forecast of what would come next was dramatically mistaken, but the eruption of new movements that rely, as most of them do, on the direct experience of the Divine rather than on creeds and philosophies seems to corroborate the death-of-God theologians' diagnosis while it completely undercuts their prescription. The fact is that atheism and rationalism no longer constitute (if they ever really did) the major challenge to Christian theology today. That challenge comes not from the death of God but from the "re-birth of the gods" (and the goddesses!).

As the twenty-first century begins, a momentous change *is* underway, and it is not just a "religious" one. No thoughtful person, believer or non-believer, can ignore it. In the last few years I have focused a good deal of my attention on the astonishing growth of Pentecostal Christianity in large part because it provides such a useful x-ray, a way to understand the much larger mutation of religion of which it is an expression. In turn, change in the nature of religiousness provides an essential key to understanding the other big change or changes.

Many people, of course, have tried to fathom the meaning of the current religious revival, and some have even focused on the Pentecostal movement as a prime example. Earnest sociologists, puzzled psychologists, and diligent anthropologists have all taken their turns. But the picture they paint is often confused and contradictory. They point out that Pentecostalism seems to spread most quickly in the slums and shantytowns of the world's cities. Is it then a revival among the poor? Well, they concede, not exclusively. Its message also appeals to other classes and stations. Pentecostals vary in color and gender and nationality. They may be teenagers or old folks, though young adults lead the way. They may be poverty stricken or perched somewhere in the lower ranges of the middle class; there are not many well-to-do. They are what one writer calls the "discontents of modernity," not fully at home with today's reigning values and lifestyles. Another scholar even describes the movement as a "symbolic rebellion" against the modern world. But that does not quite jibe either, for the people attracted to the Pentecostal message often seem even more dissatisfied with traditional religions than they are with the modern world that is subverting them. For this reason, another writer describes them as providing a "different way of being modern." Both may be right. They are refugees from the multiple tyrannies of both tradition and modernity. They are looking for what it takes to survive until a new day dawns. Is there anyone who does not find a little of this wistfulness within?

But how much does all this tell us? Are sociological or psychological analyses really enough to explain such a truly massive *religious* phenomenon? One historian has called the Pentecostal surge the most significant religious movement since the birth of Islam or the Protestant Reformation. But these previous historic upheavals have for centuries defied attempts to explain them in exclusively secular categories, however sophisticated. The present religious upheaval, of which Pentecostalism is such a vivid example, also seems to slip through such conceptual grids. What does it mean?

As I have tried to reflect theologically on the significance of the new religious movements, it has become clear to me that they represent a clear signal that a "Big Change" is underway. Indeed even the most skeptical observers are beginning to concede that—whether for weal or for woe— something quite basic is shifting. It is a change, furthermore, that is not confined to some special religious or spiritual sphere. Granted, there are many reasons to doubt whether such a metamorphosis is actually at hand. It is true that in philosophy and literary criticism something called postmodernism is the rage of the journals. But intellectuals like to imagine themselves on the cutting edge, and postmodernism could be one more pedantic self-delusion. Gurus and crystal gazers talk about a New Age, but they sound suspiciously like the aging hippies who thirty years ago were hailing the imminent dawning of the Age of Aquarius. The "new world order" that President Bush's Desert Storm was supposed to introduce has turned out to be something of a mirage, and elsewhere in the international political arena we seem to be reeling backward to an era of ethnic and tribal bloodletting, not moving into anything very new at all. There is every reason to heed the skepticism of Ecclesiastes about whether there is ever any "new thing under the sun." Still, the question stubbornly persists. Do the Pentecostal movement and the global religious stirring of which it is undoubtedly a part point to something larger and more significant?

I think so. As a lifelong student of religions—Christian and non-Christian, historical and contemporary, seraphic and demonic—I have come to believe two things about them. My first conviction, which is widely shared among my colleagues today, is that religious movements can never be understood apart from the cultural and political milieu in which they arise. I do not believe religious phenomena are "caused" by other factors, economic or political ones, for example. Still, they always come to life in close connection with a complex cluster of other cultural and social vectors. You have to look at whole configuration.

I have also come to a second working premise, one that is not as widely shared among my colleagues. It is that although religion neither causes nor is caused by the other factors in a complex cultural whole, it is often the most accurate *barometer*. It can provide the clearest and most graphically etched portrait, in miniature, of what is happening in the big picture. Freud once said that dreams are the royal road to the unconscious. This may or may not be the case. But I am convinced that religion is the royal road to the heart of a civilization, the clearest indicator of its hopes and terrors, the surest index of how it is changing.

The reason I believe religion is such an invaluable window into the whole edifice is that human beings, so long as they are human, live according to patterns of value and meaning without which their life would not make sense. These patterns may be coherent or confused, elegant or slapdash, rooted in ancient traditions or pasted together in an ad hoc way. People may adhere to them tightly or loosely, consciously or unconsciously, studiously or unreflectively. But the patterns exist. They are encoded in gestures, idioms, recipes, rituals, seasonal festivals and family habits, doctrines, texts, liturgies, and folk wisdom. They are constantly shifting, mixing with each other, declining into empty usages, bursting into new life. But they are always there. Without them human existence would be unlivable. And they constitute what, in the most inclusive use of the term, we mean by *religion*—that which binds life together. Even that most famous of atheists, Karl Marx, after all once said that religion is "the heart of a heartless world."

Naturally, just as it takes practice and experience to "decode" dreams, it also requires the combined efforts of many people—insiders and outsiders, observers and participants—to understand what the densely coded symbols and practices of religion tell us about their culture. Religions always contain a mixture of emotional and cognitive elements, often fused into powerful yet compact bits of highly charged information. Understanding them requires a particular form of what the anthropologist Clifford Geertz calls "close reading," one that brings historical and comparative methods together with both intuitive and critical perspectives. But the result is worth the effort. Knowing the gods and demons of a people and listening to their prayers and curses tell us more about them than all the statistics and case histories we could ever compile.

The twentieth century began with wildly disparate predictions. It was to be the "Christian century" in which science, democracy, and Christian values would triumph. Or it would be the century that would witness the final demise of superstition, obscurantism, and indeed, religion itself. For both parties of forecasters, paradoxically, "secularization" became a central focus, sometimes almost an obsession. The religious party saw it as an awful threat. The modernizers welcomed it as a deliverance. It now turns out that both predictions were wildly wrong, and the myth has faded. As the next century begins we are left with another question: What is the inner meaning of the massive transformation we are living through, a change within which the current religious mutation is an integral dimension, a sure sign, and perhaps even the determinative impulse? So far only faint harbingers of the new era are discernable. If the qualities of most of the new religious movements presage anything, we may expect a world that prefers equality to hierarchy, participation to submission, experience over abstraction, multiple rather than single meanings, and plasticity rather than fixedness. There will, of course, be countercurrents and backlashes—some of which we also see foreshadowed in various examples of fundamentalism, religious terrorism, and reaction. But the overall profile has, however dimly, begun to emerge. And the myth of secularization is dead.

Ultimately, of course, only the future will disclose what the future will be. But in the meantime, exploring the present, unanticipated, worldwide explosion of new religious movements, decoding their hidden messages, and listening to their inner voices will give us some valuable hints.

12

The Conciliar Ecumenical Movement

Transcending Imperial Globalism and Parochial Tribalism

ULRICH DUCHROW

There is no longer any future for the divided churches.
—Ernst Lange

The twentieth century seen in the light of church history has been called the ecumenical century. The first half was marked by several vigorous ecumenical movements. These led, fifty years ago, to the founding of the World Council of Churches (WCC). The Roman Catholic Church, while not joining the WCC, was moved by the spirit of ecumenism, especially in the aftermath of the Second Vatican Council (1962-65). After the divisions between East and West at the beginning of the millennium, in 1054, and then within the Western church five hundred years ago at the time of the Reformation, the ecumenical progress in this century must be characterized, without exaggeration, as truly epochal.

What is unsettling is that today, on the threshold of the new millennium, great dangers are emerging for the ecumenical movement. Some Christian churches are withdrawing into a "reconfessionalization," while others flag in their ecumenical commitment. This showed itself as early as the 1970s at the Vatican and has become stronger during the pontificate of John Paul II. Since the fall of the Iron Curtain, a movement of withdrawal has set in among the Orthodox churches who were members of the WCC. The Georgian church has already left the WCC community, and the Russian and Bulgarian churches threaten to do the same, pressuring the other Orthodox churches to do so as well, unless the WCC radically revises its constitution to become a non-binding dialogue-center for the Christian confessions. The mainstream Protestant churches find themselves under pressure from evangelical and charismatic groups to surrender their ecumenical and prophetic engagement and withdraw into an individualistic piety. Added to this is the impoverishment of broad strata of the population through the globalization of neo-liberal economic and social policies prevailing since the 1980s, which has reduced the revenues of the churches and curtailed their contributions to the WCC, setting it on the brink of a financial crisis.

While these trends of reconfessionalization, reprovincialization, and reprivatization are weakening the ecumenical movement, the new context of globalization—affecting the economic, social, political, and cultural life of peoples—demands of the churches as never before the capacity to act in common. At stake in the present crisis, then, is not only the momentum maintained until now toward the greater unity of the churches, but also their witness, mission, and credibility in today's world. It is therefore of great importance to recall the history of the ecumenical movement in this century, secure its fruits, and meet the new century not in the spirit of regression but with a new vision.

The Rise of the Ecumenical Movement amid the Collapse of Liberal Capitalism, 1910–1945

The World Missionary Conference at Edinburgh in 1910 is regarded as the starting point of the ecumenical movement in this century. True, there were anticipatory developments in the nineteenth century, especially in the YMCA and the International Student Movement. The key figure linking this prehistory with the World Missionary Conference was John R. Mott. He played a leading role in the founding of the World Federation of Christian Students in 1895 and later became the chair of the World Missionary Conference.[1]

The nineteenth-century missionary movement cannot be understood apart from the colonial policies of the European powers. Under the hegemonic leadership of England, the principle of free trade (laissez-faire) had become supreme in the capitalist world market and thereby fostered internationalism in various areas and different forms. The free missionary societies used trade and colonial relations to further their own activities and, conversely, were used by the economic and political forces of colonialism. At the end of the century the missions became aware of this contradiction.

The discussion of this issue at Edinburgh intended to exclude the divisive questions of faith and ecclesiology. In response, Bishop Charles Brent called upon the gathered churches to start planning for a world conference on precisely these points. This was the starting point for Faith and

Order,[2] which was to become a pillar of the ecumenical movement, alongside the continuing missionary endeavors that in 1921 came together as the International Missionary Council.

The spirit of competition incarnate in the free-market system promoted hostile relations among the nations and fostered a new militarism, leading to two world wars. The militarization of the nations, together with a certain militarization of the churches themselves, especially in Germany, stirred up the forces for peace within the Christian communities. In the face of the looming confrontation between Germany and England, Christian efforts at reconciliation eventually led, in 1914, the year of the outbreak of the war, to the founding of the World Alliance for Promoting International Friendship through the Churches. In 1919 the World Alliance was the starting point for the Life and Work movement,[3] which became the third pillar of the WCC. The 1919 Conference actually endorsed a statement made by Archbishop Nathan Söderblom that summarized the several aspirations of the ecumenical movement in such a way as to anticipate the foundation of a WCC.

Söderblom was the key figure of Life and Work, which held its first world conference in Stockholm in 1925.[4] At that time the world was still suffering from the social consequences of the war, and liberal capitalism was generating ever greater injustices and moving toward its world-shaking crisis of 1929. The Stockholm Conference, attended by high-ranking officials, paid special attention to the church's relation to God's plan for the world; its relation to economic, social, and moral questions; and its role in the interrelations of nations.

Already at that time three basic theological stances came into conflict. One reflected the American Social Gospel and the biblical promise of God's coming reign. Another represented "Christian realism," the moral effort to attain the best possible results within the framework of the system; under the influence of Reinhold Niebuhr this was to become for a time the prevailing stance of the ecumenical movement. A third position, embraced especially by German neo-Lutherans, urged a dualistic separation of church and world and was apt to favor the church's adaptation to the prevailing political conditions.

Despite these differences, the conference agreed to continue its support of the Life and Work movement. The next world conference took place at Oxford in 1937 on the interrelation among church, community, and state.[5] Meanwhile the context had altered dramatically. The world economy of laissez-faire capitalism had collapsed, leaving social devastation in its wake. By way of reaction, the nations sought to reconstruct their national economies now regulated by the state in three different ways: in Russia, in the form of national communism; in the Western countries, as economic Keynesianism (the New Deal in the United States); and in Germany, in the form of National Socialism. In this situation the Oxford Conference produced the first critical analysis of the economic order on a world level.

The Oxford Conference opted for a method that involved "middle axioms."[6] This means that instead of deriving behavioral norms directly from biblical concepts like love or the reign of God, one must find mediating concepts, reflecting the biblical imperatives, that can be applied to the concrete economic, political, and social conditions and thus provide norms for a Christian social ethics. The mediating concept of "the responsible society"—that is, the free and open society committed to the common good, as worked out especially by J. H. Oldham—came to play a determining role in the social ethics of the WCC, from Amsterdam in 1948 until 1966. This concept called for the rejection of communism and liberal capitalism alike and favored the socially responsible and democratically regulated market economy that was being set up in the Western nations. The Oxford Conference, following the Barmen Declaration (1934), inspired by Karl Barth, denounced as idolatry the deification of nation and race by German National Socialism.

Faith and Order held its first world conference at Lausanne in 1927,[7] at which two distinctive concepts of unity came into confrontation. The Anglicans favored the model of an organic union, while the Reformed churches looked for some form of federation. The Orthodox, at the most, cast minority votes for the record. A second world conference held at Edinburgh in 1937 proposed another model, that of intercommunion, that is, sharing in the same eucharist.

The two movements—Faith and Order, and Life and Work—jointly appointed an unofficial consultative group in 1933 that was to work out a proposal for the formation of a world council. This proposal was later supported by the conferences at Oxford and Edinburgh. In 1938 an appointed committee drew up a preliminary constitution for this world council. The chair of this committee was Archbishop Temple of York, and its secretary was General Willem A. Visser't Hooft, who was to become the first and long-term secretary general of the World Council of Churches.[8]

The establishment of the WCC was delayed by the catastrophic events of World War II.

The World Council of Churches in the Welfare Capitalism of the Cold War, 1948–1966

The World Council of Churches was founded at Amsterdam in 1948.[9] Since many churches feared that the World Council of Churches would become a kind of "super-church," it was fortunate and theologically meaningful that the founding assembly at Amsterdam designated the council as "a community of churches." Its doctrinal basis was drawn from existing texts of the YMCA and Faith and Order:

The World Council of Churches is a community of churches that acknowledge our Lord Jesus Christ as Lord and Savior.

On this the 147 Protestant and Orthodox churches could agree.

Some of the churches wanted the WCC to express its ecclesiological neutrality. A declaration to this effect, adopted by the Central Committee in
Toronto in 1950,[10] states that the WCC is not a "super-church, that it does
not imply a particular ecclesiology, that it does not demand of the churches
to modify their own self-understanding, and that it is not committed to a
particular vision of ecclesial unity." Within these terms, the declaration continues, the member churches of the WCC give witness of their common
faith in Jesus Christ and seek the unity which is Christ's will for his followers. The member churches are committed to entertain fraternal relations,
engage in dialogue, learn from one another, and recognize in each other
elements of "the true church" (*vestigiae ecclesiae*). While this declaration is
in principle still valid today, it has been questioned by recent reflections
proposing that it encourages static categories and protects the existing ecclesiastical order.[11]

In dealing with this issue, yet without resolving the difficulties, the Third
Plenary Assembly of the WCC at New Delhi in 1961[12] made a new proposal
resulting in some progress. At New Delhi, the East European and Russian
Orthodox churches became members of the WCC, and official Roman
Catholic observers, five in number, participated for the first time. The
Vatican Council convoked by Pope John XXIII also had a fruitful influence
on theological reflection and the formation of concepts. A process of
thought and study began that led to a concept of unity expressed in the
language of conciliarity, combining both openness and obligation. Here is
the first part of a longer statement:

> We believe that the unity which is both God's will and his gift to his
> Church is made visible as all in each place who are baptized into Jesus
> Christ and confess him as Lord and Savior are brought by the Holy
> Spirit into one fully committed fellowship.[13]

This unity statement points in the direction of conciliarity and thus ini-
tiates a new phase of the ecumenical movement.

New Delhi is also important on other grounds. It agreed to accept the
Orthodox insistence on a trinitarian expansion of the WCC's foundational
formula:

> The WCC is a fellowship of churches which confess the Lord Jesus
> Christ as Lord and Savior, according to Scripture, and therefore seek
> to fulfil together their common calling to the glory of the one God,
> Father, Son, and Holy Spirit.

In relation to issues of Christian world responsibility since Amsterdam in 1948, it is important to recall the context of the aftermath of World War II. In 1945, the United Nations Organization was founded as the successor to the League of Nations. The ecumenical movement, and more especially the World Council of Churches, must be understood as in some way part of a wider secular movement that tried to learn a lesson from the two world wars and regulate relations among the nations through principles of justice and human rights.

At Amsterdam, the East-West conflict thrust itself into the foreground. Among the delegates, it is worth remembering, were the American secretary of state, John Foster Dulles, and the Czech anticapitalist theologian, Josif L. Hromádka. In the report of the third section, the assembly recommended that the churches reject the ideologies of communism and capitalism alike and endorse instead "the responsible society." This recommendation actually reflected the socioeconomic order that was gaining ascendancy in the West, even if the assembly did not recognize this at the time. We recognize this clearly in retrospect, after the end of the period of socially regulated capitalism. This period had begun after the shock of the Great Depression, was sustained during World War II, enjoyed the support of labor and social democracy, and succeeded in creating great wealth for the West. The presence of rival communism demanded that capitalism demonstrate its own social concern. In this period, then, Christian ethical responsibility for economics and politics expressed itself within the framework of a restrained capitalism.

At the Plenary Assembly in New Delhi in 1961, it even seemed as if this historical compromise would be extended to the Third World. The 1960s have been called the decade of development. Optimists understood this to mean that the development model which had produced the prosperous West could be extended to the entire world. Even if New Delhi shared some of this optimism, it clearly recognized the problems that rapid technological and social change would create in the Third World.

The Influence of Liberation Theology in a Context Defined by the Regression to Liberal Capitalism, 1966–1983

The 1960s were marked by unrest and new beginnings in the whole of society. The churches participated in this phenomenon in their own way. The salient event was Vatican Council II. Its *Decree on Ecumenism* aimed at the restoration of Christian unity, and its *Pastoral Constitution on the Church in the Modern World* defined the liberating role the church is sent to play in the world.

In politics and economics, at the same time, began the process that would eventually lead to the imperialistic policies of neo-liberalism. Alarmed by the revolution in Cuba, the United States, which in the course of World War II had taken over England's hegemonic function in the capitalist world, had begun, on a broader front, to halt the economic and political emancipation of third-world countries. It waged a merciless war of annihilation against the revolution in Vietnam. Already at the Bretton Woods Conference, in 1944, the United States had blocked the adoption of the Keynesian sketch of a worldwide, socially regulated market economy, as its interests lay with liberalization to the advantage of its own powerful corporations and banks.[14]

While in the West the realization of what was happening emerged only slowly, perceptive observers of the Third World clearly recognized the signs of the times. Thanks to their presence at the World Conference for Church and Society, held at Geneva in 1966, the WCC swung to a new approach in theory and practice largely defined by liberation theology.[15] This began a new phase in its history. For the first time, representatives—men and women from Asia, Africa, and Latin America—assumed a significant leadership role. They called for a discussion of the theology of revolution. What they meant by this was the right of resistance in situations of modern tyranny and, in more general theological terms, the meaning of the revolutionary nature of Jesus' message in the context of the new world community.

At the Plenary Assembly at Uppsala in 1968 this new departure prevailed in all areas under the motto, "Behold, I make all things new." The influence of Vatican Council II was reflected in the understanding of unity as "a conciliar community" of all Christians in all places. A joint Rome-Geneva working group was set up, and later the Roman Catholic Church became a full member of the Faith and Order Commission. The report of section 1 submitted at Uppsala, "The Holy Spirit and the Catholicity of the Church," spoke of the church as "a sign of the future unity of humanity." Thereby the course was set for a theologically grounded bond between the hitherto separate movements of Faith and Order, and Life and Work.

The report of section 2, "Renewal in Mission," produced a similar theological bond. It combined the concept of mission with the renewal of humanity in a just society. In the Plenary Assembly, this provoked the protest of conservative Evangelicals, who wanted mission to be restricted to the preaching of individual salvation and the numerical growth of the churches. From this protest emerged the Lausanne movement, a worldwide counter-movement to the WCC, although a strong minority within it defended social ethics as an indispensable dimension of Christian faith and life.[16]

At the WCC, the new social engagement was accompanied by the emergence of a new spirituality. In the traditional Western churches the encounter with the demonstrative worship of Africans and Afro-Americans, and the experience of the Orthodox liturgies, produced a renewal in the area of divine worship. The ecumenical treasury of hymns and songs, the growing importance of the eucharist, and the many new liturgical forms went hand in hand with the new political commitment.

Since Uppsala, the WCC has adopted as its principal approach the method of liberation theology that understands all dimensions and functions of the church in a contextual manner. How did this new departure work itself out in the 1970s?

In regard to Christian unity, the Commission for Faith and Order meeting in Louvain in 1971 made the following statement.

> By conciliarity, we understand the convening of Christians—locally, regionally, or worldwide—for common prayer, consultation, and decision, in the belief that the Holy Spirit can use such a convergence for its own ends: for the reconciliation, renewal, and reformation of the Churches, inasmuch as it is leading them to the fullness of truth in love.[17]

At Louvain, ecclesial unity was understood as a conciliar community and as such had an essential theological relation to the church's mission to serve the reconciliation of humanity in justice and peace.

This liberationist understanding of ecclesiology raised several points of conflict related to racism and socioeconomic injustice in a class society. The Commission for Faith and Order eventually addressed a third point, the unjust structures of patriarchal society. St. Paul fixed upon these three points when, in the context of a patriarchal Roman Empire, he proclaimed: "There is neither Jew nor Greek, there is neither slave nor free, there is neither male nor female: for you are all one in Christ" (Gal 3:28). This message raises the troubling question whether the church can be credible— indeed, even be church—if it does not eradicate racism from its midst and does not take a public stand against the structural injustices in society between men and women, and among the nations. From Uppsala onward, these three perspectives defined the focal points of WCC programs and activities.

Immediately after Uppsala the WCC adopted the Program to Combat Racism.[18] The ecumenical movement as early as the Stockholm Conference of 1925 had denounced racism. Now, in 1969, the Central Committee of the WCC took a further practical step. It created a special fund in support of social and educational development for the struggling victims of racism. The recipients included the liberation movements in southern Africa. This support led to enraged attacks not only by the forces that defended apartheid in South Africa, Namibia, and the then Rhodesia, but also by religious and secular institutions in Europe and North America. Media campaigns were waged against the WCC in the following years. The German churches refused to contribute to the special fund from their church tax income and restrained local congregations that offered their support from doing so.

On the other hand, broad support for the explicit partisanship of the WCC was forthcoming from the community level of the churches. Women's organizations, followed later by other groups, organized boycotts of South African produce and of banks that supported apartheid. More especially, the Lutheran World Federation, at its Plenary Assembly in Dar-es-Salaam, on the basis of an antecedent ecclesiological study, offered the strongest repudiation of apartheid in the Protestant tradition by declaring it to have a "status confessionis," meaning that it contradicts the Christian gospel and that by supporting it a community excludes itself from the Christian church.[19] This was an echo of the Barmen Declaration of 1934 against the so-called German Christians who supported National Socialism. In 1982 the World Alliance of Reformed and Presbyterian Churches declared support for apartheid to be heresy.

In the 1970s the WCC also opened itself to feminist theology, understood as an area of liberation theology. Its Division on Women held a number of separate consultations on this subject and then produced, in conjunction with Faith and Order, an extensive study document for the churches.[20]

The Commission for Church and Society continued with the topic of the scientific and technological world, already addressed in Geneva in 1966, and decided to hold a world conference in Boston in 1979 under the title "Faith, Science, and the Future." As early as 1969, in the altered climate between Rome and Geneva, it was possible to found a new joint working group called SODEPAX,[21] an abbreviation of "Society, Development, and Peace." As its first topic SODEPAX addressed the question of poverty, and did so with competence, clarity, and forthrightness, so that, after its first three-year mandate, under pressure from the Vatican, it was put on the back burner.

On the question of the mechanisms of impoverishment, at the behest of the Uppsala Assembly, the WCC had already created its own instrument, the Commission of the Churches' Participation in Development (CCPD).[22] The commission followed the approach of Latin American liberation theology and appealed to the formulation of the Latin American Bishops' Conference of 1968 at Medellín by calling for a preferential option for the poor. The Plenary Assembly at Nairobi in 1975 adopted this formula and spelled out its theoretical and implications for the churches.[23]

In a process of study and consultation the newly founded commission made "the church in solidarity with the poor" the central issue and developed it from a biblical, historical, theological, and social scientific perspective. The biblical message is clear: Yahweh with Jesus of Nazareth stands unambiguously on the side of the poor and challenges all forms of unjust power. According to Matthew 25:31-46, people encounter the Messiah in the poor and will be judged according to their solidarity with the poor. Instead of objects of charity, the poor are seen as bearers of evangelization, a theme that was developed at the World Missionary Conferences at Bangkok in 1973 and Melbourne in 1980.

The earlier concept of "the responsible society" was now replaced by a concept that integrated the liberationist perspective, namely, "the just, participatory, and sustainable society." The new concept produced considerable tension at the WCC since the Commission for Church and Society wished to retain the older categories and continue to appeal to the social responsibility of technical experts, political leaders, and economic magnates. By contrast, the CCPD supported social movements and the self-organization of the poor, without giving up the critical dialogue with the prevailing powers. A study of the transnational corporations undertaken by the CCPD led to a statement of the WCC's Central Committee in 1982 that the globalized market and the behavior of the transnationals are irreconcilable with "a just, participatory, and sustainable society." Statements of this kind, including the demand for a change of the lifestyle and organizational structures of the churches, brought upon the WCC the same sort of attacks it had suffered after launching its Program to Combat Racism. In the report of the Central Committee, *Nairobi to Vancouver 1975-1983*, we are told that the preferential option for the poor produced many tensions because it calls into question not only contemporary society but also structural elements within the churches themselves.[24]

The Conciliar Process for Justice, Peace, and the Integrity of Creation in the Context of Neo-liberal Global Capitalism, 1983–

In the 1970s the ecumenical movement continued along the line of the new departures of the 1960s. However, a massive restoration was beginning to occur in the political, economic, and ideological order. In retrospect, it appears that, on the economic level, the globalization of the financial markets was the decisive factor.[25] It led to the collapse of the political regulation of currency (1971-73) and later of the credit system. In the aftermath, more and more states of the Third World and Eastern Europe went deeply into debt. Then, in 1979, the United States introduced monetaristic economic policies that allowed interest rates to be determined by the market, which immediately led to an increase in interest rates. When President Reagan indebted the United States with his massive armament program, the interest rates were pushed even higher and produced a dramatic debt crisis, which reached its first climax in the bankruptcy of Mexico in 1982 and has since squeezed the life forces out of most countries of the South and the East. Meanwhile, the economies of the Western industrialized countries, weakened especially by the tax-avoiding flight of capital to the globalized market, also became excessively indebted, causing increasing cutbacks in welfare and social programs.

Politically, under the leadership of the United States, the West tried to weaken or even crush all movements for social change. The World Bank and the International Monetary Fund imposed structural adjustment policies upon the indebted countries, which caused increasing misery among the poor. It is only in our day that the universally accepted neo-liberal dogma of liberalization, deregulation, and privatization seems to be shattered by a fundamental global crisis showing itself in a sequence of regional crises (Mexico, Southeast Asia, Russia, Latin America, and others).

Yet at the grassroots, new movements for social change have emerged. During the period of rearmament in the Cold War, the peace movement mobilized important sectors of the population, especially in Germany, West and East, with active Christian participation. To stand for peace against nuclear weapons was demanded by the gospel. Recalling the concept of "status confessionis" of the 1934 Barmen Declaration, I introduced the idea of "processus confessionis" to open the door to the participation of wide sectors of the church. For the same reason, we later spoke of "the conciliar process" rather than "the council."

Against the ongoing destruction of the earth's surface through industrial development and the exploitation of nature, ecological movements were formed in all parts of the world, again with active Christian participation. And against apartheid and other forms of oppressive regimes and structures, social justice movements spread at the community level, often with the support of church circles.

Since the beginning of the 1980s, an ecumenical network for justice, peace, and the integrity of creation has been active in West Germany. Then, in 1983, the Plenary Assembly of the WCC at Vancouver called for the creation of "the conciliar process for justice, peace, and the integrity of creation." The sociopolitical engagement of the church is here theologically linked to its ecclesiology, that is, to its search for ecclesial unity in obedience to Christ. It is significant that the Faith and Order Commission had delivered to the assembly its report on baptism, eucharist, and ministry, which provided a eucharistic vision that related the unity of the church to the reconciliation of humanity.

The conciliar process has roused a great echo, particularly in Europe. Within its framework the first truly ecumenical meeting since the Reformation took place in Basel in 1989. It brought together the Protestant-Orthodox Conference of European Churches and the Conference of Catholic Bishops Conferences in Europe. The Convocation of the WCC on the topic of justice, peace, and the integrity of creation, held in Seoul, Korea, in 1990, convened—due to a decision of the Vatican—only Roman Catholic observers. The second European Ecumenical Assembly, held in Graz in 1997, was again ecumenical in the full sense, since the universal level claimed by the pope alone was not addressed.

At the same time, it has become increasingly clear that the source of the threat to which all dimensions of the conciliar process were exposed was the globalization of the free-market economy and its ideology of competition. After the turn to neo-liberalism in the 1970s and the counterrevolutions of the Reagan and Thatcher administrations in the 1980s, the collapse of the communist experiments in Eastern Europe in 1989 produced a political rupture in the West that made it impossible to regulate the agent of capital—banks, transnationals, and mass media—in democratically, socially, and ecologically responsible fashion.

In this situation the WCC prepared a program for the Plenary Assembly at Harare that was to play a central role in the future: "Churches and Social Movements in the Face of Globalization and Exclusion." This program proceeds from the recognition that the current destructive tension between imperialistic globalization and violent tribalization can only be overcome through a process of renewal on the level of civil society. While economic and political institutions are engaged in death-dealing conflicts, social movements and nongovernmental organizations are being formed in all parts of the world that wrestle—usually dealing with single issues—for the social, cultural, economic, democratic, and ecological rights of human beings.

The WCC is now seeking a new role in the field of civil society. In the early 1990s, it supported and wove together regional ecumenical networks and social alliances, for example, Kairos Europe, Kairos USA, People's Plan 21 in Asia, the Organizations of Indigenous Peoples in Latin America, and the Ecumenical Decade for Women's Emancipation. Cooperation was sought, not only with other faith communities and the United Nations, but also with groups of civil society and secular nongovernmental organizations.

The insistence on the equality of men and women and the liberationist approach to social issues are the reasons the Russian church and other Eastern European Orthodox churches wish to withdraw from the WCC. It must be said that since the 1970s some denominations and church groups have disagreed with the WCC's position that churches have a joint responsibility for the world and hence decided to create their own parallel interdenominational structures. The Vatican, too, has engaged more and more in bilateral doctrinal dialogues, without integrating these exchanges into the multilateral framework of the WCC—which would give them general ecumenical meaning. And the Lutheran World Federation has developed the formula "unity in reconciled diversity" as a counter-concept to the WCC's "conciliar community" to protect the status quo of confessional institutions.

It would be tragic if the ecumenical movement became a mirror of what is happening in society and reacted to economic globalization only by confessional tribalization and parochial provincialization. Never has the vision, developed in the framework of the WCC, of the responsible, conciliar community of Christians in all places been more important than in today's age of destructive globalization. The WCC can meet the world-wide community of Christians only in cooperation with the other life-serving forces of civil society "to the glory of God, Creator, Redeemer, and Fulfiller of God's creation."

Notes

[1] For the Edinburgh Conference and John R. Mott's part in it, see Kenneth Latourette in *A History of the Ecumenical Movement,* ed. Ruth Rouse (London: SPCK, 1967), 355-62.

[2] For the formation and the early years of Faith and Order, see Tessington Tatlow, in Rouse, *A History of the Ecumenical Movement,* 407-45.

[3] For the formation and early history of Life and Work, see Nils Karlström, in Rouse, *A History of the Ecumenical Movement,* 509-51.

[4] On Söderblom's presence at the Stockholm Conference, see W. A. Visser't Hooft, *Genesis and Formation of the World Council of Churches* (Geneva: WCC, 1982), 12-20.

[5] On the Oxford Conference, see Nils Karlström, in Rouse, *A History of the Ecumenical Movement,* 587-93.

[6] For J. H. Oldham's definition of "middle axioms," see Michael Kinnamon and Brian Cope, eds., *The Ecumenical Movement: An Anthology of Key Texts and Voices* (Grand Rapids, Mich.: Eerdmans, 1997), 277.

[7] On Lausanne, see Visser't Hooft, *Genesis and Formation,* 21-23.

[8] For a detailed report of these events, see W. A. Visser't Hooft, in Rouse, *A History of the Ecumenical Movement,* 697-708.

[9] See *The Message and Reports of the First Assembly of the World Council of Churches* (London: SCM Press, 1948).

[10] On the Toronto Declaration, see Visser't Hooft, *Genesis and Formation,* 70-85.

[11] See Ulrich Duchrow, *Conflict over the Ecumenical Movement* (Geneva: WCC, 1981), 309-12.

[12] *The New Delhi Report* (London: SCM Press, 1962).

[13] Kinnamon and Cope, *The Ecumenical Movement,* 88.

[14] See Ulrich Duchrow, *Global Economy* (Geneva: WCC, 1987), 71-83.

[15] *Christians in the Technical and Social Revolutions of Our Time: Official Report, World Conference on Church and Society* (Geneva: WCC, 1967). For significant sections of the report, see Kinnamon and Cope, *The Ecumenical Movement,* 290-98.

[16] This minority promoted its viewpoint in the review *Transformation.*

[17] *Foi et constitution: Louvain 1971,* the special issue of *Istina* 3 (1971), 413. On the importance of Louvain for the future orientation of the WCC, see Erich Lange, *And Yet It Moves: Dreams and Reality of the Ecumenical Movement* (Geneva: WCC, 1979), 93-102.

[18] *Breaking Down the Walls: WCC Statements and Action on Racism* (Geneva: WCC, 1986); *A Long Struggle: The Involvement of the WCC in South Africa* (Geneva: WCC, 1994).

[19] See *In Christ—A New Community,* Proceedings of the Sixth Assembly of the Lutheran World Federation (Geneva, 1977), 179. Also Ulrich Duchrow, *Global Economy: A Confessional Issue for the Churches?* (Geneva: WCC, 1987), 98-99.

[20] *The Community of Women and Men in the Church* (Geneva: WCC, 1982).

[21] See Thomas Stransky, "SODEPAX," in *Dictionary of the Ecumenical Movement,* ed. Nicholas Lossky et al. (Geneva: WCC; Grand Rapids, Mich.: Eerdmans, 1991).

[22] On the work of the CCPD, see *Uppsala to Nairobi 1968-1975*, Report of the Central Committee (New York: Friendship Press, 1975), 139-52; and *Nairobi to Vancouver 1975-1983*, Report of the Central Committee (Geneva: WCC, 1983), 160-69.

[23] *Breaking Barriers, Nairobi 1975*, Report of the Fifth Assembly of the World Council of Churches (Grand Rapids, Mich.: Eerdmans, 1976), 101.

[24] *Nairobi to Vancouver 1975-1983,* 132.

[25] See Ulrich Duchrow, *Europe in the World System, 1492-1992* (Geneva: WCC, 1992), 25-38.

13

The Impact of Vatican II

ROBERT J. SCHREITER

The Church Engages the Modern World

The Second Vatican Council is undoubtedly the most significant theological event for the Roman Catholic Church in the twentieth century. It forms a watershed in the flow of theological thought: commentators and theologians regularly divide the century into the pre–Vatican II and post–Vatican II eras. Central to that division was the council's attempt to engage the modern world after a century in which it had seen itself as a bulwark against that very same world. Moreover, coming to fruition as it did in the 1960s, it intersected with powerful social and cultural influences that magnified its effects in many parts of the world.

In this chapter the significance of that encounter will be explored in three parts. The first part looks at the context in which Vatican II took place. Had the council happened earlier or later in the century, its effect would have been different. Second, some of the signal insights of the council will be noted, especially their impact both on the church itself and on the larger world. Finally, an assessment of the council's legacy at the end of the twentieth century will be proposed in light of the world's moving in many places beyond high modernity to some form of postmodernity. What will the enduring legacy of the council mean in quite changed circumstances?

A Council to Address the Modern World

When Pope John XXIII announced on July 25, 1959, his intention to convoke an ecumenical council, he caught both the Roman Curia and the larger church by surprise. Typically in the course of history, councils had been held as a response to an immediate threat to the well-being of the church. Thus, the Council of Trent convened in 1545 to counter the rising Protestant Reformation of the church in Europe. Vatican I began in 1869 to reassert the church's position over against the forces of liberalism and other consequences of the Enlightenment. But Pope John XXIII, in his announcement and then in his speech at the opening of the council in 1962, sketched out a different vision of what the council should be. Rather than giving voice again to the negative and pessimistic reading of the modern world (people who were "always forecasting disaster," as he put it), he emphasized the positive aspects. The church should contribute to the unity of humankind and present its teachings in ways understandable to people who live in the modern world. There would be no condemnation of errors but rather a positive engagement of the modern world.

Just what is meant by "modern world" here? There are many definitions that could be brought forward. Modernity arises out of the consequences of the Enlightenment, which proposed an emancipatory program for humankind based on reason and democratic participation of people in the decisions that affect their lives. Néstor García Canclini sees the modern project as having four dimensions. It is first of all *emancipatory*, in that it allows for a secularization of knowledge, meaning that knowledge is no longer beholden to arbitrary authority. One of the consequences of this emancipatory dimension is an increasing individualism and, with spheres of knowledge becoming autonomous, a greater pluralism. Second, it is *expansive*, in that it seeks to expand knowledge through scientific discovery and the spread of a capitalist form of economy. The growth of technology and what is known as globalization (more about which will be said below) is part of this dimension of the modern project. Third, it is *renovating*, in that it seeks constant improvement and innovation. Closely connected with this is the notion of progress as a value. Fourth, it is *democratizing*, in that it believes in the basic value of dignity of each human being. It places great store in education and specialized knowledge (as in engineering and medicine) to further future development.[1]

The church in the nineteenth century had reacted strongly against modernity, seeing it as rejecting many of the privileges and prerogatives that the church had enjoyed. It had attacked some of these values directly in Pius IX's encyclical *Quanta cura* in 1864, with its attendant *Syllabus of Errors*. At the turn of the twentieth century it had condemned historical-critical scholarship as undermining ecclesiastical authority. Pope John XXIII's determination to meet modernity with an ecumenical council, then, was a reversal of this nineteenth-century papal policy.

It did not happen entirely suddenly, however. At the papal level his predecessor, Pius XII, had signaled the way by reopening the door for critical biblical scholarship in his 1943 encyclical *Divine afflante spiritu*. The same year he issued *Mystici corporis*, an encyclical on the church that paved the way for a more biblical understanding of the church as well as new relations with nonbelievers. In 1946 his *Mediator Dei* encouraged liturgical reform.

Alongside papal renewal of the church, a scholarship based on histori-cal-critical studies of the church's rich tradition paved the way for rethink-ing many aspects of church life. A renewal of interest in the theology of the first six centuries of the church as well as the Middle Ages was led by such formidable figures as Henri de Lubac, Yves Congar, and M.-D. Chenu. They provided an alternative vision of what the church could be to that pro-posed by the Council of Trent and the Counter-Reformation. Although all of these theologians were silenced at one time or another during the 1940s and 1950s, their work had a tremendous impact by laying the patristic and medieval foundations for a genuine and authentic renewal of the church by retrieving the best of its traditions.

Liturgical reform, too, benefited from historical study by such figures as Josef Jungmann and the monks of Maria Laach. Liturgical reform pressed for a greater participation of all the members of the church, seeing the liturgy as not just the work of the clergy, with laity as passive observers. The question of using local languages as the medium of worship, instead of Latin, was raised the most insistently since the time of the Reformation in the sixteenth century.

Not only theological movements dealing with the inner workings of church life were setting the stage for the work of the council. Pope Leo XIII had formulated a Catholic social teaching in his 1891 encyclical *Rerum novarum*. This encyclical paved the way for social justice becoming a central category of Catholic teaching. Pius XI continued this work in his 1931 en-cyclical *Quadrigesimo anno*. Along with social justice, Leo XIII's work of-fered a new vision of engagement with the world, not only in religious mat-ters, but in the struggle for a more humane and just treatment of workers, and indeed of all people. It offered the foundation for an empowerment of the laity that had not been seen before by offering them a participation in the mission of the church to the world. In many ways it was seventy years of social teaching and lay involvement that really set the stage for the church engaging in a new relationship to the modern world.

The council convened for its first session in 1962. Three sessions were to follow, with the council being concluded in December 1965. That the council took place when it did—in the decade of the 1960s—also contributed to its impact. In Asia and Africa the colonial period of empire was coming to an end. The decline of empire could be noted already with the close of World War I (1918), but it was during the aftermath of World War II that Euro-pean powers began relinquishing their hold on colonies. The process be-gan in the 1940s (with independence for India), but accelerated from the mid-1950s into the 1960s. The experience of this newfound freedom fu-eled an optimism in many countries that a new political order could be established that would bring justice, peace, and prosperity to the colonized peoples. At the Bandung Conference in 1955, the so-called non-aligned nations (that is, aligned with neither capitalism nor communist socialism) called themselves a "Third World" that offered an alternative to what then existed. In Latin America a similar optimism that poverty and oppression could be struggled against and overcome could be found.

North America and Europe found themselves caught up in optimism as well. The economic rebuilding of Europe after World War II was beginning to bear fruit. Discussion of the possibility of Europe being united in a common market was in the air. In the countries of Eastern Europe talk of a new socialist humanism began in Poland and Czechoslovakia. The United States had become the leader of the capitalist world during the period after World War II and enjoyed an economic boom that seemed not to end. Belief in both Europe and North America that the poorer countries of the world could be aided by the surplus of the North's wealth in schemes of "development" became part of the common parlance of the period.

By the mid-1960s, as the council was ending, social movements in Europe and North America, encouraged by the optimism of the times, set out to further the emancipatory projects of the Enlightenment and modernity. In the United States, the Civil Rights movement portended the overturning of the racism that had so deeply scarred that country. Women in the United States took up again the struggle for equality and inclusion, continuing the movement that had led to women's suffrage earlier in the century. The bulge in the population of youth in both Europe and North America gave the whole era of the later 1960s an adolescent feel, as youth urged the overthrow of oppressive structures and moral boundaries.

In many ways it appeared that the project of emancipation and improvement set forth by modernity was coming to fruition. The world would be a better place for humanity, where the gaps in economic prosperity could be overcome by development and human rights would be respected.

To be sure, these lofty goals were not entirely realized; more will be said about them in the third part of this chapter. But the heady optimism of that decade intersected with the optimism Pope John XXIII breathed into the council and Paul VI, his successor, continued. This had the effect in North America and Europe of strengthening the zeal for reform and envisioning new possibilities among the poor countries of the world. One only has to look at Eastern Europe (for example, its most Catholic country, Poland) to see in some measure what the reforms of the council would have looked like had the larger environment not been so welcoming of reform, so keen on progress, so eager to engage in experimentation.

A final factor should be noted in the setting of the council, evident among the bishops in the first session. Many of the bishops were weary of the heavy-handed workings and the highly centralized and often authoritarian manner of the Roman Curia. Some of them certainly welcomed the opportunity of an ecumenical council to undo this constricting pattern and to allow more power and decision-making to flow to bishops in their local churches. When the Curia tried to control the agenda of the council at every level during the first session, the bishops rebelled and demanded that their own agenda be respected and discussed. One sees in this the same democratic spirit—demanding participation and a voice—that is part of modernity's project. Some observers have postulated this as central to the agenda of many bishops coming to the council.[2]

With all of this, the scene was set for the council. The forces of modernity, with its interest in emancipation, participation, pluralism, improvement, and renovation, were met squarely by the fathers of the council. Given the environment of what might be called the high point of modernity at the time, the "fresh air" that John XXIII wanted to let into the church through an open window turned out to be of considerable strength and velocity.

What the Council Achieved

In the course of its four sessions from 1962 to 1965 the council produced sixteen documents. Not all aspects of these documents, or even all of the documents themselves, can be reviewed here. Rather, those documents that brought about the most change will be highlighted, especially regarding the continuing impact that they have had on the church. A focus will be on their interaction with the modern world, especially to the values and interests that were outlined in the first section of this chapter. The documents will be grouped according to themes, although something of the chronology of the council itself will be respected.

One can read the council as having put a seal of approval on some movements in the church (such as the biblical renewal), thus bringing some previously controversial issues to a settlement; one can read others (such as the *Pastoral Constitution on the Church in the Modern World, Gaudium et spes*) as inaugurating a vision and an agenda that we are still trying to achieve. Both of these perspectives will be kept in mind as the documents of the council are examined for their meaning to theology in the twentieth century.

The Liturgy

After the revolt of the council fathers against the agenda proposed by the Roman Curia, the first document to be issued was the *Constitution on the Sacred Liturgy (Sacrosanctum concilium)*. A number of different factors were at play in taking this document first rather than, say, the dogmatic constitution on the church. For one, the historical and pastoral work on the reform of the liturgy, which by that time had stretched over several decades, was in many ways already well advanced. This work needed to be affirmed and adopted at the highest level of the church. But there were deeper, theological reasons at work beyond this seemingly pragmatic one. To move from the Tridentine notion of liturgy as largely expressive or representational of transcendent realities, back to a more patristic model of liturgy comprising the full, active, and conscious participation by all the baptized in the praise

and worship of God, would mean a profound shift in sensibility and awareness on the part of all believers and mark a decidedly different stance toward the larger world. To engage the laity as more than spectators or to
consign them to a parallel piety alongside that of the liturgical ministers
presented a different vision of the church itself. The church could no longer
be considered an alternative society consisting chiefly of the clergy, with
the laity largely uninvolved. The church would be, through such participation, where the assembly itself was the subject actively worshiping God (not
just the ministers) gave a whole different idea of who the church was, both
internally and to the outside world. In other words, the theme of participation and then acknowledgment of the dignity and worth of each person
would ring clearly in the very heart of the church—in its principal activity,
the praise and worship of God.

The decision to have the presider at the liturgy face the people, something that came in the texts implementing the *Constitution on the Sacred Liturgy,* also had a seismic impact. Heretofore, the action of the priest and the
worship of the people had been clearly separated, as the communion rail-
ing had signified in much church architecture. Now that barrier seemed
out of place, and railings were removed in many churches. The liturgical
action no longer was directed to some place beyond the people and the
priest but happened in the very midst of the assembly. That lay readers and
eucharistic ministers were to become commonplace flowed naturally from
this rearrangement of symbolic space, for liturgy became the celebration
of the entire People of God. Despite attempts in the subsequent decades to
reintroduce a sense of separation between priest and people, the liturgical
experience in such symbolic space militated against any return to the old
sense of division. This had its effect not only on the self-consciousness of
priest and people, but it also changed many people's theology. Their understanding of God and the presence of God also underwent a transformation. God seemed to draw nearer and be less forbidding. It became harder
for many preachers to speak about sin and judgment in what had become
an intimate space.

Although the *Constitution on the Sacred Liturgy* itself may not have envisioned that the eucharist would be celebrated completely in vernacular languages, it became harder to retain any Latin in the liturgical rites. The
move to local languages placed the final stamp on the new sense of participation, confirming an engagement with people's sense of themselves as
free, participating agents in their own future.

The Church

While the *Constitution on the Sacred Liturgy* set the stage, as it were, for a
renewed understanding of the church, it was the *Dogmatic Constitution on
the Church (Lumen gentium)* that became the charter for renewal and reform.
Although the document reflects the struggle of the bishops to come to a

single understanding of the church, it nonetheless represents a significant departure from the understanding of the church that had prevailed for four centuries.

Five significant developments stand out. First of all is the efforts to come to a new understanding of the church itself. This is evidenced in the tension one senses in reading chapters 2 and 3 of the constitution. Chapter 2, on the church as the People of God, presents a vision of a people on pilgrimage together into the reign of God, a theme echoed in chapter 7. Chapter 3, on the hierarchical nature of the church, sets out to balance the vision of chapter two by reasserting a traditional view of hierarchy within the church. Many of the post–Vatican II tensions play themselves out around the intersection of these two views. People in a culture of modernity read in the image of the People of God perhaps a more democratic, egalitarian vision of the church than the text allows. In the United States, hearing the phrase "People of God" seemed to many to be reminiscent of "We, the people," the beginning words of the U.S. Constitution. But it was something of an inevitable reading, given the context in which the church found itself in the latter half of the twentieth century.

However one reads the tension between these two visions, what was affirmed was that the church is a mystery, that is, a pathway to salvation ordained by God. It stands as more than a human or divine institution, an idea that had been enshrined in Catholic ecclesiology since the time of Robert Bellarmine (1542-1621), who called the church a "perfect society." Moreover, the constitution calls the church a sacrament, mirroring forth the divine reality in the world.

Second, alongside what appeared to some to be competing understandings of the church, a new understanding of the relation of the local churches to the universal church unfolded, an understanding of the church as a communion of particular or local churches in communion with and under the leadership of the church of Rome. Within that communion, each local church (understood as a diocese) represented the fullness of what it means to be church, even though it does not represent the entire church. This recovery of a patristic understanding of the church stands as one of the major achievements of the council. Building on this theological foundation, the council goes on to articulate a collegial understanding of the relationship of the bishops to one another and to the pope, that is, that their relationship is one of mutuality and respect. Bishops are therefore not "branch managers" of a transnational organization but are the leaders of communions that are in turn in communion with one another and with the head of this collegium, the bishop of Rome. Such thinking opened the way for reimagining how decisions were to be made, and through Paul VI's promulgation of a plan for a regular meeting of a synod of bishops, how the church itself might come to be led and governed. The latter was not to be, however, when it became clear that the synods would be only advisory to the pope, not to have a share in governance of the worldwide church.

In a third development, the Roman Catholic Church repositioned itself vis-à-vis the other Christian churches. In a debated but finally accepted move, the council defined the church of *Lumen gentium* as "subsisting" in the Catholic church (no. 8), rather than a simple identification of the church of Christ. This was elaborated in the *Decree on Ecumenism (Unitatis redintegratio)*, which was issued on the same day as *Lumen gentium*. With this, a whole new relationship to the other Christian churches was opened up; before they had been rejected as having no part in the "true church." By speaking of its own relation to the church of Christ in this way, a space was cleared for ecumenical relations that had not been there before.

A fourth significant development can be found in the fourth chapter, on the laity. As has been noted, a sense of lay involvement both within the church and in witness and ministry in the world had been growing steadily for seven decades prior to the council. In 1965 the council issued the *Decree on the Apostolate of the Laity (Apostolicam actuositatem)*, which acknowledged and confirmed the calling of the laity to full status within the church.

Finally, the council, in its *Decree on Religious Life (Perfectae caritatis)*, in 1965, called for a renewal of religious institutes by retrieving the charism of their founding figures and repositioning them in the modern world. This set off a ferment in religious institutes that led to considerable experimentation with new forms, based on reading original charisms in modern contexts. Many religious institutes recommitted themselves to ministries of seeking justice— again, building upon decades of Catholic social teaching—giving it a focus in their activities that had not been there previously.

All in all, these developments in reenvisioning the church—as a mystery, not a perfect society; as a communion of communions, not a center and periphery; not identified as the sole representation of the church of Christ; with a place for the laity; and with renewed religious institutes—fundamentally reshaped how the Roman Catholic Church might live in the modern world.

The Church in a Pluralist World

One of the features of modernity, with its concern for autonomous spheres of knowledge, is that it fosters the growth of pluralism, that is, different and sometimes competing views of the world. The council engaged that pluralism on a number of different fronts.

One of those fronts was the question of freedom of conscience. In the wider world, at least in the West of that time and in many of the so-called developing countries, freedom of conscience had come to be seen as a human right. Human rights had been a hallmark development of Enlightenment thinking, already evident at the end of the eighteenth century in declarations arising out of the American and French revolutions. By 1948 the newly formed United Nations had made a universal declaration of human rights.

While Catholic social teaching defended many human rights, the question of freedom of conscience and its attendant aspect, freedom of religion, had not made its way into official Catholic teaching. The adage "error has no rights" better portrayed official thinking. But that was to change in 1965 with the council's *Declaration on Religious Liberty (Dignitatis humanae)*.

Much of the groundwork for this declaration had been done by the American theologian John Courtney Murray, S.J. Indeed, this declaration was certainly the major U.S. contribution to the work of the council. Murray's concern had been finding a theological way for U.S. Catholics to live in a religiously plural, largely Protestant culture. But concerns about religious liberty were important too for Catholics living as minorities in countries where the pluralism was non-Christian, and also for those who were living in atheistic states under Soviet hegemony.

Dignitatis humanae not only made the religious freedom of the individual part of official church teaching, but it also represents one of the most fundamental reversals of the church's stance toward the modern world. Pius IX in his *Syllabus of Errors* had condemned such ideas as the separation of church and state, or that there could be more religions present in the state than Roman Catholicism. In *Dignitatis humanae*, the reverse position was taken.

Another major development was the attitude of the church to other religions. Already in *Lumen gentium* (no. 16) a more positive attitude had been taken to the possibility of salvation outside Christianity. Throughout the century the church had been moving away from the exclusivist position of "no salvation outside the church" that had characterized the church since medieval times. But in *Lumen gentium*, and again in the *Decree on Missionary Activity (Ad gentes)* the door is left open for God's saving activity through other religions, without defining how such activity occurs. The influence of the work on what is called the theology of religions by such figures as Yves Congar and Karl Rahner is in evidence here.

In its *Declaration on the Relation of the Church to Non-Christian Religions (Nostra aetate)* the council addresses other religions specifically, but especially Judaism. Pope John XXIII had begun a change by eliminating the reference to the "perfidious" Jews from the intercessions on Good Friday. But *Nostra aetate* sets out to reverse a long history of anti-Semitism and blaming all Jews for the death of Christ. Moreover, it rejects the belief that the New Covenant inaugurated by Christ means Jews have been "rejected or accursed" by God, and it condemns "all hatreds, persecutions, displays of anti-Semitism leveled at any time or from any source against the Jews" (no. 4). *Nostra aetate* has been the platform upon which a wholly new approach to Catholic-Jewish relations is being built.

The reference to other traditions (Buddhism, Hinduism, Islam) is rather summary, but in all instances there is an attempt to make a positive statement about each religion. The positive evaluation of these traditions made possible the prospect of interreligious dialogue at the highest level and put a stamp of approval on attempts already under way.

The attempts to deal with religious pluralism at the council, therefore, set a new agenda for the church, one that proposed closer contact without resolving the theological issues of the relation between the salvation offered in Christ and the offers made in these other traditions. It remains, however, one of the great accomplishments of the council that these dialogues have been initiated and, especially, that such a resolute stand has been taken against anti-Semitism.

The Mission of the Church to the World

A renewed sense of the church entailed more than internal reform and renewal and a revised set of relationships with other communions and religions. The question had to be raised about just how the church would engage the world itself as a modern world. Two documents addressed that issue in a special way: The *Decree on the Church's Missionary Activity (Ad gentes)*, and the *Pastoral Constitution on the Church in the Modern World (Gaudium et spes)*, both issued at the final session of the council.

The decree on missionary activity presented a theology of mission that made mission more than a peripheral activity engaged in by a few specialists; being missionary was the very identity of the church itself. Mission is born in the action of the Trinity, whereby God is made known to us through the Incarnation and the sending of the Holy Spirit. The church "is by its very nature missionary" (no. 2) as the extension of God's saving work through the Son and the Spirit.

What is remarkable is how different such a vision of mission is from seeing mission as forays into a world marked by depredation and sin, attempting to rescue a few embattled souls. Here again we see a more positive engagement with the world on the part of the church, whereby the church strives to share its message of salvation in Christ with the larger world.

The optimism about engaging the world is most evident in the final document of the council, *Gaudium et spes*, captured so well in its opening words: "The joy and hope, the grief and anguish of the men of our time, especially of those who are poor or afflicted in any way, are the joy and hope, the grief and the anguish of the followers of Christ as well. Nothing that is genuinely human fails to find an echo in their hearts" (no. 1). The church seeks solidarity here with what it calls "the whole human family." The document goes on to outline a vision of the human, based upon the dignity of each human person in the image and likeness of God. It discusses justice as an essential quality for all (no. 29). It notes the rightful autonomy of earthly affairs (no. 36)—again a far cry from *The Syllabus of Errors*—and what the church has to contribute to the modern world. Its concern with human culture and its development (nos. 53-62) shows how deeply it is engaged with the world, and what it might become. *Gaudium et spes* was promulgated as a pastoral constitution, a new genre in conciliar documents. It sought to address the world pastorally, not polemically, and embodies the spirit that Pope John XXIII had hoped would suffuse the entire council.

Where We Have Come: The Impact of Vatican II

Scores, even hundreds of books have been written about Vatican II and will no doubt continue to be written. Some thirty-five years after its conclusion, it is perhaps still too early to trace its full impact.

In this final section, something of the course of the implementation of the council will be noted, followed by an assessment of the impact of Vatican II as seen at the end of the twentieth century.

As has already been noted, the council concluded at a time of great euphoria. Modernity was at its height; belief in the possibility of a grand project to reform society was strong. Catholics plunged into the task of implementing the work of the council with great enthusiasm. A group of theologians who had been influential at the council founded the international journal *Concilium* to continue the renewal in theology that the council had endorsed and itself so powerfully done. In North America and Europe, interest in experimentation to find more adequate and appropriate forms for worship, a greater lay voice in the church, the reform of religious institutes, and the quest for justice energized many people. In Latin America, the meeting of the bishops at Medellín in 1968 signaled a new commitment to the poor and to the cause of their liberation from poverty and oppression. In Asia, interest in interreligious dialogue rose dramatically. In Africa, the missionary role was being reevaluated in light of the teaching of *Ad gentes*. The energy and ferment in the church was palpable.

Alongside the agenda for social justice, another issue made itself felt, first in Africa and then throughout Asia and Oceania, beginning in the late 1960s. The council had sent two messages that came together in a powerful way. One message was the need to adapt the church to local circumstances in so-called mission countries. The church since the time of Pius XI had been noting this need. But the other message coming from the council, regarding the importance of culture and cultural development, provided a theological underpinning for such adaptation, which carried it further than a mere pragmatic concern. By the end of the 1970s this new emphasis was being called *inculturation*. The theme of culture was to become an integral part of the message of Pope John Paul II, especially in his travels. While great attention has been given to this theme, many have been disappointed that so little inculturation has been allowed.

The euphoria created by the council became more muted, perhaps inevitably so, as the decades rolled on. Some theologians who had been supportive and in some instances instrumental in the work of the council felt that the zeal for reform and renewal had gone too far in coming to terms with modernity. They pulled back from the reform and expressed concern about the church's identity, fearing it was becoming diluted in its accommodation to modernity, and that the agenda of the world was setting too much of the agenda for the church. The international journal *Communio* was introduced to counteract what was felt to be the overly progressive tone of *Concilium.*

That the synods of bishops were to be but advisory to the pope, and not have the authority to legislate for the church, came as a disappointment to those who had hoped that the council would not be the end of the reform but an impetus to continuing reform. Nonetheless, the early synods, especially those on justice and evangelization, produced remarkable documents.

During the long pontificate of Pope John Paul II, the concern for justice continued to be voiced loudly, although liberation theology, one of its most notable media, was put under great pressure. Some of the more progressive elements in the reform appeared to be increasingly contained. A special synod was convoked in 1985 to create a kind of official interpretation of Vatican II. The People of God theme as an ecclesial image was replaced with the theme of the church as *communio,* to be sure an ancient image of the church dating back to patristic times, but one now ideologically tinged to reassert the importance of hierarchy. A new universal catechism was also developed and published, the first such catechism to be issued since the time of the Council of Trent, to clarify the teaching of the church amid the plurality of voices and theologies. A more conservative look to the church became more and more apparent from the late 1980s, both in episcopal appointments and the emergence of groups seeking some of the uniformity and clarity that the turbulence of the post-conciliar years had obscured.

In parts of the church the debate between progressive and conservative grew acrimonious. Shortly before his death in 1996, Joseph Cardinal Bernardin of Chicago launched the Catholic Common Ground Initiative as a forum where increasingly polarized positions might be aired in a calm fashion.

Where is the impact of the council at century's end? Again, the distance of thirty-five years from the council's closing may be too short a time to make an adequate assessment. Historically, the influence of the most important previous councils took a century to be completely felt. To interpret the impact of the council merely as a swing from euphoria to a more sober, even pessimistic view may prove to be shortsighted. What might be more useful is to look at (1) how the context has changed, (2) what some of the limits of the council itself have been, and (3) what seems to be enduring despite swings from euphoria to a more sober view.

The Changed Context

The optimism of the 1960s and its impact upon the immediate reception of the council have already been noted. That optimism contributed to the impact the council had in coming to terms with modernity. It coincided with perhaps the high point of modernity itself. Some date the turn from that high modernity to 1973, with the OPEC oil embargo and the report of the Club of Rome on the limits to growth.

The end of the century, nearly four decades later, presents a very different picture, which has to have some effect on how the council is received. The pulling down of the Berlin Wall in 1989, and the consequent collapse of a bipolar world political and economic system, has left world order in a more confusing state than prevailed in the 1960s. The speed of communications technology has created the phenomenon known as *globalization,* whereby there is at once an expansion and compression of time and space. This phenomenon results in an intensification of the encounter between the global and the local. The global—symbolized by a single system of neoliberal capitalism and the cultural production of consumerist products—appears to be sweeping away local difference in one great homogenizing wave. The global sweep also betokens a lack of control over key aspects of one's life, such as employment, location, and career path. But the global does not succeed in obliterating the local. In a paradoxical way, it intensifies the local. That intensification is seen in acts of resistance that try to reclaim the space for the local. At times it leads to the invention of a new local tradition as an antidote to the omnivorous nature of the global, as difference gets highlighted in an outsized way. It is evident in the seventy-some wars being fought on the planet at any given time (most of them between groups within national boundaries rather than between countries), the rise of fundamentalism to reassert a more stable identity, and the reappearance of religion as a major factor in public life.[3]

Accompanying globalization is an ever-greater assertion of what is called *postmodernity.* Postmodernity refers to a condition that signals the end of some aspects of the modern project. Most notably, the pluralism of contemporary societies makes it impossible to sustain what are called "master narratives," that is, a common interpretation of history that is shared by a society. One is confronted instead with a host of "little" narratives that create and maintain smaller communities. With this comes an experience of fragmentation of society and even of personal identity. What holds the plurality of views together is harder to see; perhaps it is the economic and cultural wave of globalization. With the disappearance of the master narratives goes also optimism about grand projects that will change society fundamentally for the better. Progress itself does not seem to have a clear goal but is mainly marked by the speed of change.

Postmodernism in itself creates a more somber view of the world. It looks back on the optimism of modernity and sees not just the great technological progress but also a blood-stained century in which more than 110 million people have died in wars alone. It sees some of the optimism as hubris about the perfectibility of humankind.

What does this changed context mean for the reception of the council? The optimism of a document like *Gaudium et spes* might seem a little overdrawn at century's end. And much of the quest for clarity and yearning for a more unified and triumphant church standing against the darkness of the current age would probably have come about in some measure no matter what leadership had been in place in the church. Moreover, for the generation born after the council, now entering adulthood, establishing some patterns of order and continuity are not ideologically driven, as they are often interpreted, but simply represent a quest for an experience of stability in a very unstable world. Older Catholics who remember pre-conciliar times often internalized more order than they realized and so find less need for those external patterns that so fascinate many of the young today. Studies have shown that most post-conciliar Catholics' views do not differ much from those of the conciliar period (except among post-conciliar priests in the United States, who tend to be more conservative than their peers). The difference is not so much in beliefs but interest in the practices that give coherence and build solidarity in Catholic communities.

Limits of the Council

Another danger in assessing the council's impact is loading it with more freight than it can bear. It is important to note what the council could and could not do as much as what it did or what it seemed to promise. It is worth pointing to two limits that the council necessarily had in order to bring this into focus.

First of all, the council was convoked to deal with problems of the modern world and the church's relation to that world. In retrospect, it is clear that the "modern world" it was addressing was that of Europe and North America. Even though there was representation from all continents, the agenda was really aimed at those two continents and their problem of secularization. That it did not deal as well with the problems of other continents (although it laid the groundwork for such work) is simply due to the fact that there was only so much one council could do.

Second, if the council was convoked to deal with the problems of the modern world, what happens when the world passes out of modernity? This is a major part of the challenge to the impact of the council today. This issue is being raised both on the right and on the left of postmodernity. What strategy should the church employ? A return to premodernity? A reassertion of modernity? Burrowing into a niche of postmodernity? This is where we stand at century's end. In my opinion, the council met the agenda for modernity successfully. It is now challenged to meet a changing time.

The Enduring Impact of the Council

A retreat to premodernity is not really an option. Any such retreat will not take the church back to its premodern stance; it will only be an imagined and selective reconstruction of it. Nor should it be satisfied with its niche in the postmodern world as an option for those who might prefer it. In a fragmented world, the church needs more than ever to show forth its catholicity by creating a unity that respects diversity but is not overwhelmed by it.

And here returning to the council continues to be of benefit. The modern agenda has not been completely set aside, neither in the world nor in the church. There are values and ideas that are needed as much as ever. The theme of participation, which so marked especially the *Constitution on the Sacred Liturgy,* becomes doubly important in a world where a global economy threatens to exclude people. The attempt to balance the local and the universal church in a world where the local and the global collide remains a fresh theme. The vision of the dignity of the human person set forth so boldly in *Gaudium et spes* has lost none of its validity. The respecting of conscience and the dialogue among religions at a time when violence is legitimated by an appeal to religion has more urgency now than at the time of the council. And a concern for the world as a whole, in its joy and its hope, its grief and its anguish, rather than retreating from it, will always stand as a theological tenet of a church that hopes to be a sacrament to and for the world of God's love and grace.

Notes

[1] Néstor García Canclini, *Hybrid Cultures: Strategies for Entering and Leaving Modernity* (Minneapolis, Minn.: University of Minnesota Press, 1995), 12-13.

[2] For one eye-witness's account, see Edward Schillebeeckx, *Theologisch Testament* (Baarn: Nelissen, 1984), 40ff.

[3] See, for example, Douglas Johnston and Cynthia Sampson, eds., *Religion: The Missing Dimension of Statecraft* (New York: Oxford University Press, 1994).

14

The Impact of Marxist Ideas on Christian Theology

GREGORY BAUM

If this were an essay on the impact of Marxism on the Christian church, it would have to describe the oppression inflicted by Marxist governments upon the churches in Eastern Europe, China, and other parts, and the hostility to the churches exhibited by Marxist political parties in Western European countries. Such an essay would have to honor the sacrifices made by believing Christians under Marxist rule who remained faithful to their religious commitment. If this were an essay on Marxist-Christian dialogue, it would have to report on the efforts made by Christians to negotiate agreements or enter into conversation with Marxists. Such a report would include the *Ostpolitik* of the Vatican,[1] that is, the diplomatic effort of the Vatican to negotiate agreements with communist governments that would protect the survival of the Catholic church in these countries. It would also include the organizations of Marxist-Christian dialogue, the best known among them being the *Paulus Gesellschaft* in Germany, which, in the sixties, brought into conversation of mutual respect Christian theologians and Marxist thinkers of Eastern Europe.[2] If this were an essay reflecting on believing Christians who came to regard themselves as Marxists and actively supported a Marxist government or a Marxist political party, it would have to deal with theologians such as Giulio Girardi,[3] who supported the Italian Communist Party, or with groups like Christians for Socialism,[4] founded in Chile in 1972, which supported the Marxist government of Salvador Allende. If this were an essay on the reaction of the Christian church to Marxist socialism, it would have to treat the condemnation of Marxism by the popes and bishops of the Catholic church and the critical statements made by the other Christian churches. Nor does this essay raise the question whether the collapse of communism in Eastern Europe in 1989 has had an effect on theological reflection. A discussion of all these topics would require an entire book.

The topic of this essay is quite different. What I wish to examine is the impact of Marxist ideas on Christian theology or, more precisely, on Christian theologians who were impressed by certain ideas of the Marxist tradition, who tested these ideas with the truth of the gospel, and who then adapted or modified them so as to be of service in their theological exploration of Christian revelation. The approach of this essay, as the reader shall notice, is systematic rather than historical. Dom Hélder Câmara believed that just as Christians were at one time impressed by the ideas of Plato and Aristotle and made use of them in their theology, so Christians of his generation were influenced by ideas derived from Marx.[5] While Plato and Aristotle were regarded as heathens by the church and their work contained positions diametrically opposed to Christian teaching, these thinkers provided ideas that appealed to Christians, were rethought by them, and were found helpful in the interpretation of Christian revelation. Such a procedure is not without danger. The Reformers of the sixteenth century thought that the medieval church had swallowed too much of Plato and Aristotle, and in doing so obscured rather than illumined the biblical message. It is also possible to swallow too much of Marx. Yet what interests me in this essay is the impact of Marxist ideas on Christian theology that wants to remain true to itself and faithful to the gospel. I have in mind the rich literature of political theology in Europe and North America and of liberation theology in Latin America. In this essay I pay special attention to the startling evolution of Roman Catholic social teaching. A parallel evolution has taken place at the World Council of Churches, which is summarized in Ulrich Duchrow's article in this volume.

The theologians who have allowed themselves to be influenced by Marxist ideas have also felt the need to be critical of these ideas and to explain how Christian thought differed from them. An impressive example of this approach is Nicholas Lash's *A Matter of Hope: A Theologian's Reflections on the Thought of Karl Marx* and Arthur McGovern's *Marxism: An American Christian Approach*, two books that offer an appreciative and critical reading of Marx and Marxism respectively.[6] Even under the conditions of discrimination existing in Communist East Germany, the Lutheran bishop Albrecht Schönherr, an important thinker of the East German church, repeatedly made the double affirmation that Christianity was separated from the official Marxism by an unbridgeable gulf and that, at the same time, Christians were challenged by, and had much to learn from, certain Marxist ideas.[7] While these theologians responded positively to the challenge of certain Marxist ideas, they also warned against being "insufficiently critical"[8] of them. In this essay I shall follow their example. In spite of the errors of any consistent Marxist ideology, the authoritarianism exhibited by most Marxist political parties, and the totalitarianism of Marxist-Leninist regimes, I am persuaded that many ideas of Marx and his followers have had a creative impact on the intellectual life of the West, including Christian theology.

Moral Outrage as Starting Point of Reflection

Karl Marx was deeply outraged by the conditions of the working class created by the Industrial Revolution. This outrage was shared at the time by many conservative thinkers and romantic novelists and poets. Yet Marx made outrage the starting point of his scientific investigation. Emile Durkheim, who had little use for the scientific analysis provided in *Das Kapital*, honored the outrage felt by its author. "It is passion that has been the inspiration of these systems: what gave them life and strength is a thirst for a more perfect justice, pity for the misery of the working classes, and a general feeling for the distress of contemporary society."[9] Some writers have likened Marx to the ancient prophets of Israel, who in the name of God's justice condemned the oppression and exploitation of the poor. What Marx added to the prophets was that, as a child of the Enlightenment, he made his outrage the starting point of critical, scientific investigation. For him, distress over the misery of others gave rise to thought.

Making moral outrage the starting point of reflection differed from the traditional Christian response to the distress of the poor, which expressed itself in acts of charity and the corporal works of mercy. Marx's approach also differed from that of the classical philosophical tradition, which regarded astonishment or wonder, not moral outrage, as the starting point of reflection.

One may well ask why Marx was so scandalized by the exploitation of workers and the dehumanizing culture created by the capitalism of his day? Why did he feel so strongly that people should be dedicated to the transformation of society? He wrote, "Philosophers have only interpreted the world in various ways; the point is to change it." Behind the outrage and the imperative to act stands an ideal of a non-alienating society and an ethical commitment to justice and human dignity. Marx was haunted by a utopian vision. The only Marxist thinker who clearly recognized the utopia behind Marx's thought was Ernst Bloch, who argued that the vision of a truly humane society was ultimately derived from the biblical promises.[10] Marx himself did not formulate his ethical convictions, nor did he marvel that in this cruel and unjust world these same convictions also existed in the hearts of other people. By contrast, Christian theologians do marvel at the capacity of people to be moved by the suffering of others, to transcend their personal self-interest, and to act on behalf of the unjustly treated. Theologians attribute this capacity to divine grace.

To begin rational reflection with outrage over the massive suffering inflicted upon human beings has appealed to many Christian theologians. The various forms of liberation theology have followed this approach. The Latin American bishops at Medellín began their statement on justice by referring to the misery inflicted upon the masses as "an injustice that cries to heaven."[11] Outrage was the starting point of their theological reflections.

According to Edward Schillebeeckx, outrage over the sins that cry to heaven has repeatedly raised the moral conscience of humankind, including the church. He designates as "contrast experiences"[12] the overwhelming feeling that the massive harm done by society is totally unacceptable, that it must be stopped, that it can be stopped, and that all energies must be oriented toward its cessation. This is how humankind and the church have learned that slavery must be abolished and that torture must be outlawed. In this manner recent popes have also learnt to condemn colonialism and imperialism. An example is the outrage over North-South relations that "cry to heaven," expressed by Pope John Paul II in a speech given during his visit to Canada in 1984: "Poor people and poor nations—poor in different ways, not only lacking food, but also deprived of freedom and other human rights—will sit in judgment on those people who take these goods away from them, amassing to themselves the imperialistic monopoly of economic and political supremacy at the expense of others."[13]

Since outrage can also give rise to bias, a prejudiced analysis, and the desire for revenge, Christians do not want to surrender themselves to outrage in a manner that brackets the call for love and justice. Christians have become painfully aware that the outrage over the crucifixion of Jesus, the Son of God, has prompted the church almost from the beginning to create a biased myth, indifferent to love and justice, that blamed the Jewish people for this deed and invalidated their inherited religion, a myth that has had terrible consequences in history.

Seeing Society from the Perspective of Its Victims

Marx looked upon industrial capitalism from the perspective of its victims. Because he concentrated his analysis on the harm done to the working class, he arrived at an evaluation of industrial society that was quite different from that made by social thinkers who focused on the achievements of that society and who trusted in the progressive dynamism built into it. The perspective from which observers look upon a society influences what they see and how they evaluate it. This Marxist insight has influenced a great many social scientists who do not regard themselves as Marxist at all. They argue persuasively that the social sciences, while following an objective methodology, are never exclusively objective; they are inevitably guided by a subjective element, that is, the perspective from which they approach their object. Every perspective is historically conditioned. The conscious or unconscious solidarities of social scientists influence the questions they ask, the data they regard as pertinent, the paradigm they choose for organizing their data, and thus their final conclusions. The Frankfurt School, a team of scholars who regarded themselves as critical Marxists, argued that social science research that is not guided by an emancipatory commitment disguises rather than reveals the uncomfortable truths about society. Following this line of thought, many social scientists defend the idea of engaged scholarship.

Christian theologians have listened to this argument with sympathy, and this for two reasons. First, they recognize that many parts of the Bible are written from the perspective defined by solidarity with the poor and oppressed, especially the story of the Exodus, the message of the Hebrew prophets, and the preaching of Jesus Christ. Contemporary authors agree that the men and women in Palestine to whom Jesus preached the good news were, on the whole, the marginalized people, overtaxed by the empire, threatened by the Hellenization of their culture and, on top of all that, excluded from the official religion.[14] Jesus brought good news to the poor. Second, modern theologians, remembering the writings of the church fathers, have lamented the separation of knowledge and love characteristic of modern rationalism. Theology sees itself as guided in its search for truth by the love of God and the longing for God's approaching reign. Theology is always engaged scholarship. Doing theology out of solidarity with society's victims seems to many Christians in keeping with the biblical witness, the example of Jesus in particular, and with the theological tradition according to which Christian truth becomes fully available only through the continual conversion to greater love. Following this line of thought, Gustavo Gutiérrez has called theology the second step, the first step being an act of love, that is, solidarity with society's victims.[15] The same approach has also inspired feminist theology, black theology, and other theologies operating out of an emancipatory commitment.

The question theologians have asked themselves is whether Marx was correct in designating society's victims. Marx and, after him, European Marxism defined these victims as the working class. Marx anticipated that capitalist society would eventually be made up of two antagonistic classes, the bourgeoisie and the proletariat. He did not foresee the emergence of an ever-growing sector of office employees, nor did he realize that technological development and the unionization of labor would create a many-leveled working class. Marx, moreover, was insensitive to the particular plight of peasants, whom he expected to become agricultural laborers. Nor did Marxism pay adequate attention to the feminist perspective. The inadequacy of the Marxist analysis became even more obvious in parts of the world where industrialization was in an early stage, where industrial laborers were few, and where the great majority of the population were the poor living in subsistence economies on the land or under conditions of misery in the shantytowns of the large cities. Third-world Marxism came to differ drastically from Marxism in the industrialized countries.

Christian theologians realized that if the Marxist analysis was incorrect, the political action guided by it would keep certain sectors of the population in the margin and possibly create new forms of injustice. At certain moments some Christian theologians did accept the Marxist analysis, thought of themselves as Marxist Christians, and joined a Marxist political project. I referred to this at the beginning of this article. Yet these were brief episodes. Christians in Latin America and other parts of the world rewrote the Marxist option for the proletariat as "the preferential option for the poor."

The Latin American Bishops' Conference at Puebla (1979) defined the option for the poor as the double commitment to read society from the perspective of the poor and to give public witness of solidarity with their struggle for justice.[16] The *Puebla Document* called upon the entire church to be converted to this option as the contemporary form of discipleship. The option for the poor differs from the option for the proletariat inasmuch as it embraces all marginalized people, that is, people prevented from participation in the wealth and power of society. In Latin America the great majority of the population refers to itself as "the people" or "the poor." In the developed world, Christians have wrestled with the question of who in their country are "the poor." In his encyclical *Laborem exercens* (1981), written at the time when the Polish union movement Solidarnosc tried to transform Polish communism, John Paul II described the necessary option as solidarity of and with labor: "There is a need for ever new movements of solidarity of the workers and with the workers."[17] In their pastoral letter on economic justice, the American Catholic bishops defined the poor largely in economic terms and demanded that the government protect their material and social well-being, while the Canadian Catholic bishops argued in their pastoral statements that in their society the option for the poor meant solidarity with the various social movements in Canada demanding justice, peace, and the protection of the environment.[18]

The Concept of Structural Sin

Responding to the social preoccupation of French Marxists, Henri de Lubac and Marie-Dominique Chenu developed in the 1950s a theological approach that brought out the social dimension of the Christian message.[19] Divine redemption aimed at the transformation of people as well as their societies. Later, in the 1960s, Johann-Baptist Metz, in dialogue with the thought of the Frankfurt School, developed what he called "political theology," that is, the systematic theological effort to recover the social dimension of Christian doctrine, which an individualistic reading of the gospel had obscured.[20] Metz was accompanied in this endeavor by two Protestant theologians, Jürgen Moltmann and Dorothee Soelle.[21] Sin, conversion, and new life, the basic concepts of the Pauline message, had to be rescued from the privatized understanding dominant in Christian piety and the dominant theology.[22] It was important to recognize that sin had personal as well as social meaning.

Social sin is above all structural. There are institutions created by humans that have destructive consequences on people's lives, consequences that are independent of the personal intentions of those now in charge of these institutions. The dehumanizing consequences are often disguised by an ideology that persuades people to accept the status quo without questioning it. The notion of social sin played an important role in liberation theology and the teaching of the Latin American bishops that analyzed the plight of the poor in Latin America as a result of internal class oppression and external economic neo-colonialism.[23] The task of the church, according to the bishops, was to raise the consciousness of the population—they called it "concientización"[24]—that is, to awaken all classes of society to the structural sin that produces poverty and misery among the poor, the great majority.

This theology of sin soon influenced the social teachings of the papacy. According to Paul VI, Christian communities must "analyze with objectivity the situation of their country" so that they come to understand their pastoral mission.[25] The preaching of the gospel, according to the 1971 World Synod of Bishops, must include the call to "social justice and the transformation of society." Why? Because the Paschal Mystery of Christ promises "the redemption of the human race and its liberation from every oppressive situation."[26] The concept of structural sin was eventually taken over by Pope John Paul II, especially in his encyclical *Solicitudo rei socialis* (1987), in which he denounced as sinful structures the political, economic, and ideological imperialism sustained by the West and the East. "'Sin' and 'structures of sin,' . . . are categories that are seldom applied to the situation of the contemporary world. Yet one cannot gain a profound understanding of the reality that confronts us unless we give a name to the root of the evils that afflict us."[27]

At the same time, Christian theologians do not sever the concept of social sin from that of personal sin. The two are interrelated. "Human limitations and personal sins compounded have created social sins, and conversely social sins create an environment that promotes personal sins in all classes."[28] The wounds inflicted on the victims, who are the sinned-against, tempt them to transform their struggle for justice into a campaign of hatred and revenge. Liberation movements need to remain self-critical.

The Ideological Dimension of Religion

Marx's critique of religion is well known. "Religious suffering is the expression of real suffering and at the same time the protest against real suffering. Religion is the sigh of the oppressed creature, the heart of a heartless world, the soul of soulless conditions: it is the opium of the people." Marxist commentators have stressed the ideological role played by religion, yet they have neglected Marx's awareness that religion can also be the source of social protest. By ideology Marxists refer to the ideas, symbols, customs, and institutions that legitimate the economic structures of exploitation and oppression. The dominant culture, including religion, Marxists argue, blesses the existing order and reconciles people with the unjust institutions built into this order. Wrestling for social reconstruction is never simply a political struggle; it is at the same time a cultural struggle raising people's awareness of the ideological dimension of their culture.

While Christian theologians reject the idea that culture and religion are nothing but ideological formations, they willingly admit that culture and religion often play an ideological role. Matthew Lamb coined the word *sacralism* to designate the use of religion to legitimate injustice.[29] Christian theologians have recognized that an exclusive emphasis on the rewards in the world-to-come and patience and obedience as the virtues for the present world distorted the full Christian message and made religion into a kind of narcotic. Political theology and the various liberation theologies have instituted the critique of ideology—"Ideologiekritik," in the language of the Frankfurt School—as a necessary step of theological reflection. To uncover the emancipatory meaning of God's revealed word, they engage in a critical reading of Christian doctrine and piety. The contemporary emphasis in theology, supported by the church's official teaching, is that the biblical message is good news already for the present world, and that while patience and obedience have their place, the call to the love of God and neighbor summons the believing community to stand against injustice and support the reconstruction of society.

Prior to Pope John XXIII, Catholic social teaching was based on a particular understanding of the natural law and made no reference to the scriptures. As a consequence, social justice appeared as a natural virtue, not directly related to the supernatural virtues of faith, hope, and love. In this context it was possible to think of oneself as dedicated to Christ and striving after holiness, without adopting a political perspective critical of injustices such as discrimination, exploitation, and oppression. To overcome this ideological inheritance, Catholic social teaching, following political and liberation theology, has learned to relate the call to social justice to the imperative of the gospel. In the contemporary understanding, Christian life includes taking a critical a look at society, entering into solidarity with the marginalized and excluded, and, if political involvement is impossible, at least supporting a culture of resistance and hope.[30]

In wrestling with the ideological dimension of religion, some Christian thinkers have interpreted the Christian message by bracketing the Resurrection and the Age-to-Come. This phenomenon is found especially in the middle classes of Western society, where Christians are grateful to God for a meaningful and interesting life and in old age are quite ready to enter an eternal sleep. By contrast, in liberation theology, which is the product of the poor and the marginalized who live frustrated lives and often die young, the resurrection of Jesus holds a central place and is interpreted as the rehabilitation of all the victims of history. Faith in the resurrection of Jesus summons these Christians to act courageously in this world.

The Human as Worker

According to Marx, humans differ from animals because humans have to create the conditions for their survival by labor. Animals act according to instinct, while humans are guided in their actions by intelligence. To interpret the human as worker was at odds with the philosophical tradition of antiquity and modern times, which defined human beings in terms of their spiritual or rational dimension. Philosophers were representatives of a culture that looked down upon manual labor and assigned it to the lower sector of society. Marx argued that humans create their world by labor and in doing so constitute themselves. Labor is a creative activity. At the same time, the master/servant relationship in the process of production marks the entire society and produces material conditions under which work ceases to be creative and instead becomes alienating. Alienating labor was a particular characteristic of industrial capitalism.

While the scriptures depicted Adam as a farmer and honored manual labor throughout its pages, the church's theological tradition, influenced as it was by Hellenic thought, looked upon reason and the spirit as the defining element of human being and had next to nothing to say about human labor. It was Christian piety in the guilds and monasteries that continued to give religious meaning to manual work.

It was only in the twentieth century, as a response to Marx's understanding of labor, that we find in the church the development of a theology of work, from M.-D. Chenu's *Pour une théologie du travail* (1955) to Pope John Paul II's bold encyclical *Laborem exercens* (1981). The pope, while an enemy of communism, had no hesitation about listening to Marx's ideas and modifying them to make them fit into his own theology of work. Invoking the creation of Adam, John Paul II defined the human as worker. Humans produce their world by labor and in doing so enter into their own self-realization. The pope distinguishes between the objective pole of labor, that is, the object produced by it, and the subjective pole of labor, that is, the self-realization of the worker, and boldly affirms the preeminence of the subjective pole. The division of labor and the conditions of labor must be such that they rescue the workers from oppression, exploitation, and alienating labor and instead serve their creative self-development. The organization of labor in society, John Paul II argues persuasively, is "a key, probably the essential key" to the entire social question.[31] Christians, faithful to the gospel, must make an analysis of the economic system in terms of its effect on workers and society as a whole.

John Paul II condemns any economic system, socialist or capitalist, that looks upon the worker simply as an instrument of production. Justice demands that workers be treated as responsible subjects of work and as true makers with claims on the work of their hands. At the same time the encyclical insists—against Marxism—that the labor movement and the movement of the excluded are not expressions of class struggle; they express rather the struggle for social justice, which should be supported by people of all classes committed to an ethical vision of society. John Paul II thus calls for "solidarity of labor and with labor."

The Concept of Praxis

Since, for Marx, reflection begins with outrage over the suffering inflicted upon the working class and solidarity with its struggle for emancipation, he believed that the entry into truth must be preceded by taking sides, that is, by practice, by commitment, and by action. Here practice precedes theory. On this basis, Marx criticized Feuerbach and philosophers in general. Their indifference to the plight of the exploited and oppressed majority gave their theories an abstract character, the impact of which left the damaging society unchallenged. "Philosophers have only interpreted the world in various ways," Marx wrote. "The point is to change it." For Marx—at least, for the Marx of the early writings—truth liberates; it supports the social forces of emancipation. Truth is to be tested by its weight and power in history. The path to truth is initiated by the practice of solidarity and guided by the ongoing interaction between theory and practice, that is, between theoretical knowledge and practical experience. This interaction is called *praxis*. Truth here is the praxis oriented toward human liberation.

While Christian theologians disagree with this purely secular understanding of emancipation and the Promethean character of Marx's proposal, they find the notion of praxis very enlightening. Christian faith surely is a praxis. It begins with action, the surrender to God's word, and continues through an ongoing interaction between its cognitive and agapic dimensions. Seeing faith as praxis, as discipleship, rescues it from a purely cognitive understanding as well as from an understanding that neglects the cognitive dimension. Living faith, then, is the praxis that supports the healing and redemption of the world.

Many theologians—this writer among them—regard theology itself as a praxis. For them, theology is not the rational exploration of divine revelation to increase its intelligibility; for them, the task of theology is not to provide abstract knowledge independent of the historical situation of the believing community. Instead, according to these theologians, theology is a rational exercise that follows upon the option for the poor and searches for an understanding of God's revelation that discloses its redemptive and liberative power. Theology as praxis is historically rooted; since history changes, praxis theology must move forward, through the interaction of the cognitive and agapic dimensions of faith, in an effort to formulate God's revealed word of rescue and hope addressed to people in the present.[32]

A Critique of Modernity

In the dialogue with modernity Christian theologians have always kept a critical distance. This is true also of the theologians influenced by the ideas of Marx. In particular, these theologians reject the veneration of reason as the single organ of human liberation and refuse to endorse the idea of necessary progress. Not only do these theologians lament, with the Frankfurt School, the collapse of Enlightenment reason into instrumental rationality (reason dealing with means), but they are also keenly aware that even substantive rationality (reason dealing with ends) can be grounded on false presuppositions and be in need of redemption. Only reason grounded on love and solidarity—which is a fruit of divine grace—is a reliable guide in the struggle for emancipation. Postmodern thinkers have a point when they suspect that the arrogant affirmation of the universality of reason hides the wish to dominate the world.

For similar reasons the same theologians are also ill at ease with theories of necessary progress, whether liberal or Marxist. While they believe that God is graciously at work among human beings, enlightening and empowering them to struggle against oppression and build a more just society, they also recognize that any social progress that is achieved remains vulnerable to human sin and may in time take on oppressive features. Relying on God's redemptive presence, these theologians entertain a view of history that supports the human struggle for justice, peace, and ecological responsibility; yet they refuse to draw the conclusion that this divinely sustained struggle leads to the definitive emancipation of humankind within history. They share the postmodern suspicion of all grand narratives that promise a happy ending in time. The theologians offer a message of unshakable hope because they hold that after every failure God's presence stirs up new struggles to create a more just and more responsible society. They recognize, of course, that ultimate liberation lies beyond history.

Conclusion

The collapse of communism was a great relief for the peoples of Eastern Europe. Marxism was a failure not only because, under the impact of Leninism, it produced oppressive, totalitarian regimes, but also because the centralized command economy that it had set up led to complete bankruptcy. The deadly experiment has demonstrated that markets are necessary, the remaining question being how they can be guided by society so as to serve the common good.

The collapse of communism has led to a new world order. Because of the absence of an alternative, capitalism, it would seem, is now able to show its ugly face, promote a global economy based on competition and the quest for gain, and become indifferent to the growing sector of people excluded from society's wealth—massively in the poor countries, and significantly in the rich ones. A single, unchallenged military superpower is now protecting the ongoing globalization of the self-regulating market system. Thanks to the power of the large corporations and the international financial institutions, national governments have lost the capacity to protect the material and cultural well-being of their citizens. The dominant neo-liberal ideology persuades people that the ideas of Marx have lost their relevance.

In my opinion the ideas of Marxism discussed in this article have, in one way or another, become part of the Western intellectual tradition and hence are not likely to lose their validity. The modification of these ideas in the light of faith has greatly enriched theology and helped to enroll theology in the service of God's coming reign.

Notes

[1] Eric Hanson, *The Catholic Church in World Politics* (Princeton, N.J.: Princeton University Press, 1987), see index under "Ostpolitk."

[2] See Peter Hebblethwaite, *The Christian-Marxist Dialogue* (New York: Paulist Press, 1977), 17-37.

[3] Giulio Girardi, *Marxisme et christianisme* (Paris: Desclée, 1968).

[4] See Hebblethwaite, *The Christian-Marxist Dialogue*, 57-73.

[5] Dom Hélder Câmara, "What Should St. Thomas, the Aristotle Commentator, Do If Faced with Karl Marx?" lecture given at the University of Chicago, October 29, 1974, *Jesuit Project for Third World Awareness: Resource Services* 1, issue 12 (1974).

[6] Nicholas Lash, *A Matter of Hope: A Theologian's Reflections on the Thought of Karl Marx* (Notre Dame, Ind.: University of Notre Dame Press, 1982); Arthur McGovern, *Marxism: An American Christian Approach* (Maryknoll, N.Y.: Orbis Books, 1980). See also David McLellan, *Marxism and Religion* (New York: Harper & Row, 1987); Wayne Stumme, ed., *Christianity and the Many Faces of Marxism* (Minneapolis, Minn.: Augsburg Publishing House, 1984); Alasdair MacIntyre, *Marxism and Christianity* (Notre Dame, Ind.: University of Notre Dame Press, 1984).

[7] Gregory Baum, *The Church for Others: Protestant Theology in Communist East Germany* (Grand Rapids, Mich.: Eerdmans, 1996), 40-42.

[8] Even Cardinal Ratzinger, in his 1984 Instruction warning of the abuse of Latin American liberation theology, only complained that some theologians made an "insufficiently critical" use of Marxist ideas. See Gregory Baum, *Theology and Society* (New York: Paulist Press, 1987), 105.

[9] From Emile Durkheim's *Le socialisme*. See *Emile Durkheim: Selected Writings*, ed. Anthony Giddens (New York: Cambridge University Press, 1995), 157.

[10] Ernst Bloch, *Geist der Utopie* (Frankfurt am Main: Suhrkamp, 1971 <1923>).

[11] "Justice," "Medellín Documents," *The Gospel of Peace and Justice*, ed. Joseph Gremillion (Maryknoll, N.Y.: Orbis Books, 1976), 445. The expression "an injustice that cries to heaven" was used by Paul VI in *Populorum progressio,* no. 30. See *Catholic*

Social Thought: The Documentary Heritage, ed. David O'Brien and Thomas Shannon (Maryknoll, N.Y.: Orbis Books, 1992), 247.

[12] *The Schillebeeckx Reader*, ed. Robert Schreiter (New York: Crossroad, 1987), 54-56.

[13] See Baum, *Theology and Society*, 96.

[14] Gerd Theissen, *Sociology of Early Palestinian Christianity* (Philadelphia, Pa.: Fortress Press, 1978).

[15] Gustavo Gutiérrez, *A Theology of Liberation* (Maryknoll, N.Y.: Orbis Books, 1973), 11.

[16] "The Final Document," nos. 1134-40, in *Puebla and Beyond*, ed. John Eagleson and Philip Scharper (Maryknoll, N.Y.: Orbis Books, 1979), 264.

[17] *Laborem exercens*, no. 8 (O'Brien and Shannon, *Catholic Social Thought,* 363).

[18] For the interpretation of "the option for the poor" by the American bishops, see their 1986 pastoral letter "Economic Justice for All," especially nos. 87ff., which outline what society must do to provide justice for the poor (O'Brien and Shannon, *Catholic Social Thought,* 599-61). The 1982 pastoral statement of the Canadian bishops, "Ethical Reflections on the Economic Crisis," interprets "the option for the poor" as the call to Christians "to follow Jesus by identifying with the victims of injustice, by analyzing the dominant attitude and structures that cause human suffering, and by actively supporting the poor and oppressed in their struggles to transform society" (*Do Justice! The Social Teaching of the Canadian Catholic Bishops*, ed. E. F. Sheridan, [Montreal: Éditions Paulines, 1987], 399).

[19] Henri de Lubac, *Catholicisme: Les aspects sociaux du dogme* (Paris: Cerf, 1953); M.-D. Chenu, *Pour une théologie du travail* (Paris: Seuil, 1955).

[20] Johann-Baptist Metz, *Theology of the World* (New York: Seabury, 1973).

[21] See Dorothee Soelle, *Political Theology* (Philadelphia, Pa.: Fortress Press, 1974); and Jürgen Moltmann, "Towards a Political Hermeneutic of the Gospel," *Religion, Revolution and the Future* (New York: Scribner's, 1969).

[22] Gregory Baum, *Religion and Alienation* (New York: Paulist Press, 1975), 197-213.

[23] See "Peace," nos. 1-10, "The Medellín Documents," in Gremillion, *The Gospel of Peace and Justice*, 455-57.

[24] "Justice," no. 17, "The Medellín Conference," in Gremillion, *The Gospel of Peace and Justice*, 452.

[25] *Octogesima adveniens,* no. 4, in O'Brien and Shannon, *Catholic Social Thought,* 266.

[26] "Justice in the World," Introduction, in O'Brien and Shannon, *Catholic Social Thought,* 289.

[27] *Solicitudo rei socialis*, no. 36, in O'Brien and Shannon, *Catholic Social Thought,* 419-20.

[28] Baum, *Religion and Alienation*, 204.

[29] Matthew Lamb, *Solidarity with Victims* (New York: Crossroad, 1982), 18.

[30] Reflecting on the contemporary political impotence and the postmodern deconstruction of the self, David Tracy has formulated Christian spirituality in terms of resistance and hope: "On Naming the Present," *On the Threshold of the Third Millennium*, special edition of *Concilium* (Philadelphia, Pa.: Trinity Press International, 1990), 66-85.

[31] *Laborem exercens*, no. 3, in O'Brien and Shannon, *Catholic Social Thought,* 355. For an analysis of the encyclical, see Gregory Baum, "Laborem exercens," in *The New Dictionary of Catholic Social Thought*, ed. Judith A. Dwyer (Collegeville, Minn.:Liturgical Press, 1994), 527-35.

[32] See Lamb, *Solidarity with Victims*, 61-99.

15

The Women's Movement and Theology in the Twentieth Century

SUSAN A. ROSS

From the inauguration of the movement for women's emancipation the Bible has been used to hold her in the "divinely ordained sphere," prescribed in the Old and New Testaments. . . . So long as tens of thousands of Bibles are printed every year, and circulated all over the habitable globe, and the masses in all English-speaking countries revere it as the word of God, it is vain to belittle its influence.

—Elizabeth Cady Stanton, *The Woman's Bible*

The bible is not simply a religious but also a profoundly political book as it continues to inform the self-understandings of American and European "secularized" societies and cultures. Feminist biblical interpretations therefore have a critical political significance not only for women in biblical religion but for all women in Western societies.

—Elisabeth Schüssler Fiorenza, *Bread Not Stone*

A century separates Elizabeth Cady Stanton, the founder of the Women's Rights movement, and Elisabeth Schüssler Fiorenza, the foremost feminist biblical theologian of the late twentieth century. Their positions, however, are strikingly similar, and they serve to illustrate both the progress that has been made, as "women-defined theologies"[1] have affected the discipline of theology, and the barriers to women's equality yet to be overcome. In this essay I will focus largely, though not exclusively, on the women's movement in theology in the United States, primarily from the perspective of Roman Catholic theologians. While no one essay can do justice to this vast and continually developing topic, my hope is that some of the crucial issues that emerge as the twentieth century comes to an end will be clarified.

Historical Context

While the twentieth century is the focus of this book, one must go back, at least briefly, to the nineteenth century to understand the impact of the women's movement on theology, as well as on other disciplines. The year 1998 marks the 150th anniversary of the Seneca Falls Convention, which began the organized struggle in the United States for women's rights. Led by Elizabeth Cady Stanton and others, Seneca Falls marks the start of the "first wave" of the women's movement, which culminated in the Nineteenth Amendment to the U.S. Constitution, ratified in 1920, which finally granted women the right to vote. British women also struggled for the right to vote and in the early years of the twentieth century engaged in hunger strikes to draw attention to their situation. In the seventy-two-year period between 1848 and 1920, the women's movement in the United States also focused on women's roles in religion, and such events as the ordination of Antoinette Brown Blackwell by the Congregational church in 1853, the publication of Elizabeth Cady Stanton's *The Woman's Bible* in 1895, and the activism of Margaret Sanger on birth control issues (to the dismay of the churches) in the early years of the twentieth century witness to the concerns of women in religion.

The Woman's Bible was prescient in terms of its awareness of such interpretive issues as the male authorship of the Bible, the role of the Bible in underscoring women's subordinate roles in family and society, and the importance of highlighting women in the Bible who played prominent roles. It is generally acknowledged that the "first wave" of feminism ended at about the time the Nineteenth Amendment was passed. The battle for women's suffrage had been won, but in fact the war for women's rights was ongoing.

This became evident in 1930, when the Anglican Communion voted at its Lambeth Conference to allow married couples to use contraceptives. Their decision was followed on December 31 of that year by Pope Pius XI's encyclical *Custi connubii* (*On Chaste Marriage*). Pius reiterated the teaching that the primary purpose of marriage was procreation, and thus any form of birth control other than "natural" methods was intrinsically immoral. He further argued that the women's movement threatened to deprive women of "their most noble office as wife and mother and companion" and that women were to submit to their husbands' authority in marriage (no. 26). The encyclical, however, also gave rise to a flood of literature on the goodness of marriage, although not without emphasizing both the hierarchical character of the church and of marriage.[2] Pius XI's conception of all women as mothers (nuns were understood as "spiritual" mothers) and as "essentially different" from men has been reiterated by his successors and remains the basis for official Vatican teaching on women, as will be developed below.[3]

The publication in 1952 of Simone de Beauvoir's *Le Deuxième Sexe* is widely acknowledged to have inaugurated the "second wave" of the women's movement in the West. While de Beauvoir's existentialist individualism and her embrace of a somewhat disembodied concept of the person would later come under criticism by feminist scholars, there is no question that her statement, "one is not born, but rather becomes, a woman," had a profound and lasting effect on the understanding of what it means to be a woman.[4] That "femininity" was, in the terms later used by academics, a "social construction," and not an innate quality, challenged the notion that all women (as well as all men, in a different way) shared a fixed nature and flew in the face of traditional concepts of womanhood that had long been held by the religious and cultural traditions of the West: that women were weaker, that their true destiny was motherhood, and that they were to submit to the authority of men. Yet such ideas have proven to be remarkably long-lasting; in 1998 the Southern Baptist Convention of the U.S. passed a statement that women were to "submit graciously to their husbands' servant leadership."[5]

In 1960 a graduate student at the University of Chicago Divinity School (who was also a single mother) published an essay in the *Journal of Religion*.[6] In it, Valerie Saiving (Goldstein) argued that the prevailing Christian understanding of sin as pride more adequately addressed the experiences of men, who were, on the whole, more in a position to experience this sin than were women, who were already encouraged by culture and religion to be self-sacrificing. Thus the virtue of Christian love as *agape* (sacrificial love) was appropriate for men, who more likely needed to be other-centered. Women, on the other hand, needed to develop a stronger sense of self. Saiving was arguing that women's *experience* was distinctively different from men's, and thus women's senses of "sin" and "grace" were also distinctively different. Saiving's essay did not become well known for another fifteen years, but her ideas were fundamental to what later came to be known as feminist theology.

In 1963 Betty Friedan published *The Feminine Mystique*, a book that would jump-start the women's movement in the United States. Friedan identified "the problem which has no name," the problem being that women—and in this case Friedan meant white, middle-class women—felt a deep sense of emptiness and meaninglessness about their lives.[7] Friedan argued that women needed to gain a greater sense of personal identity and autonomy. The 1960s were also marked by liberation movements for former European colonies and for American blacks, by the Second Vatican Council, by the Vietnam War, by student movements in France and the United States, and by a series of violent incidents—the Los Angeles, Newark, and Detroit race riots, the assassinations of John F. Kennedy, Robert F. Kennedy, and Martin Luther King Jr.

The women's liberation movement, as it came to be called, also left its mark on U.S. culture. Drawing on the "rap groups" developed in the Civil

Rights movement, the "consciousness-raising group" became a means for women—again, largely white and middle-class women—to develop a sense of awareness about their own life situations, including their dependence upon men for their name and identity and the inequities they faced in education, the job market, and religion. Most of all, these groups accentuated women's sense that they were not alone—that their experiences were shared by countless other women. Inspired by the slogan *The personal is the political* and by acting in solidarity with other women, they began to address these issues, both in society and at home. The women's movement had a powerful effect on Western culture, and on non-Western cultures as well, in its drive for women's right to vote, for reproductive rights, for equal treatment in employment and health care, and for changes affecting marriage and divorce laws.

The women's movement inevitably led to the push for women's ordination. If women were to be considered equal to men, the arguments against women's ordination seemed increasingly as discriminatory as the barriers to women's suffrage. Already in 1918 Methodist women had been "officially granted the same rights and conditions as male local preachers"; in 1956 the Presbyterian church began to ordain women. In 1970 Lutherans found that on biblical grounds "the case both for and against ordination is found to be inconclusive" and subsequently ordained women; Episcopalian women forced the issue by having four retired bishops ordain a group of eleven women in 1974. The church's General Convention formally approved the ordination of women in 1976. The Church of England approved women's ordination in 1992. But this issue has remained divisive among many traditions and has led to some groups of churches withdrawing from national conventions, as well as Episcopal priests and Lutheran pastors leaving their own traditions and requesting ordination in Roman Catholicism.[8] The Roman Catholic Church has maintained its official position against ordaining women, which I will discuss below, but not without considerable dissent.

By the mid 1970s the literature of the women's movement was increasing, and the discipline Women's Studies had emerged on college and university campuses, alongside Black Studies, Chicano and Latin American Studies, Native American Studies, Asian and Asian American Studies, and other interdisciplinary approaches to race, ethnicity, and gender. The U.S. Supreme Court decided in 1973 that women's constitutional "right to privacy" included the right to obtain an abortion, and the issue of reproductive rights has been in the center of public and religious debate in the United States ever since. The women's movement has since been credited—or blamed—for dramatic changes in family life, including a rising divorce rate and increasing numbers of working women. The first United Nations International Women's Conference took place in Mexico City in 1975 and has been followed by conferences in Nairobi, Stockholm, and Beijing; the decade 1976-85 was designated the United Nations Decade for Women. The

1995 Beijing conference confirmed the international character of the women's movement but also illustrated the gap between official government policies and grassroots women's organizations. Clearly, the last forty years of the twentieth century have witnessed enormous changes in the lives of women across the globe.

The Women's Movement and the Study of Theology

As it has affected theology, the women's movement has developed in its approaches and concerns. The first stream, so to speak, can be identified as one of initial awareness and concern to reveal the male-centeredness of the historical tradition and what it actually said about women. Elizabeth Clark and Herbert Richardson's anthology *Women and Religion: A Feminist Sourcebook of Christian Thought*, first published in 1975, presented selections from important religious thinkers from ancient Greece to the recent present.[9] Included were Thomas Aquinas's (in)famous statement, quoted from Aristotle, that women were "misbegotten males"; passages from the *Malleus Maleficarum*, the "Hammer of Witches" used in the late Middle Ages to identify women "who were more prone to witchcraft"; Luther's comment that women were created for procreation; and Karl Barth's statement that man is to woman as A is to B. Mary Daly's first book, *The Church and the Second Sex*, drew on de Beauvoir's own title. Daly documented the treatment of women by the institutional church and concluded with an optimism that, once past discrimination was recognized, women would take their rightful place alongside men.[10] Just a few years later Daly repudiated the position she had taken in this book and declared herself a "post-christian feminist philosopher."[11] Uta Ranke-Heinemann's 1990 book, *Eunuchs for the Kingdom of Heaven*, also documented this history, but in a much less sympathetic way than did Daly's first work.[12] This initial development led to the realization that merely documenting women's absence from history did not solve the problem of *why* women were absent, but it raised profound questions about how and for whom history is written.

A second stream of this process was (and is) the concern to address the historical record by restoring women to their place in history. This development is actually more of an ongoing process, along with movements in the "new histories," to see the past from the eyes of those who formerly have been excluded from having place or voice in determining what constitutes "history." Such a process involves not only "rewriting" the past but also reconstructing the present. Scores of women have been "discovered" or "rediscovered," thus changing prevailing notions of what constituted medieval piety, or of the nature of women's historical leadership. Notable here is the work of scholars such as Carolyn Walker Bynum, whose many books have transformed notions of femininity and masculinity in medieval piety, the significance of the body, and the meaning of life after death[13]; Elisabeth

Schüssler Fiorenza, whose work on the early church has challenged understandings of the inevitability of patriarchy in the early Christian community's
formative years[14]; and Ann Taves, whose work on nineteenth-century women
illustrates the complex roles that women have played in family and public
life.[15]

Feminist biblical interpretation has been one of the most productive
areas in feminist theology.[16] Since the Bible serves as the canonical text for
Judaism and Christianity, its interpretation is crucial, not only for the Protestant tradition's biblically centered theology, but also for Roman Catholicism. In Judaism, the rich practice of biblical midrash has inspired new
feminist rereadings of ancient texts. Both Protestant and Catholic scholars
have challenged appeals to the Bible's revelatory character as they expose
its androcentrism, its misuse by religious authorities in justifying structures
of oppression such as slavery and sexism, and the distorted way in which it
ignores and misrepresents women's participation in religious history
through the choices of lectionary readings. But, as the introductory quotes
to this chapter illustrate, feminist biblical scholars take very seriously the
Bible's profound influence on Western culture. They seek to use this power
not only to expose its abuses but also to uncover its rich emancipatory possibilities. Schüssler Fiorenza's reconstruction of the active role of women
in Christian origins and Phyllis Trible's focus on women's "texts of terror"
show how women's struggles and survival offer hope and inspiration for
the present, as their suffering is remembered and restored to history.

A third development in the way in which the women's movement has
affected the study of religion can be identified in the ways in which feminist
scholars have challenged and restructured prevailing models of the disciplines. That is to say, when feminist scholars engage the method and questions of biblical, historical, systematic, and moral theology, the issue is not
so much what women can contribute to the (already existing) question or
issue—the "add women and stir" approach—but rather how women are
transforming the discipline itself. For example, Rosemary Radford Ruether's
Sexism and God-Talk: Toward a Feminist Theology takes on the traditional structure of a systematic theology but recasts theological themes within a context that imaginatively rewrites the creation story and addresses such issues
as Christology and eschatology from a feminist perspective.[17] Elisabeth
Schüssler Fiorenza's *In Memory of Her* is not only a work of sophisticated
biblical criticism but also a challenge to the "objectivity" of the academy,
particularly as it is found in biblical studies, in its argument that all scholarship has an ideological bias. Elizabeth Johnson's *She Who Is* retraces the
lines of the doctrine of God and suggests that a retrieval of the Wisdom
tradition can aid in expanding the human vision of the divine.[18] These works
take their starting point from the tradition—biblical criticism, doctrines of
systematic theology—but then turn the tradition on its side (or head) by
challenging basic presuppositions and method (for example, the objectivity of biblical scholarship, the assumption that God is male).

A fourth development in the scholarship of women and religion has been the emergence of the voices of women "on the margins": African and African American, Latina and Latin American, Asian and Asian American women have challenged the work of European and Euro-American women as sufficiently representative of the voices of all women. Arguing that the dominance of white women mirrors the dominance of white men and white culture, nonmajority women have developed distinctive approaches to women and religion. Ada María Isasi-Díaz, a Cuban American theologian, has coined the term *mujerista* as an alternative for U.S. Hispanic women to "feminist"; African American women have taken up Alice Walker's term *womanist* as their way of expressing identity.[19] The challenges of these theologies to (white) feminist theology have been not only in terms of nomenclature but of substance. For example, both womanist and *mujerista* theologies have argued that (white) feminist theology places too much emphasis on the individual, in contrast to their more family- and community-oriented foci; that feminist Christologies that criticize an emphasis on the sacrifice of the cross miss the ways in which the suffering Jesus can be a source of hope to oppressed peoples; that the issue of inclusive language for God may not adequately address the traditional piety of oppressed and formerly enslaved people.[20] More important, these theologies raise the question of the adequacy of conceptions of "experience," arguing that the "social location" one occupies will largely determine the way in which one conceives of the world, and thus, of self and God. Thus, it is, some argue, fundamentally mistaken to talk about "women's experience," as if there were universals shared by all women.[21]

What has been the effect of the women's movement on the discipline of theology? There are many ways in which this question could be answered. I will, however, focus on the following issues. First, the women's movement has profoundly affected the theological conception of the human person, and thus of theological method; second, it has challenged traditional ideas of moral theology, particularly regarding human sexuality; third, it calls for major recasting of Christian doctrines, in particular the doctrines of God, of Christ, and of church.

Theological Anthropology

Until relatively recently—around the time of Vatican II—theological anthropology was treated under the rubric of the "doctrine of man." Human nature was understood to be relatively static, in that humans shared, over time and across cultures, a stable set of characteristics: rationality, the quality that raised humans above animals; an openness to God; and an inclination to sin. While human beings were either male or female, and thus had different biological capacities that also played a part in their vocational

choices, "man" was treated generically. The women's movement has fundamentally challenged this idea of "man."

First, the women's movement participated in the general emphasis of
the secularization of the 1960s by placing great weight on the normative
and revelatory qualities of human "experience," although some of these
issues would later be called into question. Recall that Valerie Saiving argued that "the temptations of woman as woman are not the same as the
temptations of man as man."[22] As mentioned earlier, Saiving's real contribution was to show how doctrines of sin and grace derived, in large part,
from the experiences of *men,* who found that their own situations of human power and sinfulness led them to an arrogance which needed correc-
tion from a corresponding self-sacrificial doctrine of grace and love.
Women's experiences, she argued, were, on the whole, not experiences of
power and arrogance but rather of too often putting others before oneself,
of "diffuseness and triviality," thus necessitating a different approach to sin
and grace.[23] Human experience was revealed to be "socially located"—that
is, gender, as well as race, class, and ethnic background, were seen to shape
one's understanding of reality, thus challenging universalist understandings of "man" or of "the human" as adequate for all people. Thus the
women's movement, along with other movements for liberation, challenges
the normative character of the white, Western (and often also celibate)
male as the prime "author" or "subject" of theology, highlights the significance and problematic character of experience, and raises social location
as key in interpreting any theological statement.

Along with this, the women's movement has challenged the idea that
rationality and autonomy are the "highest" qualities of human nature, and
that women should strive for the kind of "detached" rationality celebrated
by some philosophers and theologians. That all human beings have rational capacities is not denied by feminist scholars; rather, autonomy and rationality, they argue, need to be balanced by an emphasis on human relation and emotion. Again, feminist scholars have turned to women's
experiences as grounds for a criticism of an androcentric picture of the
human. Carol Gilligan's influential book *In a Different Voice* challenged ideas
of moral development pioneered by Harvard psychologist Lawrence
Kohlberg by suggesting that differences in the ways that boys and girls are
raised may help to account for why boys scored higher overall on tests mea-
suring moral development, which tended to privilege principle-based moral
reasoning, where girls tended to score lower.[24] The "different voice" of rela-
tionship-based moral reasoning that Gilligan proposed was more characteristic of girls and women, and could, she argued, complement more traditional approaches.

While Gilligan's ideas continue to raise questions among psychologists,
theologians, and sociologists, her work has had the effect of stressing the
relational quality of human life. Human existence, feminist theorists have

argued, is profoundly relational as well as situational, and excluding women's experiences from normative conceptions of the person has had the effect of truncating our ideas of what it means to be human. Thus Beverly Wildung Harrison emphasizes the role of anger in the work of love, and Margaret Farley sees personal commitments at the center of human life.[25] While it can be argued that an emphasis on the power of emotion and relation in human life is not altogether new in the Christian tradition, both the influence of the detached Enlightenment subject and women's absence in the theological and philosophical literature on the person have undeniably contributed to a narrowly defined understanding of the self.[26] *Mujerista* and womanist theologians, as well as postcolonial women and men, have also challenged the picture of "rational man" as the normatively human; they stress the importance of family and community, the role of struggle in daily life, and the impossibility of prescinding from concrete concerns for health and well-being, civil rights, and human dignity when considering the question of human nature.[27]

A third dimension of theological anthropology that feminist, womanist, and *mujerista* theologians have stressed is the embodied character of the human person. Along with the understanding of the human person as primarily rational has been an implicit, and sometimes explicit, functional dualism: mind over body, male over female, human over animal, north over south, reason over emotion. As Rosemary Radford Ruether discussed in her 1975 book *New Woman, New Earth*, such dualisms link together women, Jews, people of color, and the earth, and classify them as more sexual, more physical, more emotional, and thus in need of control by "rational man."[28] Such a picture of the human is profoundly distorted and incomplete. All human beings, men as well as women, eat, sleep, need shelter, have sexual drives, become ill, experience emotion, think, eliminate; in short, we are all embodied. While embodiment is to some extent differentiated by sex—women conceive and bear children, menstruate, and tend to live longer than men; men grow facial hair, have the capacity to impregnate, and tend to have greater upper-body strength than women, for example—no one sex is more embodied than the other.[29] Indeed, the central focus of the Christian faith is on the incarnation of God in the body of a human person. Yet the fact that all human beings experience themselves and their relationships to others and to God *through their bodies* has tended to be forgotten in a tradition that still carries with it an ambivalence about body and sexuality.

Feminist scholars have sought to remind us that we are "body-selves" as well as "mind-selves," and that sexuality is a gift from God. Far from being a barrier to relations with God, as traditional prohibitions of sex before eucharist and requirements of clerical celibacy have suggested, human embodiment and the natural world are the very avenues to encounter God, as the Christian sacramental tradition should (but does not always) celebrate.[30] Feminist scholars have thus argued that the opposition to the ordination of women rests, in large part, on a fear of women's bodies and of sexuality. Women cannot truly represent God, in this line of thinking, because an association of God with embodiment and sexuality would threaten the careful separation of the two that the Western Christian tradition has long struggled to maintain. To rethink the significance of embodiment and sexuality, especially from the perspective of women's experiences, means, ultimately, to take seriously the idea that women are made "in the image of God."[31] Below, I will consider some of the doctrinal implications of this point.

A further implication of the importance of embodiment is a new perspective on the natural world. The dualism that pits "man against nature" also relies on a concept of the person that abstracts humans from their natural environment and privileges technological development over concern for environmental effects. It is not at all odd that nature is frequently referred to in feminine pronouns. The attitude toward animals, the earth, sea and sky, mirrors the cultural attitude that has been prevalent toward women. The feminist concern for embodiment seeks to link together all of creation in an interdependent whole.[32]

Moral Theology

As Lisa Sowle Cahill has noted, "All feminist theology is, virtually by definition, feminist ethics."[33] The ethical implications of thinking of women as subjects, of the significance of relationships in human life, and of embodiment, are many. For Roman Catholic moral theology, the last thirty-plus years of the twentieth century have been marked by a particular focus on moral theology, especially on sexuality. And at the center of this concern is a focus on women's reproductive sexuality. While other urgent issues—the threat of war and nuclear weapons, social and economic justice, racism, capital punishment—have also claimed the attention of moral theology, few issues have received as much attention from both the secular press and the Vatican in the last thirty years as has sexuality.

In the late 1950s, when the birth control pill became widely available, it became possible for the first time ever for women to have nearly complete control over their reproductive capacity.[34] Along with the growth of the women's movement in the 1960s, and easy access to birth control with the liberalization of laws, new attitudes toward sexuality emerged. At the same time, the question of the moral permissibility of birth control for Catholics was considered by a papal commission established at Vatican II. On July 30, 1968, Pope Paul VI issued the encyclical *Humanae vitae*, which maintained the church's traditional ban on all "artificial" forms of contraception. But the debate on sexuality was just beginning.

In response to *Humanae vitae*, a group of theologians at the Catholic University of America in Washington, D.C., signed a statement that, in their judgment, it was permissible for Catholics of good conscience to dissent from the church's teaching.[35] Many Catholics had anticipated a different response, since the majority of the "birth control commission" had recommended a change in church teaching. But the Vatican vigorously rejected arguments for change, and what followed has been a thirty-year struggle between the Vatican and those in the church who disagree with church teaching. Much of the focus of these disagreements has been on matters relating to women's sexuality.

In the literature on sexuality that precedes Vatican II, marriage is, of course, the only context for licit sexual expression. The primary goal of marriage was affirmed as the procreation of children, and the bride-bridegroom relation in marriage was understood to be hierarchical, like that of the clergy and laity.[36] In an often-quoted article by the renowned moral theologian John C. Ford, the sacramental concept of the marriage bond was understood to transcend any kind of emotional relationship that the spouses might have.[37] The discussion of marriage in the pastoral constitution, *Gaudium et spes,* revolutionized the Catholic discussion of marriage by including as one of the primary ends of marriage the unity (that is, the love) of the partners. In *Humanae vitae,* the argument of Paul VI was that the unitive and procreative ends of marriage were inseparable.

While this shift in the theological language about marriage was not a direct consequence of the women's movement, the council nevertheless affirmed the equality of women and men, with the usual qualifications about women's "particular nature."[38] And as women gained a voice in the world, and in the church, with the new emphasis on the laity and clergy together as the People of God, sexuality emerged as a way for women, and the laity as a whole, to challenge traditional authority structures in the church. What has happened is that, by the early 1990s, some 87 percent of Catholics in the United States "believed the church should permit couples to make their own decisions about forms of birth control."[39] To a great extent, it appears that the Catholic hierarchy has conceded the battle over the issue of birth control, but the issues of abortion and, to some extent, new reproductive technologies remain central moral issues. While these issues are complex and involve multiple moral dimensions, such as the role of conscience, economic resources, and the like, at their heart is women's concern to have a voice in responsible moral decision-making.

A number of theologians have observed that in some serious moral issues such as the use of nuclear arms, capital punishment, and economic justice, varying degrees of moral pluralism are not only tolerated but encouraged.[40] Yet, when it comes to other life-and-death issues involving women and sexuality, there is no moral pluralism; indeed, sanctions against such pluralism have been invoked and used against those who have argued for it, as occurred with the "Vatican 24."[41] The moral gravity and complexity of abortion are not questioned by those feminist theologians who argue for an increased emphasis on women's moral agency; rather, the issue is the extent to which women's voices and experiences are included (or excluded) in discussions of its moral status.

Thus the question of moral theology is also a question of theological method—that is, the significance of experience—and in this case, of women's experiences, as a necessary source for an adequate understanding of human sexuality. Those who argue for changes in church teaching on such issues as the moral status of non-procreative sex, of committed homosexual unions, of artificial reproductive techniques, are also arguing for the legitimacy of people's experiences of these issues as having moral value, alongside, and perhaps distinct from, church teachings. While the debates in moral theology have often focused on women's sexuality, they have wider implications; that is, they challenge hierarchical notions of relationship (spousal, ecclesial) with a more egalitarian model and propose that human experience—particularly women's experience—provides a necessary theological source.

Moreover, feminist and other liberation theologians argue that such questions need to be placed in their broader social and economic context so that issues of power and privilege can be identified. The women's movement has claimed that "the personal is the political," and thus it challenges the structures that perpetuate ideas that women and children are property, that women's place is in the home, and that the family is sacrosanct from public scrutiny. These attitudes underlie such serious issues as domestic violence, sexual harassment, and job discrimination. Feminist theologians challenge the churches to condemn the sin of sexism, to recognize that even sex in canonically licit unions can be sinful and unjust, and to be more sensitive to the complexity of issues that often surround pregnancy.[42] In addition, feminists challenge church leaders to practice in their own structures the very issues they preach in the public sphere: the right to form unions, equal pay for equal work, and the right to have a voice in (church) governance.[43]

Doctrinal Issues

When it comes to the basic Christian doctrines, none of them has been untouched by feminist critique and reconstruction, along a continuum that ranges from the radical critiques of Mary Daly and Daphne Hampson, to the goddess spirituality of Carol Christ, to the sympathetic retrievals of the tradition by Elizabeth Johnson and Catherine LaCugna. Daly's rejection of the Christian tradition as fundamentally misogynistic and "necrophilic" ("If God is male, then the male is God"; Christ is "a dead man on a dead tree"[44]) laid down a gauntlet to later feminist writers who have continued to struggle with the tradition's overwhelmingly male language and images for God.[45] Elizabeth Johnson's *She Who Is*, as mentioned above, has used the tradition itself as the basis for a transformed conception of God through a retrieval of Wisdom literature. Catherine LaCugna has developed an understanding of the Trinity as fundamentally relational and as a more appropriate model of the divine than the impassible God of Hellenistic philosophy.[46] For these theologians, God's gender is not an issue to be taken lightly, as the powerful influence of language and image on human consciousness is revealed.

Christology has also been profoundly influenced by the women's movement. Rosemary Radford Ruether's bold question— "Can a male savior save women?"—sums up the issue: Is Jesus' maleness essential to his role? The answer from feminist theologians has been a resounding no. The significance of Jesus' life, death, and resurrection lies not in his maleness more adequately representing God to humanity, but rather in his embrace of particularity, his concern for the poor and downtrodden, his unbending loyalty to God even to death, and his glorified presence remaining in the world through the Spirit. In Roman Catholicism, the most contested christological issue has to do with the prohibition of women's ordination. According to official Vatican teaching, the example of Jesus choosing only men to be his apostles, the appropriateness of this choice given the theological significance of human sexuality (that is, the "spousal" relation of God to humanity, husband to wife, clergy to laity), and the church's long tradition all work together to make the male-only priesthood an intrinsic part of divine revelation, basic to and an unchanging part of Catholic faith.[47]

Feminist scholars, on the other hand, argue that selective biblical interpretation, a failure to take into account the social and historical context of biblical times, a deep and unacknowledged fear of women, and a resistance to transforming hierarchical church structures are the more likely explanations for the Roman Catholic Church's not ordaining women. They point to Jesus' inclusive and anti-hierarchical approach to social custom, women's equality before God, the deprivation of the church when women's gifts are excluded, and the needs of the present day, arguing that the issue of the ordination of women is really an issue of justice—for women, and for the church as a whole. Along with issues relating to sexuality, women's ordination remains deeply divisive in the church; throughout the 1990s, it has been one reason for faculty dismissals from seminary faculties and serves as a litmus test for possible episcopal appointment.[48]

It is difficult to separate the issue of women's ordination from ecclesiological and sacramental issues, as they are intimately connected both theologically and pastorally. The promise of the Vatican II church—the People of God—remains, in many ways, unfulfilled, as the Vatican has kept tight reins on episcopal appointments, national bishops' conferences, and even local parish councils. Given the decline in numbers of ordained clergy, as well as inspired by the post–Vatican II church, women have increasingly stepped into pastoral work and are, in many places, serving as parish leaders when clergy ("sacramental ministers") are unavailable.[49] Parishes are finding that women bring a richness of experience and talent to pastoral work, and some parishioners, as well as many pastoral ministers, find themselves frustrated by the strictures placed on the non-ordained by the Vatican.[50] Yet there are also many women and men who find themselves bitter and alienated from the church on this issue, and they join other Christian traditions that welcome the ministry of ordained women—or they leave the church altogether. Thus the issue of the ordination of women has wide repercussions.

Conclusion

While in some ways progress on women's issues in the churches seems frustratingly slow—witness the 1998 Southern Baptist Convention's statement and the Vatican's position on women's ordination—the women's movement has had dramatic effects on theology, as we have seen. Nevertheless, certain issues remain unresolved. One of these is the extent to which "women's experience" constitutes a distinct category for theological attention. As womanist, *mujerista*, some non-Western women, and postmodern feminists have argued, one can no longer speak of the "modern subject," given the decentered nature of the person and of global societies. Thus generalizations about women are prone to the same sorts of problems that were once made of "man." They represent a position that is no longer viable, that is, a universalistic picture of "woman" as essentially identical across time and culture. Yet other feminist thinkers such as Lisa Sowle Cahill, Cristina Traina, and Martha Nussbaum argue convincingly that without some explicit focus on women's particular needs— for example, prenatal health care, support for child care—the real and concrete issues that women and children struggle with will be lost among a competition of postmodern subjectivities. Their critical retrieval of Aristotelian and Thomistic natural-law theories provide one possible way of honoring both real and cross-cultural human needs with the diversity of a global society.[51]

A second unresolved issue is to what extent the women's movement challenges the basic character of the Christian tradition; for example, how one is to speak of God, the hierarchical character of the Roman Catholic Church, and the celibate clergy. Inclusive language—not only for humanity, but also for God—has been a particularly contentious issue; it has come to symbolize for some the "radical" concerns of feminists who want to turn Christianity into "goddess worship."[52] Inclusive translations of the Bible, even when approved by national bishops' conferences, have been overridden by the Vatican, prompting discussion not only about language but also about episcopal jurisdiction and collegiality.[53] Some feminist critics of hierarchy charge that hierarchical structures were explicitly rejected by Jesus and are inherently sinful. Clearly, feminist theologies propose profound changes in Christian thought and practice, yet not all feminist theologians agree on the extent of the need for changes. Feminist theologies will continue to challenge the church to be faithful to its mission while struggling to balance ideals with the need for pragmatic solutions.

In my judgment, feminist theologies represent the continuing movement of self-correction in the church. Historically, religious reform movements have struggled to define the church from the perspective of a fresh interpretation of the tradition's roots. The women's movement has always had both religious and political ambitions, and it seeks to transform the tradition to one that is inclusive of women's concerns. Like other reform movements, some groups have opted out of the tradition—for example, goddess spirituality, Wicca—while the ones that remain differ in the extent to which they believe that the existing tradition needs transformation: should women be ordained? or should the whole clerical-ministerial system be changed? The twenty-first century may not provide all the answers. But the impact of the women's movement on theology in the twentieth century cannot be ignored.

Notes

¹ The term is Janet Kalven's, of The Grail, a women's spiritual center in Ohio.

² See Susan A. Ross, "The Bride of Christ and the Body Politic: Body and Gender in Pre–Vatican II Marriage Theology," *Journal of Religion* 70/3 (July 1991): 345-61.

³ See John Paul II, *On the Dignity and Vocation of Women (Mulieris dignitatem)* (August 15, 1988).

⁴ Simone de Beauvoir, *The Second Sex*, trans. and ed. H. M. Parshley (New York: Vintage Books, 1974 <1952>), 301.

⁵ *The New York Times* (June 10, 1998), A1.

⁶ Valerie Saiving, "The Human Situation: A Feminine View," *Journal of Religion* 40 (1960), 100-12; reprinted in Carol P. Christ and Judith Plaskow, *Womanspirit Rising: A Feminist Reader in Religion* (San Francisco: Harper & Row, 1979), 25-42. See also Judith Plaskow, *Sex, Sin and Grace: Women's Experience and the Theologies of Reinhold Niebuhr and Paul Tillich* (Washington, D.C.: University Press of America, 1980).

⁷ Betty Friedan, *The Feminine Mystique* (New York: Norton, 1963).

⁸ The Episcopal Synod of America represents a group of conservative members who oppose the ordination of women as well as the blessing of same-sex unions.

⁹ Elizabeth Clark and Herbert Richardson, eds., *Women and Religion: A Feminist Sourcebook of Christian Thought* (San Francisco: Harper & Row, 1975).

¹⁰ Mary Daly, *The Church and the Second Sex* (New York: Harper & Row, 1968).

¹¹ See the two subsequent editions of this book: 1975, "With the Feminist Postchristian Introduction," and 1985: "New Archaic Afterwords by the Author"; see also Mary Daly, *Beyond God the Father: Toward a Philosophy of Women's Liberation* (Boston: Beacon Press, 1973).

¹² Uta Ranke-Heinemann, *Eunuchs for the Kingdom of Heaven: Women, Sexuality, and the Catholic Church*, trans. Peter Heinegg (New York: Doubleday, 1990).

¹³ Carolyn Walker Bynum, *Jesus as Mother: Studies in the Spirituality of the High Middle Ages* (Berkeley and Los Angeles: University of California Press, 1982); idem, *Holy Feast and Holy Fast: The Religious Significance of Food for Medieval Women* (Berkeley and Los Angeles: University of California Press, 1987); idem, *Fragmentation and Redemp-*

tion: Essays on Gender and the Human Body in Medieval Religion (New York: Zone Books, 1992).

[14] Elisabeth Schüssler Fiorenza, *In Memory of Her: A Feminist Theological Reconstruction of Christian Origins* (New York: Crossroad, 1982); *Bread Not Stone: The Challenge of Feminist Biblical Interpretation* (Boston: Beacon, 1984); *But She Said: Feminist Practices of Biblical Interpretation* (Boston: Beacon, 1992); *Jesus, Miriam's Child, Sophia's Prophet: Critical Issues in Feminist Christology* (New York: Continuum, 1994).

[15] Ann Taves, *Household of Faith: Roman Catholic Devotions in Mid-Nineteenth Century America* (Notre Dame, Ind.: University of Notre Dame Press, 1986).

[16] For feminist biblical interpretation, see the work of Elisabeth Schüssler Fiorenza (note 14 above); also Sandra M. Schneiders, *The Revelatory Text: Interpreting the New Testament as Sacred Scripture* (San Francisco: Harper & Row, 1991); Phyllis Trible, *Texts of Terror: Literary-Feminist Readings of Biblical Narratives* (Philadelphia, Pa.: Fortress Press, 1984).

[17] Rosemary Radford Ruether, *Sexism and God-Talk: Toward a Feminist Theology* (Boston: Beacon Press, 1983).

[18] Elizabeth A. Johnson, *She Who Is: The Mystery of God in Feminist Theological Discourse* (New York: Crossroad, 1992).

[19] See Ada María Isasi-Díaz, et al., "*Mujeristas*: Who We Are and What We Are About," *Journal of Feminist Studies in Religion* 8/1 (Spring 1992), 105-25; Cheryl Sanders et al., "Christian Ethics and Theology in Womanist Perspective," *Journal of Feminist Studies in Religion* 5/2 (Fall 1989), 83-112; *Inheriting Our Mothers' Gardens: Feminist Theology in Third World Perspective*, ed. Katie G. Cannon, Ada María Isasi-Díaz, and Kwok Pui-lan (Philadelphia, Pa.: Westminster Press, 1988).

[20] For representative treatments of some of these issues, see Ada María Isasi-Díaz, *Mujerista Theology: A Theology for the Twenty-First Century* (Maryknoll, N.Y.: Orbis Books, 1996); Jacqueline Grant, *White Women's Christ and Black Women's Jesus* (Atlanta, Ga.: Scholars Press, 1989); *Feminist Theology from the Third World*, ed. Ursula King (Maryknoll, N.Y.: Orbis Books, 1994).

[21] Mary McClintock Fulkerson, *Changing the Subject: Women's Discourses and Feminist Theology* (Minneapolis, Minn.: Fortress Press, 1994).

[22] Saiving, "The Human Situation," 38.

[23] Ibid.

[24] Carol Gilligan, *In a Different Voice: Psychological Theory and Women's Development* (Cambridge, Mass.: Harvard University Press, 1982).

[25] Beverly Wildung Harrison, "The Power of Anger in the Work of Love," in *Making the Connections: Essays in Feminist Social Ethics*, ed. Carol S. Robb (Boston: Beacon Press, 1985); Margaret A. Farley, *Personal Commitments* (San Francisco: Harper & Row, 1986).

[26] Thomas Aquinas, for example, makes an argument for the importance of anger in moral thinking (cf. *Summa Theologiae*, IIaIIae, Q. 158) as well as the inherent relationality of human life across generations (see *ST* IIaIIae, Q. 154, 2). But Aquinas also thought that women were deficient intellectually (*ST* I, Q. 93). Similarly, see Jean-Jacques Rousseau's *Emile: Or On Education*, trans. and ed. Allan Bloom (New York: Basic Books, 1979), on the education of young people and what was appropriate for women and men.

[27] For an example, see Isasi-Díaz, *Mujerista Theology*.

[28] Rosemary Radford Ruether, *New Woman, New Earth: Sexist Ideologies and Human Liberation*, rev. ed. (New York: Continuum, 1995).

[29] There has been considerable discussion on the pliability of sex and sex roles by some postmodern thinkers. See Judith Lorber, *Paradoxes of Sex* (New Haven, Conn.: Yale University Press, 1991); Judith Butler, *Gender Trouble: Feminism and the Subversion of Identity* (New York: Routledge, 1990); and idem, *Bodies That Matter: On the Discursive Limits of "Sex"* (New York: Routledge, 1993).

[30] See Susan A. Ross, *Extravagant Affections: A Feminist Sacramental Theology* (New York: Continuum, 1998).

[31] See Mary Catherine Hilkert, "Cry Beloved Image: Rethinking the Image of God," in *In the Embrace of God: Feminist Approaches to Theological Anthropology*, ed. Ann O'Hara Graff (Maryknoll, N.Y.: Orbis Books, 1995), 190-205.

[32] See Rosemary Radford Ruether, *Gaia and God: An Ecofeminist Theology of Earth Healing* (San Francisco: HarperSanFrancisco, 1992); Sallie McFague, *The Body of God: An Ecological Theology* (Minneapolis, Minn.: Fortress Press, 1993); Elizabeth Johnson, *Women, Earth, Creator Spirit* (New York: Paulist Press, 1993); *Ecofeminism and the Sacred*, ed. Carol J. Adams (New York: Continuum, 1993); and Carolyn Merchant, *The Death of Nature: Women. Ecology, and the Sexual Revolution* (San Francisco: Harper & Row, 1980).

[33] Lisa Sowle Cahill, "Notes on Feminist Ethics," *Theological Studies* 51/1 (March 1990), 50.

[34] See John A. Noonan, *Contraception: A History of Its Treatment by the Catholic Theologians and Canonists* (Cambridge, Mass.: Belknap Press, 1965).

[35] See Charles E. Curran, Robert E. Hunt, et al., *Dissent in and for the Church: Theologians and Humanae Vitae* (New York: Sheed and Ward, 1970); the statement can be found on 24-27.

[36] See Ross, "The Bride of Christ and the Body Politic."

[37] "Even a marriage in which there is no mutual help, no life in common, hatred instead of love, and complete separation, both bodily and spiritually, remains a true marriage in the sense that the essence of marriage is still there; that is, the partners are still married and in virtue of the essential marriage bond they are still bound to one another" (John C. Ford, S.J., "Marriage: Its Meaning and Purposes," *Theological Studies* 3 [1942], 348).

[38] See *Gaudium et spes (The Pastoral Constitution on the Church in the Modern World)*, nos. 29, 60, in *Vatican Council II: The Conciliar and Post-Conciliar Documents*, ed. Austin Flannery (Collegeville, Minn.: Liturgical Press, 1980).

[39] A 1991 Gallup poll cited in Robert McClory, *Turning Point: The Inside Story of the Papal Birth Control Commission, and How Humanae Vitae Changed the Life of Patty Crowley and the Future of the Church* (New York: Crossroad, 1995), 148.

[40] See Christine E. Gudorf, "To Make a Seamless Garment, Use a Single Piece of Cloth: The Abortion Debate," *Cross Currents* 54/4 (1985) 473-91; and William P. George, "War and Other Issues," Core Nine lecture, St. Joseph's College, Rensselaer, Indiana (March 1994).

[41] The "Vatican 24" refers to the twenty-four women religious who signed an advertisement in *The New York Times* in the fall of 1984 stating that there was a pluralism of views among Catholics regarding abortion (see Anne E. Patrick, *Liberating Conscience: Feminist Perspectives in Catholic Moral Theology* [New York: Continuum, 1996]).

[42] See, for example, Christine E. Gudorf, *Body, Sex, and Pleasure: Reconstructing Christian Sexual Ethics* (Cleveland, Ohio: Pilgrim Press, 1994); Marie M. Fortune, *Keeping the Faith: Guidance for Christian Women Facing Abuse* (San Francisco: HarperSanFrancisco, 1987); idem, *Love Does No Harm: Sexual Ethics for the Rest of Us* (New York: Continuum, 1995).

[43] See Christine Firer Hinze, *Comprehending Power in Christian Social Ethics* (Atlanta, Ga.: Scholars Press, 1995); Barbara Hilkert Andolsen, *Organization Man, Organization Woman: Calling, Leadership, and Culture* (Nashville, Tenn.: Abingdon Press, 1997).

[44] Daly, *Beyond God the Father*, 19; idem, *Gyn/Ecology: The Metaethics of Radical Feminism* (Boston: Beacon Press, 1978), 79-81.

[45] For a careful and detailed survey of feminist literature on God and Christ up to 1995, see Mary Catherine Hilkert, "Key Religious Symbols: Christ and God," *Theological Studies* 56/2 (June 1995), 341-52.

[46] Catherine Mowry LaCugna, *God for Us: The Trinity and Human Life* (San Francisco: HarperSanFrancisco, 1991).

[47] For the official documents that develop this teaching, see "Inter Insigniores," the Vatican Statement on the Question of the Admissibility of Women to the Ministerial Priesthood (December 1976); "Ordinatio Sacerdotalis" (May 30, 1994); "Response to a Dubium" (November 1995). All are available in *Origins*, the Catholic News Service.

[48] As I wrote this essay in the summer of 1998, the *National Catholic Reporter* reported that Liturgical Press had been ordered to cease distribution of Lavinia Byrne's *Woman at the Altar: The Ordination of Women in the Roman Catholic Church* (Collegeville, Minn.: The Liturgical Press, 1994) because of its advocacy of women's ordination. Liturgical Press has complied with the order but has sold the copyright to Continuum Press, a secular publisher (see *National Catholic Reporter* [July 31, 1998]).

[49] See Ross, *Extravagant Affections*.

[50] See Eight Vatican Offices, "Some Questions regarding Collaboration of Nonordained Faithful in Priests' Sacred Ministry," *Origins* 27/24 (November 27, 1997), 397-410.

[51] Lisa Sowle Cahill, *Sex, Gender and Christian Ethics* (Cambridge, Mass.: Cambridge University Press, 1996); Cristina L. H. Traina, *A Feminist Retrieval of Natural Law Ethics* (Washington, D.C.: Georgetown University Press, forthcoming); Martha C. Nussbaum, "Human Functioning and Social Justice: A Defense of Aristotelian Essentialism," *Political Theory* 20 (1992): 204-46.

[52] The Re-Imagining Conference in Minneapolis in November 1993 led to firings among women of church staffs and a strong backlash from religious groups. See Mary E. Hunt, "Re-Imagining Backlash," in *Feminist Theology in Different Contexts*, ed. Elisabeth Schüssler Fiorenza and M. Shawn Copeland (London and Maryknoll, N.Y.: SCM Press and Orbis Books, 1996), 45-51.

[53] See *National Catholic Reporter* 34/10 (January 9, 1998), 18, for a summary of the dialogue between U.S. bishops and the Vatican over the issue of inclusive language.

16

Voices from the Margins
in the United States

DWIGHT N. HOPKINS and LINDA E. THOMAS

In the 1960s and 1970s, black American, American Indian (Native American), and Latino American (Hispanic) communities irrupted throughout the United States. In contrast, the prior decade of the 1950s saw people of color or minority communities pursuing the court system as an acceptable forum of debate over discrimination or following the path of acquiescence. However, churches, student groups, and nontraditional protest organizations assumed leadership during the last half of the twentieth century. Instead of the courts being the primary arena for addressing social imbalances, the streets and other open public spaces provided the venue for disagreements over and contestation against segregation and benign neglect. Blacks, Indians, and Latino populations, in their own respective contexts, demanded the expression of their own humanity independent of norms set by the majority white community. That assertion of humanity took on at least two broad manifestations. First was an accent on culture. In this instance, oppressed minority groups claimed a return to their indigenous or syncretized cultures which existed prior to the impact of whites. Second, these newly awakened groups asserted their need for their own leadership representatives and their own access to wealth and resources. Both statements regarding an independent full humanity underscored the right of self-identity and the right of self-determination.

In addition to the shift from more acceptable court battles of the 1950s to the massive street movements of later decades, people of color were greatly affected by the national liberation and anti-colonial struggles throughout Africa, Asia, and Latin America, especially events in Vietnam, Cuba, and southern and southwest Africa. A deep sense of solidarity developed between people of color in the United States and "people of color" in the Third World. Third-world countries inspired blacks, Indians, and Latinos throughout the United States to raise their voices by any means necessary.

In response to these massive societal and global shifts, pastors, theologians, religious professors, and lay people within minority communities in the United States began to reflect on the theological meaning and implications of this renaissance of claiming and naming cultural self-identity and political self-determination. Was God providing a kairos moment for the oppressed people? What was the relation among theological faith, church witness, and the gospel message of Jesus Christ? What had Christians been called to say and do in the midst of attacks against poor people and their counter resistance for freedom? The theologies developed by blacks, Indians, and Latinos emerged by discerning the presence of God in the midst of the plight and struggle of oppressed sectors of their respective contexts.

Black Theology

Black theology is the name given to a movement created by a certain group of African American clergy in the late 1960s who felt that the gospel of Jesus Christ had a positive message about the racial condition of black people and the prospects for a God-human encounter to transform this racial condition eventually into a new society of justice on earth. Black theology was needed, argued the founders of this theological movement, because all theologies are human speech about God's relation to humanity. Since the gospel of Jesus Christ is essentially one of liberation and since the human social relations in America were characterized both by racial discrimination against African Americans and by their struggles toward freedom, then black theology of liberation was needed not only for African Americans, but for America in general.

Theologically and doctrinally, black theology holds that God created this world for all of humanity. But because of the hubris or selfishness of most of the white community, that community usurped God's created order for itself; thus sin in black theology emphasizes both personal and systemic relations and group accountability as the condition for individual responsibility. Moreover, evil manifested in the monopolization of power over resources and over divinely given rights or privileges for all of humanity. In the American context, this denial of power manifested in a disproportion of disenfranchisement for African Americans on two accounts. First, racial discrimination denied the self-identity of what it meant to be a black person, especially in the framework of the 1960s, when the definition of what it meant to be human was encoded de jure (by law) and de facto (by custom) in the identity of white Americans. The consequence for blacks was that they were not human beings—a cancellation of both their African heritage and their unique gifts of being black people on North American soil.

Second, in addition to restrictions on self-identity there were restrictions on African American people's right to self-determination. All peoples, particularly poor communities, were given the right to determine for themselves how they wanted to conduct themselves on earth—how they attempted to control the wealth, resources, and space around them. Because the *imago dei* (the image of God) grants freedom in a total manner, the first component of black theology spoke to cultural concerns; this second component touched on a political agenda. If the church was to be the church, then it should be about the business of working with Jesus in the midst of the movement to realize self-identity and self-determination in the black community.

In sum, black theology arose as a Christian movement of liberation for the transformation of personal and systemic power relations in American society at the point of racial difference.

Contemporary black theology began with the formation of the ad hoc National Committee of Negro Churchmen (NCNC) in the summer of 1966, specifically with the publication of its "Black Power Statement" in the *New York Times* (July 31, 1966). In June 1966 the Black Power challenge came forth from black students in the Civil Rights movement. For African American Christians, the question immediately became this: Is it possible to be both black and Christian if the gospel of Jesus Christ denies black people power as well as a strong sense of their own cultural roots? This stage of black theology included primarily radical black clergy who claimed that black power and black consciousness revealed the presence of Jesus Christ the Liberator. Furthermore, they asserted that the essence of Christianity was deliverance of and freedom for the oppressed on earth. With the appearance of the NCNC in 1966, black clergy, administrators, and educators began to separate the theological reflection and practice of black religion from that of the conservative and liberal theologies of the white churches. Black theology emerged both as a critique of white conservative theology's rejection of the role of the black church in the Civil Rights movement, and as a critique of white liberal theology's denial of the relation between black religion and black power. To the various perspectives of white theologians, pastors, and church administrators, black theology posed liberation of the oppressed as the normative thread throughout the Christian gospel. For the initiators of black theology, the good news of Jesus Christ was not neutral; it concerned power—those with it and those without.

In the spring of 1969 the seminal theological work that systematized black theology was written and published by James H. Cone, the father of black theology of liberation in the United States. In fact, the first two books published on liberation within North, South, and Central Americas were Cone's *Black Theology and Black Power* (1969) and *A Black Theology of Liberation* (1970).[1] In his *Black Theology and Black Power* Cone asserted that not only was black power not alien to the gospel but that it was, indeed, the gospel message for all of twentieth-century North America. Since that time, more African Americans have received Ph.D. degrees in various fields of religion and, consequently, have slowly entered the teaching academy. With the arrival of second and third generations of African American religious scholars, black theology has become a fixed institution, body of knowledge, and faith commitment within North American society and culture. Hence, black theology is not uncommon in many educational curricula. Moreover, some white churches and, mostly, black churches have become familiar with the theological themes of black theology of liberation. One of the most important theological trajectories emerging out of black theology is womanist theology.[2]

Womanist Theology

Womanist theology is the name chosen by black women in various fields of religion who wish to claim two things. First, black female religious scholars, pastors, and laywomen emphasize the positive experiences of African American women as a basis for doing theology and ethics. Black women are made in God's image, and therefore their values, voices, experiences, looks, bodies, and ways of being in the world have positive divine significance.

Second, the title *womanist theology* calls attention to the negative experiences of black women when they confront both the racism of white feminist and white male theologians and the sexism of black and white male theologians. Womanist theology grows out of black theology and therefore separates its theological claims from white feminist theologians who ignore racism. And, in this instance, African American female scholars join with their black brothers in the struggle against white supremacy in the church, society, and religious educational institutions. In other words, the reality of being black in America unites womanist and black theologies.

At the same time, African American women's female experiences in patriarchal America lay a basis for black women's coalition with white feminists. African American female religious scholars have to live out their dual status of race and gender before God. They cannot separate their reality of being a black person from their reality of being a woman. Both of these experiences go into defining who the African American woman is. To sum up, womanist theology says that there is a unique relation between God and black women. On the other hand, womanist theology struggles against discrimination caused by white supremacy and by patriarchy.

Womanist theology, moreover, takes its theological guidelines from the definition of womanism given by Alice Walker in *In Search of Our Mothers' Gardens*.[3] Walker's four-part definition contains aspects of (1) tradition; (2) community; (3) self, nature, and the Spirit; and (4) criticism of white feminism.

The history of the term *womanist theology* begins after a 1979 article (written by Jacquelyn Grant) that spoke, at that time, more about a black feminist theology. Titled "Black Theology and the Black Woman," the article called into question the most fundamental belief of black theology as a theology of liberation. It challenged this liberation assertion by showing how black theology contradicted its own claims, evidence, warrants, qualifications, and criteria.

Specifically, Grant argued that if black theology described itself as a theology of liberation, meaning that Jesus Christ was with the most oppressed and God was working for the liberation of the least in society, then why was it that black theology was at best silent about black women and at worst oppressing African American women? In this article Grant also draws lines of theological difference with white feminist theologians but states that the primary focus of her article is the development of a black woman's voice in black theology.

In searching for African American women in black theology, Grant concluded that black women are invisible. This is true either because black women have no place in the practice of God-talk and God-walk or because black men are capable of speaking for black women. Similar conclusions can be drawn about black women in the African American church and the larger society. Grant writes:

> If the liberation of women is not proclaimed, the church's proclamation cannot be about divine liberation. If the church does not share in the liberation struggle of black women, its liberation struggle is not authentic. If women are oppressed, the church cannot be "a visible manifestation that the gospel is a reality."[4]

In her 1985 article "The Emergence of Black Feminist Consciousness,"[5] Katie G. Cannon produced the first written text to use the term *womanist*. She writes:

> Black feminist consciousness may be more accurately identified as Black womanist consciousness, to use Alice Walker's concept and definition. As an interpretive principle, the Black womanist tradition provides the incentive to chip away at oppressive structures, bit by bit. It identifies those texts that help Black womanists to celebrate and to rename the innumerable incidents of unpredictability in empowering ways. The Black womanist identifies with those biblical characters who hold on to life in the face of formidable oppression. Often compelled to act or to refrain from acting in accordance with the powers and principalities of the external world, Black womanists search the Scriptures to learn how to dispel the threat of death in order to seize the present life.[6]

Cannon's scholarship introduced womanism as the innovative and new category for all black women's religious work. However, the first written text using the specific phrase *womanist theology* was written by Delores S. Williams in "Womanist Theology: Black Women's Voices," which appeared in the March 2, 1987, edition of *Christianity and Crisis* magazine. In that article Williams used Alice Walker's definition of womanism as a theoretical framework to equate black women's theology with the womanist definition.

Further defining the quilt-like configuration of womanist diversity in harmony and solidarity, Linda E. Thomas writes the following about the complementing threads and rainbow mixtures in womanist theology:

> We are university, seminary and divinity school professors. We are ordained and lay women in all the Christian denominations. Some of us are full time pastors; some are both pastor and professor. We are preachers and prayer warriors. We are mothers, partners, lovers, wives, sisters, daughters, aunts, nieces and we comprise two thirds of the black church in America. We are the black church. The church would be bankrupt without us and the church would shut down without us. We are from working class as well as middle class backgrounds. We are charcoal black to high yellow women. We love our bodies; we touch our bodies; we like to be touched; we claim our created beauty. And we know that what our minds forget our bodies remember. The body is central to our being. The history of the African American ordeal of pain and pleasure is inscribed in our bodies.[7]

In the development of theology and ethics, womanists write about a total relation to God (for example, a holistic relationship). They believe in the positive sacred-human connections at the locations of gender, race, class, sexual orientation, and to a certain degree, ecology. In fact, a holistic methodology and a holistic worldview constitute what it means to do womanist theology. Womanist theology is holistic in terms of (1) the many theological ways black women face oppression and struggle for liberation; (2) the use of many disciplines of analyses; and (3) the diverse dimensions of what it means to be a human being, that is, the spiritual, cultural, political, economic, linguistic, aesthetic, and so forth. Furthermore, from the perspective of Delores S. Williams, womanist theological method is

> informed by at least four elements: (1) a multidialogical intent, (2) a liturgical intent, (3) a didactic intent, and (4) a commitment both to reason and to the validity of female imagery and metaphorical language in the construction of theological statements.[8]

Multidialogical intent allows Christian womanists to engage in many conversations with different people from various religious, political, and social communities. The desire of womanists in these exchanges is to focus on the "slow genocide" of poor African American women, children, and men, caused by systems of exploitation. Liturgical intent means that black female religious scholars and clergywomen will develop a theology relevant to the African American church, especially its worship, action, and thought. At the same time, womanist theology challenges the black church with the prophetic and critical messages coming from the practice of black women. In a word, black church liturgy has to be defined by justice.

Didactic intent points to the teaching moment in the theology of the black church as it deals with a moral life determined by justice, survival, and quality of life ethics. All of these concerns commit us to a language rich in both imagination and reason, and filled with female stories, metaphor, and imagery.

Part of the methodology of womanist theology includes both epistemology and practice, that is to say, how we obtain knowledge and how we witness in ethics. How do womanists get their knowledge and how does knowledge relate to their practice?

In the analysis of Kelly Brown Douglas, womanist theology is accountable to ordinary women, poor and working-class black women.[9] This means that (1) womanists must teach beyond the seminaries and divinity schools and go to churches and community-based organizations to learn. Put differently, "it will be church and community-based women who will teach womanist theologians how to make theology more accessible."[10] (2) If womanist theology is accountable to church and community-based women, then womanist conversations must take place beyond the academy. It must have as its primary talking partners and primary location poor and working-class women in their families, churches, and community organizations. And (3) womanist theology must work with church women to help empower them and to help them speak their voice so that church leadership will respond or change. Black women are up to 70 to 80 percent of most African American churches and are the financial supporters and workers of the church.

Summing up the holistic dimension of the different sources in womanist theology, Emilie M. Townes states:

> Yet the anchor for womanist thought is the African-American church and its people. The history of the Black church is not only religious, it is social. The social conditions and worldviews of its people have had an intricate connection. Womanist thought reflects some of this intimacy. Examples of this can be found in the deeply spiritual and moral aspects [of sacred and secular black writers and singers]. West African religions, vodun, and folktales are mediums. Life in the church—from preacher's admonitions to choir crescendos to board meeting and power struggles—all are resources and guardians of communal memory and accountability. Academic theological discourse is also a part of womanist reflection and thought. Such are the touchstones for womanist reflection.[11]

American Indians or Native Americans

American Indian theologians link their theological voices to the invasion of their land by Christopher Columbus in 1492. For Native Americans, the United States of North America built its "manifest destiny" on top of pre-existing Indian nations. Therefore, even today, Indians remain in the territorial vicinity of their homeland. They are not immigrants, nor were they forcibly brought as free labor. Yet the initial European invasion led to white settlements and forced removal of Indians from their sacred and ancestral earth. Thus, among other issues, invasion and removal serve as important sources in the construction of an American Indian or Native American theology.

White exploiters from Europe (for example, those who became white North Americans) flooding the religious land of native peoples used several approaches. The military conquest acted to maim, destroy, and perpetuate genocide physically. Bodily violence accompanied the tactic of Christian ideological justification. White missionaries served this role well. In order to break Indians from their own traditional religions and culture, white Christians first had to use Jesus Christ to demonize Indians. Thus Christians and white culture invented disparaging titles like noble savage and nature worshipers. Unfortunately, many within the Indian communities have expressed modes of spiritual self-denial by looking down on their own sacred culture and privileging not only the gospel of Jesus Christ, but also imitating and making sacred white culture. Resisting the theft of land, the forced removal by the U.S. government and military, and the ideological justification of these dynamics by white Christians and their churches undergird a major part of American Indian theological developments. At the same time, a primary source for Indian theological themes has been the affirmation of Indianness and its unique spirituality.

Theologically, Native American religious scholars have struggled with the indigenization of Christianity. How does one embrace the core message of Jesus Christ and still maintain one's own native spirituality and culture? In response, American Indian theologians look to the best from their tribal traditions to discern native spiritual categories derived from Indian culture. George E. Tinker (Osage) writes:

Following on the renaissance of traditional tribal spirituality, many Indian clergy, lay people, and whole congregations are insisting on understanding the gospel in Indian terms, insisting on the natural indigenous categories of our tribes for structuring our faith. Hence the old ways of tribal spirituality are beginning to be as much at home in Indian churches as they are in traditional ceremonies. The values that define Indian existence, Indian community, traditional spirituality

and culture are being articulated in Indian preaching and Indian theology in our churches.[12]

The gospel message, reflected in the Bible, has a tradition of clothing its
message within the discourse understandable to potential converts. When
he felt called by God to missionize the Gentile populations, Paul pursued
this path in the Christian scriptures. For instance, Paul employed the Greek
thought form of *logos* and equated it with Jesus Christ. Likewise, drawing on
their own resources, Indian Christians create new categories of faith and
novel structures of thought that blend indigenous ways with a reinterpreta-
tion of the Christian way. Traditional prayers and native symbols are taken
more seriously in American Indian theology. Christian scholars and pastors
have sought a closer relation with indigenous healers and spiritual leaders.
Still, this process of indigenization has a ways to go, because only 10 to 25
percent of Indians are Christians. Many Native Americans are still highly
suspicious of Christianity, because it has for so long and continues in many
quarters today to equate conversion to Jesus Christ with surrendering one's
Indian way of being and thinking.

In response, American Indian theologians are taking seriously the beliefs, way of life, and worldview of their ancestors. For instance, land remains a central theological datum of investigation. Unlike white theology
in the United States, where land is perceived more as wealth for accumulat-
ing profit, Native American religious scholars are reincorporating notions
of land as sacred, and land as mother or brother. Thus creation entails a
kinship connection with the land. The centrality of land to one's religious
essence is seen in the belief that spirituality, rituals, and religion are all
rooted in land. Native peoples'

> cultures, spirituality, and identity are connected to the land—and not
> simply land in a generalized sense but their land. The act of creation
> is not so much what happened then as it is what happened here; it is
> the story of the formation of a specific land and a particular people.
> Thus, when Indian tribes were forcibly removed from their homes,
> they were robbed of more than territory. Taken from them was a
> numinous world where every mountain and lake holds meaning for
> their faith and identity.[13]

The centrality of land also surfaces the distinct perspectival difference
between space and time in American Indian theology. White theology privileges time, the linear time of God invading human history and creating a
salvation based on chronological time events. What is important for white
Christians is the exact and predictable time and day of the week when church
services start. Though Indian theologians recognize the import of time,
space occupies a position of primacy. Thus the sacredness of the land is in-
separably linked to a view of land as space. Religious leaders within Indian

communities receive their power and communion with the spiritual world by being located physically on a sacred mountain, beach, or open plain. Similarly, the four spaces of the land or four directions of creation play crucial roles in the worldview, ritual practices, and symbolical representations. All indigenous American communities utilize the four directions of east, south, west, and north in some dimension of religious ceremonies.

One distinct challenge and contribution derived from the Indian experience in America is its critique of white missionary theology and the liberation theology of other people of color in the United States. When the British invaded the "New World" with permanent settlements in 1607 (Jamestown) and 1620 (Plymouth Rock), they pictured themselves as the chosen people of God and the Americas as the "promised land." This theological perspective not only underscored attacks on Indians, but it also encouraged increased genocidal attempts. Such a biblical paradigm, from white invaders' intent, imaged Native Americans as Canaanites waiting to receive the destructive hand of Yahweh. Likewise, the liberation theologies of other U.S. minorities, especially African Americans, have adopted the biblical imperative of the Exodus story, in which Yahweh chooses the oppressed and delivers them to Canaan, a land filled with milk and honey. From the critique of Indian theologians, what other liberation theologians fail to do is to pursue the remaining details of the Exodus narrative. For, if we did, we would discover that the Canaanites were the indigenous peoples upon whom, under theological justification from Yahweh, genocide was committed. Robert Allen Warrior concludes:

> Indians, in this era of "self-determination," have verified for themselves and the government that they are the people best able to address Indian problems as long as they are given the necessary resources and if they can hold the US government accountable to the policy. But an enormous stumbling block immediately presents itself. Most of the liberation theologies that have emerged in the last twenty years are preoccupied with the Exodus story, using it as the fundamental model for liberation. I believe that the story of the Exodus is an inappropriate way for Native Americans to think about liberation.[14]

From the theological and physical vantage of Indians already living in America, the religious rhetoric of white missionaries and liberation theologians from U.S. minority communities complements each other. Yahweh, the liberator of oppressed people suffering under slavery, becomes, in the Canaan context, Yahweh the conqueror and instigator of genocide against the native Canaanite peoples. American Indians were the original "Americans." But now they have been transformed by force into the bottom of the pecking order of all U.S. minorities. In this sense, the Exodus-liberation model becomes a double attack against Indians. On the one hand, European Christian invaders employed religious language to subdue the land

and the native peoples in order to establish a white Canaan. At the same time, people of color (the natural allies of American Indians) have propagated the Exodus-liberation discourse without taking seriously American Indians being the "Canaanites" at the end of the road of liberation theologies in the Americas.

Finally, Native American theologians have plumbed their own religio-cultural narratives in order to reconfigure understandings of Jesus Christ. For instance, if Christ is perceived as the part of God expressing creativity, salvation, or healing toward humanity, then other parallel manifestations appear in Indian culture and history. One discovers such a "mythic truth" in the story of Corn Mother. It is no accident that Indian theology looks toward gender inclusivity in its reconceptualization of Christology. For Indian theology's faith and worldview, bi-gender duality stands at the center. In this Corn Mother narrative, Native Americans derive important theological themes centered on eating as a sacrament, death, and sacrifice as vicarious suffering, and the divine kinship of human beings with all of nature and with the ancestors.[15]

Latino-Latina Hispanic Theology

Latino-Latina Hispanic theology has contributed a great deal to the ongoing development of theology in the United States, especially in the areas of theological method. First, it informs us about the importance of taking seriously the fact of diversity among the human community. Doing liberation theology is contextual and particular.

> A definition of the contemporary Hispanic identity would reflect a diversity of national origins, ethnic identity, acculturation, socioeconomic status, gender, and especially religious traditions. There are as many national origins as there are Spanish-speaking Latin American countries, including Puerto Rico and the United States. Each provides a unique base of ethnic identity and cultural tradition. The diversity of socioeconomic status includes the extremely wealthy, the many who are poor and marginalized, and an emerging middle class. . . . There are newly arrived refugees, undocumented workers, and other immigrants, as well as those who have been in the United States for many generations.[16]

Though the Hispanic/Latino reality encompasses overarching similarities, still theologians from this group derive critical faith claims from their unique sociocultural location as, for instance, Cuban American, Puerto Rican American, Mexican American, and so on. Similarly, a growing diversity (and therefore an increased ecumenical thrust) is taking place among different faith communities. In addition to the well-known presence of Hispanics in the Roman Catholic Church (indeed, they are the fastest growing segment of that church), Latinos also have an increasing impact within mainline Protestant churches and Pentecostal denominations.[17]

Second, Latino theology emphasizes the importance of doing theology in community or *en conjunto*. This latter phrase underscores the collaborative dimension of theologizing. For Hispanic scholars, theology arises not from the solitary, isolated, and (supposedly) brilliant genius. On the contrary, critical reflection on the God and human connection springs from the simultaneous interaction and mutual exchanges among scholars in the academy, the church, and the community. Therefore, Hispanic theologizing calls individuals to accountability by starting their work in the barrios and areas of non-formally trained people. They also embark consciously on academic work unfolding through discussion and a dialogical paradigm in conferences. Consequently, there is a growing number of edited works compiling diverse voices.

Third, Hispanic theology is interdisciplinary, accenting both a cultural body of knowledge and a liberationist epistemology. The cultural perspective comes from the negative denigration and positive assertion of Latino culture, language, worldview, rituals, etc. The liberationist moment privileges social scientific analyses calling for fundamental transformation of systemic structures in society. Still, in both instances, religious scholars concern themselves with the practice of pastoral issues.

Fourth, Latino religious writers privilege popular religiosity or the religion of the people as the primary starting point and normative standard regarding the authenticity of a Latino-Latina, Hispanic theology of liberation. Methodologically, the theological location and origin of all theology should be embedded in the culture of the people in the neighborhood, the poor, and working folk. The everyday ways of life of the people, from below, should be the creative sources manifesting divine revelation. Doing theology means doing it from the perspective of and with those lacking the privileges of the top strata of society.

Fifth, Hispanic theologians call on the necessity to do theology as *mestizaje*—a notion of hybridity or syncretism. This concept images a tertium quid that is the creation of the Hispanic or Latino ethnic group or race. *Mestizaje* means the coming together of two or more racial stocks. For Hispanics, this included the mixing of European invaders in the Americas, the original native Indians, and the Africans brought as slaves. The mixture of these three has produced the possibility of doing theology from the rich innovations of three different sources, while discarding and critiquing the negative aspects of each.

Finally, Latino theology has dissected the notion of "bridge theology" for its local, regional, and global consequences for human solidarity and community:

One of the greatest promises of Hispanics in the United States, who understand both North American and Latin American idiosyncrasies, is that of becoming a bridge, a "border people," between the dreams and struggles of the people in the United States and the dreams and struggles of the people in Latin America and third world. [Latino-Latina Hispanic theology's] mission is to serve as a means of communication between the rich, overaffluent, and misdeveloped world of the North and the poor, exploited, and also misdeveloped world of the South.[18]

Serving somewhat as a bridge, Latina women have begun their own religious reflection as part of, yet distinct from, Latino Hispanic theology. Like their black sisters, who have created womanist theology from the faith belief and practice of black American women, Latina women have forged their unique self-naming with the category of *mujerista* theology.[19] Here, holiness emerges not only from praying and self-denial but also from the experiences of doing the gospel. When Latinas do God's work, it exemplifies an act of worship. Moreover, this doing, based on the realities of the poor, demands a liberative praxis for interpreting the Bible. *Mujerista* theology is a theology of liberation grounded in the daily struggle *(lo cotidiano)* of Latina Hispanic women. The theology grows out of the *mestizaje* of the Latina movement of the folk. The daily struggle is both the hermeneutic and the epistemology of *mujerista* theology. As a critical reflection on faith and witness, it embodies three main themes: (a) in the struggle *(la lucha)*, maintaining hope amid difficult suffering; (b) sustaining voice; allow me to speak *(permitanme hablar);* Latinas' self-expression and self-definition remain essential elements; having moral agency is crucial to theologizing; and (c) grasping Latina self-understanding originates from the community/the family *(la communidad/la familia)*. Ultimately, for *mujerista* theology, all theology needs to comprehend the poor to the point that we journey beyond handouts to solidarity, which requires an analysis of structural oppression and active participation in the liberation process. Hence, the oppressed and the oppressor must undergo a relationship of mutuality for comprehensive freedom.

Conclusion

Voices from the margins in the United States of America (blacks, Indians, and Latino-Latinas) have initiated novel ways of doing theology. They claim the right to reread the Bible from the oppressed sections of their respective communities. With that hermeneutical turn, they comprehend the core gospel message as total liberation, against both internal spiritual demons and external structural systems of destruction. God has created all humanity in freedom and to be free. However, various structural and spiritual evils usurped divine intent and brought about a destructive asymmetry within humanity. Jesus came among the lowly of the earth in order to offer liberation for the oppressed. With Jesus' ascension, God's Spirit remains to comfort and accompany the "little ones" of this world. Though deconstruction of disparate mainstream varieties of theology plays a prominent place in voices from the margins, ultimately liberation theologies from peoples of color in the United States seek to advance the divine creation, which is constructing a new humanity and a new commonwealth on earth as it is in heaven. And that final revelation will affirm the divine connection to oppressed people's right of self-identity based on indigenous sources and self-determination to reclaim their wealth and land.

Notes

[1] Cone's *Black Theology and Black Power* was reprinted by Orbis Books (Maryknoll, N.Y.) in 1997; Orbis Books reprinted *A Black Theology of Liberation* in 1986. The third book published on liberation theology (in the Western hemisphere) was Gustavo Gutiérrez's *Teologia de la liberacion, Perspectivas* (Lima, Peru: CEP, 1971).

[2] For books on the origin, development, and theological emphases in black theology, see James H. Cone, *Black Theology and Black Power* (Maryknoll, N.Y.: Orbis Books, 1997); idem, *A Black Theology of Liberation, twentieth anniversary edition* (Maryknoll, N.Y.: Orbis Books, 1990); and idem, *For My People: Black Theology and the Black Church, Where Have We Been and Where Are We Going?* (Maryknoll, N.Y.: Orbis Books, 1984). Also see Dwight N. Hopkins, *Introducing Black Theology of Liberation* (Maryknoll, N.Y.: Orbis Books, 1999).

[3] Alice Walker, *In Search of Our Mother's Gardens: Womanist Prose* (New York: Harcourt Brace Jovanovich, 1983).

[4] Jacquelyn Grant, "Black Theology and the Black Woman," in *Black Theology: A Documentary History Volume One, 1966-1979*, ed. James H. Cone and Gayraud S. Wilmore (Maryknoll, N.Y.: Orbis Books, 1993), 328.

[5] The article was first published in *Feminist Interpretation of the Bible*, ed. Letty M. Russell (Philadelphia, Pa.: Westminster Press, 1985), 30-40.

[6] Katie Cannon, in Russell, *Feminist Interpretation of the Bible*, 40.

[7] Linda E. Thomas, "Womanist Theology, Epistemology, and a New Anthropological Paradigm," *Journal of Constructive Theology* [Centre for Constructive Theology, University of Durban-Westville, Durban, South Africa] 2, no. 2 (December 1996):19-31.

[8] Delores Williams, "Womanist Theology: Black Women's Voices," in *Black Theology: A Documentary History, Volume Two, 1980-1992*, ed. James H. Cone and Gayraud S. Wilmore (Maryknoll, N.Y.: Orbis Books, 1993), 269.

[9] Kelly Brown Douglas, *The Black Christ* (Maryknoll, N.Y.: Orbis Books, 1994), 114.

[10] Ibid.

[11] Emilie M. Townes, "Introduction," in *A Troubling in My Soul: Womanist Perspectives on Evil and Suffering*, ed. Emilie M. Townes (Maryknoll, N.Y.: Orbis Books, 1993), 2.

[12] See George E. Tinker, "Native Americans and the Land: 'The End of Living, and the Beginning of Survival,'" in *Lift Every Voice: Constructing Christian Theologies from the Underside*, ed. Susan B. Thistlethwaite and Mary Potter Engel (San Francisco: Harper & Row, 1990), 142.

[13] See Jace Weaver (Cherokee), "From I-Hermeneutics to We-Hermeneutics: Native

Americans and the Post-Colonial," in *Native American Religious Identity: Unforgotten Gods*, ed. Jace Weaver (Maryknoll, N.Y.: Orbis Books, 1998), 20.

[14] See Robert Allen Warrior, "A Native American Perspective: Canaanites, Cowboys, and Indians," in *Voices from the Margin: Interpreting the Bible in the Third World*, ed. R. S. Sugirtharajah (Maryknoll, N.Y.: Orbis Books, 1991), 288.

[15] See George E. Tinker (Osage), "Jesus, Corn Mother, and Conquest," in Weaver, *Native American Religious Identity*, 134ff.

[16] See David Maldonado Jr., "Doing Theology and the Anthropological Question," in *Teologia en Conjunto: A Collaborative Hispanic Protestant Theology*, ed. Jose David Rodriguez and Loida I. Martell-Otero (Louisville, Ky.: Westminster John Knox Press, 1997), 101.

[17] For the Roman Catholic voice, see Virgilio Elizondo, *Galilean Journey: The Mexican American Promise* (Maryknoll, N.Y.: Orbis Books, 1983); idem, *The Future Is Mestizo: Life When Cultures Meet* (Bloomington, Ind.: Meyer-Stone Books, 1988). For the Protestant perspective, see Justo L. Gonzalez, *Manana: Christian Theology from a Hispanic Perspective* (Nashville, Tenn.: Abingdon Press, 1990). And for the Pentecostal voice, see Eldin Viollafane, *The Liberating Spirit: Toward an Hispanic American Pentecostal Social Ethic* (Lanham, Md.: University Press of America, 1992).

[18] Jose David Rodriguez, "On Doing Hispanic Theology," in Rodriguez and Martell-Otero, *Teologia en Conjunto,* 17.

[19] See Ada María Isasi-Díaz, *Mujerista Theology* (Maryknoll, N.Y.: Orbis Books, 1996).

17

The Ecological Crisis

STEPHEN B. SCHARPER

Reason says that destroying clean air is impractical; faith ought to say it is blasphemous.

—Joseph Sittler

The above epigraph represents both a horizon and a hope. As a pioneering Christian theological voice, Joseph Sittler, in 1961, articulated the need for a theology of the environment, one that took the destruction of the natural world at human hands as a sign, not of progress or advancement, but of ecological and spiritual crisis.[1]

Since then, a growing crescendo of Christian voices has been raised in defense of nature, especially resonant after cultural historian Lynn White's 1967 polemic, which claimed that the Judeo-Christian tradition's anthropocentric roots had laid the cultural foundations for the environmental crisis.[2] The Christian responses to this charge have consequently explored the need for a Christian ecological theology and helped spawn an emerging body of Christian organizations, reflection, and social teaching dedicated to stewardship and environmental sustainability.

Yet there is not a consensus in the Christian world, as yet, surrounding Sittler's injunction to label pollution blasphemous. The wedding of modern Christianity with modern social and economic movements, in which nature was the canvas on which the human and Christian spirit painted its dreams, is presently being challenged by a plethora of theologians, philosophers, scientists, and environmentalists, and the role of the human—and indeed the vocation of the Christian—lies in the balance. The understanding of the human artisan and of God's artistry in nature is being radically reviewed, and our relationship to the "canvas" of nature is being deeply questioned.

The environmental signs are quite distressing as a new millennium dawns. From the polar ice cap to the remote depths of the Pacific Ocean, evidence of human-engendered pollutants can now be found. We are experiencing a rate of species extinction, estimated by some at seventeen species of flora and fauna a day, unprecedented since the dinosaur age closed with a bang or a whimper (scientists aren't sure which) some sixty-five million years ago. Greenhouse gases, according to a plurality of the world's climate experts, are generating a dramatic warming effect upon the world, leading to wide swings in weather patterns, flooding, and other natural disasters of seemingly apocalyptic proportions. Indeed, 1998 was deemed the hottest year on record, and most of the leading contenders for that ominous honor have been in the 1990s.[3] Consumerism and militarization continue throughout the Northern nations and increasingly permeate nations of the South, while countries such as China rapidly replace salutary bicycles for non-emissions-tested automobiles at a disturbing rate.

Deforestation, especially among tropical rain forests, is occurring at the rate of one football field a second—an area the size of Austria each year. Moreover, according to the United Nations, thirty-five thousand children die daily owing to diseases engendered by contaminated water and food, and the growth of the human family will reach six billion, it is estimated, shortly into the twenty-first century. (As such a litany attests, one could convincingly argue that ecology now rivals economics as "the gloomy science."[4])

Were we to receive a report card from the Creator for our stewardship of the earth, one surmises it would not be a happy read, prompting a student-teacher conference the like of which has never been seen.

While the twentieth century certainly did not have a monopoly on environmental destruction or concern for nature, philosophically, theologically, or practically speaking, it did witness several significant, distinctive environmental moments which are worth exploring here.

Moment One:
The Dawn of the Environmental Movement

Rachel Carson: Recasting Our Relationship with Nature

While Joseph Sittler was sounding a tocsin for nature amid hallowed theological halls, Rachel Carson, a biologist, writer, and former editor-in-chief of the U.S. Fish and Wildlife Service, rang an environmental alarm that reverberated throughout the corridors of U.S. corporate and political power. Having achieved critical and financial success with *The Sea around Us*,[5] which settled comfortably for weeks on *The New York Times* bestseller list, Carson in 1962 launched her most influential book, *Silent Spring*, which many claim to be the single most important event in alerting the world to the hazards of environmental poisoning by pesticides, or "biocides," as she termed them. Attacked by chemical companies and threatened with legal action from powerful interests (as were *The New Yorker* and Houghton-Mifflin for publishing her work), Carson, valiantly fighting breast cancer, perse-vered with her project. Once published, *Silent Spring* became an immediate bestseller, sparking hearings in the U.S. Senate and a presidential report from the Kennedy administration resulting in a ban on DDT use in the United States.[6]

Carson argued that for humanity to think it can somehow transcend the laws of nature is equivalent to thinking it can repeal the law of gravity. In contradistinction to the reigning sense that humans were "at war with na-ture" and, in particular, with "hordes of insects" that jeopardized crops and hence human survival, Carson pushed for organic alternatives to pest con-trol in keeping with natural processes.

Sadly observing that the "current vogue for poisons" demonstrated "no humility" before the fabric of nature—"a fabric on the one hand delicate and destructible, on the other miraculously tough and resilient," Carson wrote:

> The "control of nature" is a phrase conceived in arrogance, born of the Neanderthal age of biology and philosophy, when it was supposed that nature exists for the convenience of man. The concepts and prac-tices of applied entomology for the most part date from that Stone Age of science. It is our alarming misfortune that so primitive a sci-ence has armed itself with the most modern and terrible weapons, and that in turning them against the insects it has also turned them against the earth.[7]

While Carson is generally regarded as the fountainhead of the modern environmental movement, her antecedents are many: Henry David Thoreau, the civilly disobedient naturalist and author of *Walden*; John Muir, founder of the Sierra Club and chief protagonist for the establishment of Yosemite National Park; Aldo Leopold, a visionary conservationist whose *A Sand County Almanac* is the first seedling of environmental ethics; and Albert Schweitzer, who developed an ethic of "reverence for life" as a sustainable leitmotif amid the rubble and smog of the post–World War II period, and to whom Rachel Carson dedicated *Silent Spring*.[8]

Moment Two:
Environmental Destruction as a Theological Concern

Lynn White Jr. and the Advent of Ecological Theology

Though Joseph Sittler had been calling for a serious and sustained theo-logical reflection on the environment in the early 1960s, it was not until 1967, with the publication of Lynn White's accusatory article "The Histori-cal Roots of the Ecologic Crisis," that Christian theologians were impelled to deal with the environmental onslaught and their own culpability for the crisis.

A cultural historian and practicing Christian, White asserted that Christianity is the "most anthropocentric religion" the world has ever known. Though observing countervailing trends in the writings of St. Francis of Assisi, whom White nominated as patron saint of ecology (a designation later affirmed by Pope John Paul II), White claimed that the Judeo-Christian tradition on the whole, owing to its sense of the human as a subduer of the earth with a divine injunction to have dominion over creation, provided the moral, cultural, and spiritual foundation for the birth of aggressive and environmentally harmful technologies. Why did the scratch plow first emerge in medieval Europe rather than in the great civilizations of Persia or China? For White, one need go no further than the focus on human power and redemption inherent in Western Christianity.

White's critique was perhaps meant more as a gauntlet thrown before the tradition than a Molotov Cocktail tossed within it. Nevertheless, coming as it did in the late 1960s, with an emerging cultural critique of traditional political, educational, and religious traditions, White's thesis was waved broadly by the secular environmental movement in North America, eager to distance itself from a tradition often seen more as a keeper of the status quo than as a force for progressive change. Consequently, the budding environmental movement did not readily embrace an alliance with members of one of the most effective shapers of public consciousness and action in North America, that is, the mainline Christian churches.[9]

In theological circles White's article prompted an explosion of articles and books, leading him jocularly to refer to himself as the "founder of ecological theology."[10] In the aftermath of his challenge, Christian responses adopted three main positions.[11]

First, there is what might be termed the "apologetic" or defensive response, which avers that White had insufficient biblical background or understanding of the nuances of the Christian tradition to support his statements. These responses cull from biblical scholarship and church tradition in order to defend the Judeo-Christian legacy from White's charges. They also suggest that the emergence of Western technology was a complex and multi-branched phenomenon, one that could not be facilely attributed to a single root cause. Among the most prominent of these spokespersons are philosopher Robin Attfield and theologians Thomas Sieger Derr and H. Paul Santmire[12]; Santmire's *Travail of Nature* painstakingly pours the sands of the Christian tradition through an ecological sieve, finding two parallel movements, one "spiritual" and the other "ecological," with the latter providing the seeds, Santmire claims, for a positive theology of the environment.

The constructive position, the second response, acknowledges that environmental concerns were not at the forefront of theology. While conceding that it had been a while since they last heard a sermon on safeguarding the non-human world, many in this camp intimate that there are fruits in the tradition that can be harvested, and their seeds cultivated, for a more sanguine response to nature. Theologian Douglas John Hall,[13] a contributor to this volume, who explores Christian dominion as a form of stewardship, and Jürgen Moltmann,[14] who delineates an ecological doctrine of creation from a trinitarian perspective, are but two architects of this approach. The pioneering work of John B. Cobb Jr., Jay B. McDaniel, and Catherine Keller, through the lens of process theology, has attempted to see the interconnection of the human with the non-human in dialogue with contemporary physics, economics, and animal-rights literature.

Ecofeminism, which relates the oppression of women to the domination of nature, strives to move from a cultural paradigm of patriarchy to one of mutuality and builds on a critical theological response to social injustice and sexism. Rosemary Radford Ruether (1992), Sallie McFague (1993), Heather Eaton, and physicist Vandana Shiva (1993) represent important voices in this emergent literature.[15] In addition, the nascent Latin American social ecology of Leonardo Boff and Ivone Gebara is also representative of this creative engagement with the Christian tradition in light of environmental degradation, claiming that the same cultural, political, and economic forces that render the majority of the world's peoples destitute are also rapaciously destroying the world's ecosystems.[16]

A third response to White, the "listening approach," in many ways transcends the debate, suggesting that Christianity has to listen to science, other religious traditions, and nature itself to get its bearings in a sea of environmental peril. Among the spokespersons here are Thomas Berry and his former students John Grim and Mary Evelyn Tucker. The work of Thomas Berry, a self-dubbed "geologian," is noteworthy as much for its progression as for its content. A cultural historian and Passionist priest who once served in China, Berry founded a center for world religions at Fordham University in New York, the first such center at a Catholic institution, and published important texts in the areas of Buddhism and Eastern thought.

Arguably, however, his most lasting work has come since 1970, when he established the Riverdale Center for Religious Research and published his papers on the "new cosmology." Though circulated among friends and members of the American Teilhard Association for years, they were not published in book form until the *Dream of the Earth* appeared.[17] Berry, once a "lone voice for the wilderness," is now seen as one of the progenitors of the modern religious environmental movement, and his advice is sought by U.S. President Bill Clinton; Vice-President Al Gore; the U.S. bishops; and church, civic, and educational leaders around the world. Interestingly, recognition of the importance of Berry's work has grown concomitantly with interest in Christian circles in the environmental crisis. Thomas Berry, a humble and prescient priest from the red hills of North Carolina, is now an intellectual grandfather and inspiration to several generations of religious and spiritual seekers of environmental sustainability, including many women religious congregations whose practical ecoministries combine Berry's thought with pragmatic acts of social justice.

Indeed, the spill of books, papers, conferences, and organizations around environmental issues in the Christian world has been sizable, from the National Religious Partnership on the Environment, prompted by an open letter from leading scientists to the religious community to deal with the eco-crisis, to the Harvard Conference on World Religions and Ecology spearheaded by Mary Evelyn Tucker (1998), the increasing environmental focus by the National Catholic Rural Life Conference, the Center for Respect of Life and the Environment, the North American Coalition on Religion and Ecology, and many others.[18] The formation of such groups has been accompanied by an increasing volume of Catholic social teaching on the environment, from Pope John Paul II's 1990 World Day of Peace message, the first to focus on ecological concerns, to environmental statements from bishops' conferences in the Philippines, Dominican Republic, United States, Canada, and elsewhere. There has been tremendous growth in awareness and action from Christian theological voices around the environment.[19]

Moment Three:
The Commingling of Social Justice and Environmental Concerns

Toward a Political Theology of the Environment

Intriguingly, the environmental consciousness of Christian churches was being prodded by Lynn White just as its social conscience was also being tweaked by liberation theologians.[20] Just as liberation theologians were developing a preferential option for the poor, and a critique of economic, social, and military structures that continue to lock generations of people in Southern nations in the iron grip of misery, environmental theologians were also attempting to chart a new ground for theology. They sought a new context—not only social and political but also environmental.

For many years the connections between these two views, social justice and ecology, were not readily discerned. At one gathering at the College Theology Society in Loyola Marymount University in Los Angeles, Thomas Berry and Jon Sobrino, S.J., from El Salvador, author of *Christology at the Crossroads* (1978) and a leading liberation theologian, sat together on a panel, but their worldviews remained in different places. Frustrated with Berry's presentation, Sobrino at one point wondered how Berry could equate the life of a starving child with that of a bird. Berry, on his part, noting the absence of Christian reflection on eco-destruction, was critical of certain biblical approaches to the environmental movement. He would observe later that Christians should "put the Bible on the shelf for twenty years and listen to nature."[21]

Fortunately, a confluence of sorts has begun between these two important theological streams. Leonardo Boff, the famous Brazilian liberation

theologian twice silenced by the Vatican for his views, has sought to integrate a preferential option for the poor with a preferential option for the
earth. He has drawn a compelling connection between environmental and
human rights concerns, especially in the area of indigenous cultures of the
Amazon rain forest, where a way of life is being torched along with the rain
forest itself.[22] With Mary Evelyn Tucker and John Grim, Boff has served as
editor of the Ecology and Justice series of Orbis Books, the premier publisher of liberation theology. Moreover, churches have looked increasingly
at environmental racism in North America and elsewhere as both a social
justice and an ecological issue. With the aid of the social sciences, church
groups are realizing it is no accident that toxic waste dumps and noxious,
poison-spewing incinerators are located in poorer neighborhoods in the
United States, often where the majority of citizens are black or Hispanic.
(Intriguingly, Jon Sobrino currently comments on the need of a theology
of creation, and Thomas Berry acknowledges that his work is vulnerable to
social-justice critiques.)

It is increasingly evident that environmental issues run along the same
fault lines that mark our social and political landscape. While interconnec-
tions were articulated, as mentioned, by theologians such as Joseph Sittler
and Rosemary Radford Ruether, they were made institutionally in the 1970s
by the World Council of Churches' Justice, Peace, and Integrity of Creation
Initiative, which saw all three concerns as interrelated.

In many ways the melding of political theology and ecological religious
reflection is among the most promising and hope-yielding theological developments at the crepuscule of the twentieth century. Such a convergence
points out the need for an integrated response to both human suffering
and environmental destruction, a chord sounded strongly in the Jubilee
statements of progressive Christian coalitions worldwide, who invoke the
biblical tradition in Deuteronomy of every fifty years forgiving debts, giving
the land a rest, and releasing slaves. The Canadian Ecumenical Jubilee Initiative, in particular, has stressed these three dimensions of Jubilee in terms
of debt cancelation for Southern nations, release of persons sold into pros-
titution and child labor rings, and protecting the environment. These are
sanguine new millennium resolutions, as it were.

Yet there is a growing need for the churches and theologians to take the
environmental crisis seriously. Here, we can all benefit from the example
of religious women who have done environmental audits of their property,
supported women religious in full-time environmental ministry, sponsored
community-supported organic agriculture, and led education programs
influenced by the new cosmology of Brian Swimme and Thomas Berry, which
link social justice with a love for creation.

They are practitioners of a new type of political theology, an ecological
theology of politics, as it were, that sees the context of theology with new
eyes—not just human, but non-human as well. Such a theology will have to
take seriously the tendency toward anthropocentrism in the tradition. It

must develop what I have termed elsewhere an "anthro-harmonic approach," with harmonic suggesting "of an integrated nature."[23] This perspective views the human in a mutually constitutive relationship with creation, not simply as lord and master over it. It intimates that while the human has a unique potency to both wreck and restore creation, the human is also in some ways dependent on creation for moral, spiritual, and physical well-being. In this sense, human and non-human nature share a "dialectical contingency," a fundamental integration, which must form the context for theological exploration. Just as we are not above nature, so too are we not at its service. Our biblical tradition calls us to a special concern for the systematically impoverished and destitute, and to use the fruits of our science to bring about not only a just society, but a sustainable one, where the gifts of the Creator are preserved not simply in gated communities for the affluent but in the open garden of creation, our graced home.

Notes

[1] Peter W. Bakken, Joan Gibb Engel, and J. Ronald Engel, in their assiduously researched survey of Christian Ecojustice Literature, suggest that theologian Joseph Sittler's 1961 address—"Called to Unity"—to the Third Assembly of the World Council of Churches in New Delhi marks the outset of post–World War II attempts to interweave environmental concerns, justice, and Christian faith (see Bakken, Engel, and Engel, *Ecology, Justice, and Christian Faith: A Critical Guide to the Literature* [Westport, Conn.: Greenwood Press, 1995]). For careful assessments of Sittler's ground-breaking ecological theology, see Steven Bouma-Prediger, *The Greening of Theology: The Ecological Models of Rosemary Radford Ruether, Joseph Sittler, and Jürgen Moltmann* (Atlanta, Ga.: Scholars Press, 1995); and Bruce Heggen, "A Theology for Earth: Nature and Grace in the Thought of Joseph Sittler" (Ph.D. diss., Montreal, McGill University, 1995).

[2] See Lynn White Jr., "The Historical Roots of Our Ecologic Crisis," *Science* 155 (1967):1203-7.

[3] According to the Intergovernmental Panel of Climate Change, global temperatures may rise by 1 to 3.5 degrees Celsius by 2100 owing to fossil-fuel emissions, leading not only to alarming weather patterns, but also to dramatic effects upon plant and animal ecosystems, including the northward spread of such tropical diseases as yellow fever and malaria.

[4] For up-to-date and thorough statistics on environmental issues, see the annual report of the Worldwatch Institute, *State of the World,* edited by Lester Brown.

[5] Rachel L. Carson, *The Sea around Us* (New York: Oxford University Press, 1951).

[6] When *The New Yorker* magazine printed pre-publication excerpts from *Silent Spring,* it received menacing legal correspondence from the U.S. chemical firm Velsicol, as did Houghton-Mifflin, Carson's publisher. For a cogent treatment of U.S. corporate attempts to silence *Silent Spring,* see the 1993 PBS video "Rachel Carson's *Silent Spring,*" part of *The American Experience* documentary series.

[7] Rachel Carson, *Silent Spring* (Boston: Houghton Mifflin, 1962), 297.

[8] Carson's childhood imagination was fueled by the nature-study movement, represented by botanists Liberty Hyde Bailey and Anna Botsford Comstock. Comstock's *Handbook of Nature Study* (1911), widely used by elementary-school children in North

America, taught the fundamental principles of birds, fish, and animals, and sought to instill a love of nature in children. In the case of Carson, it was apparently most successful. For further background on the movement and its influence on Carson, see Linda Lear, *Rachel Carson: Witness for Nature* (New York: Henry Holt, 1998).

[9] Max Oelschlaeger, *Caring for Creation: An Ecumenical Approach to the Environmental Crisis* (New Haven, Conn.: Yale University Press, 1994).

[10] Quoted in Thomas Sieger Derr, "Religion's Responsibility for the Ecological Crisis: An Argument Run Amok," *Worldview* 18 (January 1975): 39-45.

[11] Stephen B. Scharper, *Redeeming the Time: Toward a Political Theology of the Environment* (New York: Continuum, 1997).

[12] Robin Attfield, *The Ethics of Environmental Concern* (New York: Columbia University Press, 1983); Derr, "Religion's Responsibility for the Ecological Crisis"; H. Paul Santmire, *Travail of Nature: The Ambiguous Ecological Promise of Christian Theology* (Philadelphia, Pa.: Fortress Press, 1995).

[13] Douglas John Hall, *Imaging God: Dominion as Stewardship* (Grand Rapids, Mich.: Eerdmans, 1986).

[14] Jürgen Moltmann, *God in Creation: A New Theology of Creation and the Spirit of God* (San Francisco: Harper & Row, 1985).

[15] Rosemary Radford Ruether, *Gaia and God: Toward an Ecofeminist Theology of Earth Healing* (San Francisco: HarperCollins, 1992); Sallie McFague, *The Body of God: An Ecological Theology* (Minneapolis, Minn.: Fortress Press, 1993); Vandana Shiva, *Monocultures of the Mind: Perspectives on Biodiversity and Biotechnology* (London: Zed Books, 1993).

[16] Leonardo Boff, *Ecology and Liberation: A New Paradigm,* trans. John Cumming (Maryknoll, N.Y.: Orbis Books, 1995); and Ivone Gebara, "Cosmic Theology: Ecofeminism and Panentheism," in *Readings in Ecology and Feminist Theology*, ed. Mary Heather MacKinnon and Moni McIntyre (Kansas City, Mo.: Sheed and Ward, 1995), 208-13.

[17] Thomas Berry, *The Dream of the Earth* (San Francisco: Sierra Club Books, 1988).

[18] For a more detailed listing of such groups, see S. Scharper and H. Cunningham, *The Green Bible* (Maryknoll, N.Y.: Orbis Books, 1993), 109-11.

[19] Texts of such church statements are included in Drew Christiansen and Walter Grazier, eds., *"And God Saw That It Was Good": Catholic Theology and the Environment* (Washington, D.C.: United States Catholic Conference, 1996).

[20] See the chapters by Virgilio Elizondo and Lee Cormie in this volume.

[21] Thomas Berry, *Befriending the Earth: A Theology of Reconciliation between Humans and the Earth* (Mystic, Conn.: Twenty-Third Publications, 1991).

[22] Boff, *Ecology and Liberation.*

[23] Scharper, *Redeeming the Time.*

18

The Postmodern Debate

MICHAEL J. SCANLON, O.S.A.

By now it is obvious that the term *postmodern* is ambiguous. I will use it as synonymous with *contemporary*. From our study of history we have learned to think in eras or epochs, and thus we distinguish the ancient world from the medieval world and the medieval from the modern. I concur with the many who feel that our time is significantly different from the modern era. We no longer resonate with some of the central characteristics of modernity as fathered by Descartes—the monological, rational self, the Enlightenment presupposition of "universal reason," the panacea of science and technology, and the ideology of historical progress with "man on his own." The word *postmodern* attempts to describe our current situation in light of its difference from modernity. Used as an umbrella, it covers many different responses or reactions in the twentieth century to the end of modernity in 1914. World War I put an end to the ideology of progress that described the Promethean projects of modernity. The "postmodern debate" means that many of the ideals of modernity have become "debatable," that is, questionable, open to debate. We shall consider some of these debatable issues from a theological perspective.

In both philosophy and theology, postmodern writers clarify postmodernism in relation to the characteristic emphases of modern thought: the "turn to the subject," universal reason, historical progress, and androcentrism. For most of these thinkers Descartes is the father of modern thought to the extent that it can be identified as rationalism. The Cartesian *cogito* with its "clear and distinct ideas" provided a foundation for rational thinking in response to the failure of religious authority to provide an unquestioned framework for thought because of the divisions in Western Christendom after the Reformation. The assumption was that while religious tradition is historical and particular, reason is universal for the *animal rationale*. Confidence in human reason is closely related to another pervasive mark of modernity, its vehement critique of religion. For the reflective modernist, religion was a demonic cause of war, as verified in the seventeenth-century wars of religion. While religions divide people, reason could unite them.

In discussing postmodern critiques of modern emphases we should keep in mind Gregory Baum's cautions about "innocent critique."[1] Instructed by the important themes of critical theory, developed by the Frankfurt School, Baum insists that innocent critique of culture and society must stop. A critique is innocent when it does not critically explore the range of its own implications and possible consequences. Postmodern critiques of modernity are innocent when they jettison modern concerns without remainder—without caring to salvage the grains of truth and value in those concerns. What follows in our consideration of postmodern issues in anthropology and theology will attempt to avoid innocent critique.

Toward a Postmodern Theological Anthropology

A primary aim of the postmodern critique of modernity is to overcome the latter's focus on the self, modernity's famous "turn to the subject." To celebrate their work, some postmodern philosophers employ a rhetoric of hyperbole evident in such phrases as "the death of the subject," or "the end of the self." Their target, of course, is the foundational subject of the Cartesian *cogito* or the Kantian transcendental self, but their rhetoric appears to jettison any notion of the self whatsoever. Theological anthropology must reject this extremely "innocent" critique in fidelity to the biblical notion of the self as person, as the responsible self in relation to others. But theological anthropology has much to gain from the postmodern critique of the modern self that found its center in consciousness, in thought, in private interiority. Perhaps the most common characteristic of all postmodern anthropology is its insistence on the linguisticality of human existence. Premodern anthropology (for example, that of Thomas Aquinas) explored the essential structure of the human being in terms of "human nature" with its specific powers of intellect and will. Instructed by the contemporary emphasis on language as the key to understanding the human, we might say that human nature is the given potential for human existence, but this potential must be nurtured by a linguistic induction into the human community. It is language that makes human knowing and doing possible. Aristotle got it right—we are animals that have the *logos* (word *before* thought, making thought possible), and his social anthropology follows—as linguistic animals we are political animals (we need others to talk to). Speech makes intersubjectivity the matrix of personal subjectivity.

In his project of retrieving human subjectivity in the wake of the postmodern critique of the monological, autonomous self philosopher Calvin Schrag explores the notion of the "decentered self" within the context of communicative *praxis.*[2] This "decentered self" is, of course, the Christian ideal of losing oneself to find oneself. The "self-centered self" is a classical definition of the sinner. In a postmodern approach that refuses simply to jettison human subjectivity, the modern question, What is the self?, yields to the question, Who is the self? The "what" question is the metaphysical search for the unchanging, essential core of the human be-ing. The "who" question invites a story for an answer, a temporal narrative filled with ever-changing situations. It is the social process that is respon-sible for the appearance of the self as a kind of "multiple personality."[3] In this process the "who" emerges in its different roles, its different relation-ships, its different responsibilities. These "different selves" of our different involvements in language and life against the background of multiple so-cial memories, various customs, habits, and institutional practices revolve around a "responding center," a personal sphere of interest and concern whence things are said and done. The "who" is a shifting center of initiative and response in the ongoing human "conversation." But conversation re-quires tongues, and tongues come with bodies. For postmodern anthropol-ogy, embodiment together with temporality is an essential characteristic of the decentered self. Through the emphasis on the linguisticality of human existence the human body is rediscovered as basic symbol. Within and through our intersubjectivity the phenomenon of the decentered self de-livers its own embodied presence in the communicative performances of discourse and action. As event and acquisition the decentered subject emerges from and sustains itself within these performances. The body is the self-manifestation, the self-expression of the human person, the con-crete "medium" through which the human person becomes a reality in the world. In the sacramental economy of Catholicism, "to express" is "to ef-fect." By bodily self-expression the human being enacts itself in a lifetime. Body is the basic human sacrament through which the human person ef-fects itself in freedom in interdependence with the embodied selves of other human beings in their common commerce with the material world.

This "linguistic turn" is a further specification of historical conscious-ness that alerts us to the fact that we are shaped by the past—by history, by society, by culture, by tradition with language as *the* medium of the trans-mission of tradition. Shaped by the past, we shape the future by our com-municative *praxis*. In accord with historical consciousness the modern En-lightenment generated a tradition of universal emancipation or liberation, based on the presupposition of universal reason's ability to achieve ratio-nal agreement on universal human goods or values. Some postmodern think-ers give us an innocent critique of the Enlightenment's tradition of human emancipation through reason. They jettison this "meta-narrative" to cel-ebrate the incommensurability of our different "language games" or cul-tures. It seems to them that we are incarcerated in our diverse linguistic horizons or traditions. For the Enlightenment, tradition with all of its par-ticularity is inimical to freedom and autonomy. Tradition must give way to universal reason as the path to progress. Today we must concur with the postmodern unveiling of Enlightenment rationality as itself a tradition (a meta-narrative) and not just "pure reason." But, to avoid innocent critique, must we not try to recover the grain of truth in the Enlightenment's emancipatory thrust without reducing it to simply a modern "epistemological" movement? Rejecting the Enlightenment's claim to non-historical rationality must not mean capitulation to incommensurability without nuance. In place of an ahistorical rationality to arbitrate conflicting claims some postmodern thinkers turn to another "universal" that, however, always is pluralistic—language. The hermeneutical potential of language itself provides a way to overcome simple incommensurability. A dialogical approach to the search for truth should replace the monological methods of modernity. This approach does not lead to relativism. Through the cultivation of hermeneutical sensitivity and imagination different languages can be compared and rationally evaluated. Incommensurable languages and traditions are not windowless monads sharing nothing in common. There are always points of overlap and crisscrossing. Our linguistic horizons are always open. We may fail to understand alien traditions, but our response to this failure should be ethical—listening more carefully and enlarging our imaginations. It is quite difficult, but we must learn to live in critical openness to the cultural pluralism of our time. We will learn that it is only through engaged encounters with the "other" that we will come to a more profound understanding of our own traditions.

Discussing the issue of incommensurability leads us to a consideration of the *alterity* that has been a central theme of postmodern Continental philosophy. "'Postmodern' thinking, if it means anything at all, means a philosophy of 'alterity,' a relentless attentiveness and sensitivity to the 'other.'"[4] The most extreme and radical formulation of the problem of the "other" comes from the French Jewish philosopher Emmanuel Levinas.[5] His vocabulary immediately reveals his postmodern distance from the great ethical ideal of modernity, autonomy, which he replaces with "heteronomy"—ethical living is constant openness, constant obedience, to the summons of the "other"—especially to the oppressed, the excluded, the marginalized ("the widow, the orphan, and the stranger" of Exodus 22:21). Levinas indicts the entire tradition of Western philosophy as the effort to reduce, absorb, appropriate the "other" to the "same." Writing out of the experience of the Holocaust, he portrays the "other" as a kind of moral infinity from whose face issues the categorical command "thou shalt not kill." The primary ethical relation of the "face-to-face" can never be reduced to the "totality" of the "same" and the "other." Against the Western tradition, which emphasizes reciprocity, likeness, and symmetry in "personal" relationships, Levinas emphasizes the lack of reciprocity, unlikeness, and asymmetry wherein I, in responding to the "other" (*l'autrui*), am always responsible for (to) the "other" (*l'autrui*), regardless of the "other's" response to me.

According to John Caputo "heterology" is a common feature of postmodern thought in general, but not all heterology gives rise to ethical sensibility and responsibility.⁶ We can distinguish "heteromorphism" and "heteronomism." Levinas's thought is an extreme form of the latter, but the former is more often identified with postmodernism. Heteromorphism stems from Nietzsche, but it is far more cheerful. It is a Dionysian play with differences, with novelties that enable us to enjoy the flux that has no end. "The play plays on, spacing and outspacing itself, disseminating itself, taking a whirl of new forms, making it impossible for the circle to close and so making dialectical enclosure impossible."⁷ Here all action is *ab intra* as the strongest, noblest, best forces overflow themselves—*bonum est diffusivum sui*. Their final discharge is a glorious death, which sets in motion new energies in their endless, joyful cycles. This heteromorphic difference is represented by Deleuze, Guattari, and Baudrillard. Quite different is the other heterology, heteronomism, which replaces autonomism as the postmodern ethical ideal. Levinas is the paradigm, with Derrida and Lyotard as his disciples. Derrida's postmodern philosophy of deconstruction is totally inspired by the spirit of "heteronomy," as he constantly alerts us to the constructedness of what we call the "reality of the "extra-linguistic"—a constructedness so often destructive of the "other." "Heteronomism" is respectful, responsive, and responsible, even religious. It is a lover of one family of "re-" words, which emblematize "the look it re-turns, sends back to the other, the regard it has for the other, and the mark of its heteronomic posture and immeasurable courtesy, its re-spect and re-sponsiveness."⁸ Here all action is *ab extra*. The heteronomist is attuned to the needs and desires of the "other," who is the source of all ethical obligations. As a heteronomist, Jacques Derrida is consumed with a prophetic passion for justice, which is neither a Platonic form nor a Kantian regulative idea but an eschatological promise. Justice can never be deconstructed. Indeed, deconstruction is justice. But law, which exists to serve justice, must always be deconstructed, because it never completely coincides with justice.

For quite some time, however, Derrida was identified with heteromorphism. In his more recent writings his ethical and political concerns have come to the fore. Very interesting is the fact that these concerns emerge most clearly from his "religious turn."

Toward a Postmodern Theology

In 1641 René Descartes dedicated his *Meditations on First Philosophy* to "the wisest and most distinguished men, the Dean and Doctors of the Faculty of Sacred Theology of Paris," with the claim that "two questions—that of God and that of the soul—are chief among those that ought to be demonstrated by the aid of philosophy rather than of theology."⁹ It seems that he met with no disagreement from the divines. For some time they had accepted the need for philosophical reflection on the *preambula fidei*, as illustrated in St. Thomas's *Summa Theologiae*. For Thomas, however, the use of philosophical reflection was always in the service of theology. In his Christology, Aquinas makes it very clear that the Incarnate Word is *the* Way to God. But the Cartesian transfer of the theological task of explicating the existence of God and the relation of the world to God to philosophy opened the door to the modern metaphysical phenomenon of "ontotheology." In the strict sense ontotheology is not just the employment of philosophical categories for theological purposes. Theology only becomes ontotheology when philosophers or theologians sell their soul to philosophy's project of rendering the whole of reality intelligible to human understanding by using God to do so.[10] Thus, ontotheology consists in the pride that refuses to accept the limits of human knowledge. The current critique of ontotheology is directed not at *what* we say about God but at *how* we say it, to what purpose, in the service of what project. The modern philosophical project of total comprehension of reality would absorb God into a pseudo-explanatory system that amounts to idolatry. The modern desire to "control" the world is part of the pathology of anthropocentrism, the fruits of which have been all too obvious in the postmodern twentieth century, the ecological crisis being one clear example. The modern desire to "control" God is not limited to Enlightenment deism. To give God a necessary role in establishing the intelligibility of reality was the ontotheological approach to mastering the divine. This modern metaphysics came to an end in principle when Nietzsche, the last metaphysician, declared the ontotheological god dead.

The deconstructive labor of postmodern philosophers is usually focused on the rationalistic pretensions of modern thought. Their emphasis on gnoseological humility—on what we do not know—recalls for contemporary theologians the long tradition of apophatic or negative theology. This tradition is central to Christian mysticism wherein the profound experience of divine "alterity"—the most radical otherness there is—leads to silence, to a "fear and trembling" that overwhelms any attempt to grasp God in human language. Divine transcendence is acutely felt by the prayerful human being, aware of our creatureliness and/or our sinfulness. This divine transcendence, however, does not mean God's distance, even though the Bible portrays the sinner as one separated from God. Transcendence in reference to God means difference, not distance. Here transcendence should not be contrasted to immanence—the more immanent in, or involved with, the world God is, the less transcendent God is. Intense divine involvement with the world "requires, one could say, an extreme of divine transcendence."[11] A contrastive understanding of divine transcendence implies that God is one of the things in the world, but the Catholic tradition on primary and secondary causality should have kept us from this mistake. The more transcendent God is, the more immanent—as every mystic knew.

A negative theology needs something to negate. In ancient Christianity there is almost no formal negative theology. It took some time for Christian thinkers to reflect on the "whatness" of God. In the teachings of Jesus as reported in the New Testament there is no interest in the question, What is God? That is the Greek question, and it was only with the progressive Hellenization of Christianity that questions about the nature or essence of God came to the fore.

Among the postmodern philosophers, the deconstructor par excellence, Jacques Derrida, has been interested in the question of negative theology for quite some time. Derrida's first interpretation of apophatic theology considered it as a "hyperessentiality" in which God is presented as God beyond being or Being beyond being or God beyond God. Yet this hyperessentiality still remains within the "metaphysics of presence"—now a higher or "hyper-presence," which would also demand deconstruction. Thus, deconstruction cannot be equated with apophatic or negative theology. Deconstruction frees negative theology from the Greek metaphysics of presence by inviting it to move away from the still too philosophical notion of hyperessentiality toward biblical eschatology, especially apocalyptic eschatology.

One of the most famous of Derrida's neologisms is *différance*, which conflates two verbs, to "differ" and to "defer." To illustrate the meaning of *différance* we may apply it to the God of the Bible—a transcendent God who "differs" radically from everything in the world and whose full revelation is "deferred" until the *eschaton*, when God will be "all in all" (1 Cor 15:28). Derrida's "religious turn" is a turn to the Bible with special focus on prophetic and apocalyptic eschatology.[12] These dramatic traditions of hope appeal to Derrida because they bring together religion and ethics—for them, God is the God who promises justice, the "democracy to come" or "the gift." This God is the "Absolute Future" who will never be a "future present." Like the prayer of the early Christians, *Maranatha*, Derrida's prayer is "Come" (*Viens*). Deconstruction becomes *faith* in *the* impossible advent, a faith that begets "religion without religion."

Derrida's form of prophetic/apocalyptic religion without religion expresses itself in his distinction between the "messianic" and the "messianisms."[13] The messianic is a universal (*quasi*-transcendental?) structure of experience (the radical hope for justice that is the human spirit). It must be distinguished from the messianisms, or the historical religions, Jewish, Christian, or Islamic. For Derrida this distinction is very important, because he seems to consider all the messianisms essentially demonic. In their historical encounters with one another they have always spawned violence and war. But what is the relationship between the messianic and the messianisms? In attempting to answer this question Derrida entertains two possibilities. The messianic is as general structure of experience a "groundless ground" on which there have been revelations (Judaism, Christianity, etc.), so that the messianic becomes the "fundamental ontological" condition of the possibility of these religions. Students of Karl Rahner would find an interesting connection here. Derrida, however, submits another possibility. The events of revelation that constitute the Jewish, Christian, and Islamic are "absolute events, irreducible events which have unveiled this messianicity." With this possibility Derrida claims that these religions would not be "cases" of some religious a priori. These religions are irreducible "singularities," not particulars subsumable under a general category. But without these messianisms we would know nothing about the messianic. For Derrida, these answers remain a serious dilemma, given his deconstructive approach to transcendental thinking.

In response to Derrida's dilemma John Caputo offers the early Heideggerian notion of a "formal indication," a "kind of weak or fragile pointer to the lush complexities of the 'factical' messianisms."[14] Such a pointer does not subsume, enclose, or precontain particulars, "but merely points an indicative finger at 'singularities' that are beyond its ken." Thus, the messianic is not a "universal concept" that grasps or includes its particulars. It seems to me that Karl Rahner would find this response congenial, for his "universal" or "transcendental revelation" is also not a concept grasping particulars. For Rahner, the "universal" is a Gift, the divine Self-Gift to the world. This is not an epistemological foundationalism but a *theological foundationalism*, which fits nicely with Caputo's (and Derrida's) insistence that "the facticity or singularity" (of messianisms) is not "conceived" or "grasped" but entered into, given in to, by a certain practical or praxical engagement, which means that you can never "get" it from the outside and you can never "get into" it except by "doing" it, *facere veritatem* (Derrida's Augustinian approach to truth for deconstruction). Getting into or doing it, where *it* is God, is only thorough the *praxis* of faith, hope, and love—for God is the *cognoscibile operabile*, knowable only by doing the truth (or, maybe better, by "making" the truth by changing the world).[15]

Derrida's religious language is a testimony to the end of the secularism of modernity and the old Enlightenment. His new Enlightenment is an ethical retrieval of responsibility, an ethical stance that mediates his "religion without religion."

Coinciding with the influence on theology of the postmodern recovery of the linguisticality of human existence is a rather recent theological retrieval of "its own voice." It no longer accepts the Cartesian takeover of theology by philosophy. When it comes to the issues of the meaning of the word *God* or of discussing the existence of God, theology now turns to its own resources. For example, Christian theology no longer begins with the question of the divinity of Christ, implicitly allowing philosophy to define the word *divinity*. The words, deeds, and destiny of Jesus become the focal disclosure of the meaning of the word *God*. What is God? is no longer our question. It is replaced by, Who is God for us? This shift has enriched theology and has opened up new prospects for retrieving *the* Christian doctrine of God, the Trinity.

Theologian David Tracy holds that "at its best postmodern theology is an honest if sometimes desperate attempt to let God as God be heard again."[16] Tracy provides us with a critique of modern theology that is in no way "innocent." Modern theology gave us genuine insights into the reality of God, including panentheism and all the modern forms of relational God-talk—Hegelian, process, trinitarian, feminist. But the central meaning of postmodern contemporary thought on God is the breakthrough of God's reality, no longer constrained by the modern *logos*. Postmodernity has brought a strange return of God to the center of theology. This re-entry of "the hidden-revealed God now comes through the interruptive experience and memory of suffering itself, the suffering of all those ignored, marginalized, and colonized by the grand narrative of modernity."[17] This postmodern theology is not a new set of propositions to rival modern theology. It is "an attempt at new forms of language rendering excess, gift, desire, prayer."[18]

Two significant books on postmodern theology were published very recently.[19] Both celebrate the return of God to philosophy and theology as *postmodern* becomes *post-secular.* It seems that this discussion is just beginning.

Notes

[1] See Gregory Baum, "The End of Innocent Critique and the Postmodern Discourse," *The Ecumenist* 3, no. 3 (July-September 1996), 58-63.

[2] See Calvin O. Schrag, *Communicative Praxis and the Space of Subjectivity* (Bloomington, Ind.: Indiana University Press, 1986), and *The Self after Postmodernity* (New Haven, Conn.: Yale University Press, 1997).

[3] Schrag, *Communicative Praxis and the Space of Subjectivity*, 148.

[4] John Caputo, "The Good News about Alterity: Derrida and Theology," *Faith and Philosophy* 10, no. 4 (October 1993), 453.

[5] See Emmanuel Levinas, *Totality and Infinity* (Pittsburgh, Pa.: Duquesne University Press, 1969).

[6] See John Caputo, *Against Ethics* (Bloomington, Ind.: Indiana University Press, 1993), 53-62.

[7] Ibid., 55.

[8] Ibid., 61.

[9] René Descartes, *Meditations on First Philosophy* (Indianapolis, Ind.: Hackett Publishing Company, 1979), 1.

[10] See Merold Westphal, "Overcoming Onto-Theology," a talk given at Villanova University's Conference on Religion and Postmodernism, September 25-27, 1997 (Bloomington, Ind.: Indiana University Press, forthcoming).

[11] Kathryn Tanner, *God and Creation in Christian Theology: Tyranny or Empowerment?* (Oxford: Basil Blackwell, 1988), 89.

[12] See John Caputo, *The Prayers and Tears of Jacques Derrida* (Bloomington, Ind.: Indiana University Press, 1977), 69-116.

[13] See John Caputo, ed., *Deconstruction in a Nutshell: A Conversation with Jacques Derrida* (New York: Fordham University Press, 1997), 156-80.

[14] Ibid., 177.

[15] On the portrayal of God as the *cognoscibile operabile* (the "doable knowable"), as the object of knowledge that can be reached only by *praxis*, in Duns Scotus, see Nicholas

Lobkowicz, *Theory and Practice: History of a Concept from Aristotle to Marx* (Lanham, Md.: University Press of America, 1967), 74.

[16] David Tracy, *On Naming the Present* (Maryknoll, N.Y.: Orbis Books, 1994), 37.

[17] Ibid., 43.

[18] Ibid., 45.

[19] Graham Ward, ed., *The Postmodern God: A Theological Reader* (Malden, Mass.: Blackwell Publishers, 1997); and Phillip Blond, ed., *Post-Secular Philosophy: Between Philosophy and Theology* (New York: Routledge, 1998).

Concluding Reflections

Looking Back over the Century

GREGORY BAUM

The following theological reflections on the essays in this volume are written after my return from South Africa, where I had been invited to participate in a seminar on the theology of work organized by the Industrial Mission and held at the School of Theology on the Pietermaritzburg campus of the University of Natal. A first seminar on this topic had been organized in 1989, to which I had also been invited, but at the time the apartheid government refused to grant me a visa. Over ten years later, in 1999, after democracy had been won, a second seminar was held on the same topic, to which I had the honor of being invited again. This meeting, which impressed me greatly, strengthened my conviction that Christian theology is the response of faith to the historical events that determine the life of a community.

In 1985, under the apartheid regime, an ecumenical group of courageous theologians had published the *Kairos Document,* which repudiated both the state theology of the Afrikaans-speaking Reformed church that legitimated apartheid and the liberal theology of the English-speaking churches that disapproved of apartheid but did not summon their members to participate in resistance against it. The *Kairos Document* proposed a prophetic theology, according to which fidelity to Jesus and his message demanded active resistance to the existing order of enslavement. Resistance against great social evil was the light in which these theologians read the scriptures and the Christian tradition. Yet after the creation of the new South Africa in 1994, these theologians, rethinking their position, concluded that in the present context the Christian mission was to promote reconciliation among the various nations, parties, and tribes in their country. Fidelity to Jesus in this situation demanded of all citizens mercy and justice, forgiveness and restitution, confession of guilt and the healing of memories. In this light they now reread scripture and the Christian tradition. Their new theology became incarnate, at least in part, in the Truth and Reconciliation Commission set up by President Mandela's government.

This South African story shows that to call a theology "contextual" does not tell us a great deal about it. The Afrikaner church had an elaborate contextual theology, based on a particular reading of scripture, that presented apartheid as God's law. This theology, preached from the pulpits and taught in the education of children, eventually resulted in the excommunication of that church by the World Alliance of Reformed and Presbyterian Churches in 1982. (The Afrikaner church abandoned its support for apartheid in 1986.) The English-speaking churches had their own contextual theology. That the harsh evaluation of the South African churches expressed in the *Kairos Document* was no exaggeration was confirmed by the *Report of Truth and Reconciliation Commission*, which—in its fourth volume— examined the role played by the churches under the apartheid regime and arrived at the same devastating analysis of conformity and compliance. At the same time, the report acknowledged the minority movement in the churches and its theological expressions that boldly resisted the apartheid regime.

The South African story reveals in dramatic fashion that reading the Bible and constructing a theology based on a set of biblical quotations do not guarantee fidelity to the biblical message. The Afrikaner church used an abundance of biblical texts to defend its position. The scriptures become word of God only if—using traditional language—they are read "in the Spirit." The Bible becomes word of God when it is read with a faith that acknowledges the heart of the divine message: God's creation, redemption, and vivification of the world; and Jesus' unique path of love, justice, and peace. Reading the scriptures in this faith when confronted by new challenges or new historical events is a creative process that brings to light new insights and clarifies what fidelity to the gospel means in the here and now.

Historical Developments in Protestant and Catholic Thought

The articles collected in this volume reveal the creativity of theology in its response to historical events and offer one major example of a contextual theology of betrayal. James Reimer's article shows how some German theologians were so impressed by Hitler's national-socialist revolution that they created a contextual theology in support of it. In fact, a large part of the German Protestant church, the so-called Deutsche Christen, embraced an interpretation of Christian faith that endorsed Nazi ideology. Victor Consemius mentions in his article that in the Germany of that period to be "open to the world" was dangerous for theologians, because it tempted them to focus on positive elements in Hitler's program, thus overlooking its evil dimension.

It is no wonder that there are theologians and ecclesiastics who are suspicious of contextual theology, fearing that openness to the *Zeitgeist*, the spirit of the world, will distort the divinely revealed message. These think-ers hold that theology should articulate and explore the eternal truths re-vealed by God that by their very nature transcend human history and are thus independent of life's changing circumstances. A reply to them is the observation that there are no formulations of eternal truth that have es-caped historical conditioning. We acknowledge the contextuality of bibli-cal accounts as well as the historical character of the early church councils that defined the core of Christian dogma. This recognition does not have to lead to theological relativism. Accepting the uniqueness of these texts and the divine truth disclosed in them, theologians understand their task as inquiring what these texts meant when they were composed and what these texts and their truths mean in the contemporary historical situation.

From Victor Consemius's article we learn that in the early twentieth cen-tury the Catholic church still emphasized the conceptual character of di-vine revelation, defended the highly rational neo-scholastic theology, and was suspicious of historical criticism and the theological relevance of reli-gious experience. The condemnation of modernism revealed a trust in abstract reason transcending historical circumstances. Consemius's article also shows that this non-historical stance was adopted by the papacy under particular historical circumstances, including resistance to modern, liberal society; the protection of Catholic unity in times of social change; and the pastoral concern for the uneducated people in the church, that is, the majority of Catholics. What this analysis suggests is that all theological affirmations, even when they defend the trans-historical nature of eternal truths, are in fact contextual in character. They all reflect in one way or another the concerns, the anguish, and the hope of believers in a given historical situation. This is a topic to which we shall return.

Because of the power of the magisterium in the Catholic church, it seemed to me, when I began to plan this volume, that Catholic theology prior to Vatican Council II was obliged to wrestle with ecclesiastical deci-sions and did not respond to the events of the twentieth century, such as the two world wars and the Great Depression, with the same passionate attention exhibited by Protestant theologians. Yet the article by Joseph Komonchak on the Catholic theology of the 1930s, especially in France, shows that my hunch was based on a superficial generalization. Influential Catholic thinkers in France—Chenu, Congar, Maritain, and Mounier—rec-ognized the dangerous one-sidedness of liberal capitalism and dogmatic communism and instead proposed a Catholic interpretation of culture rep-resenting a creative middle way between the two extremes. Bernard Dupuis's article on the Russian Orthodox theologians who after the Revolution had taken refuge in France shows that their emphasis on *sobornost*, on commu-nity and solidarity, influenced the Catholic theologians with whom they were in dialogue and thus made an important contribution to the more communal understanding of church and civil society characteristic of French Catholic thought at that time. This renewal of Catholic theology in France, with its trust in the reform of the church and the transformation of society, was one of the main ecclesiastical developments that prepared Vatican Council II.

The creative Protestant theology following upon World War I is examined in the articles by Douglas Hall, Donald Schweitzer, and Gary Dorrien. They deal with what Dorrien calls "the theological giants" of the time. Neoorthodox theology developed by Karl Barth and an alternative version produced by Reinhold Niebuhr understood the word of God first of all as judgment upon the world. Reason itself was here under judgment because it lent itself to the promotion and defense of any cause, however evil. A new and original return to the scriptures—without a hint of biblicism—produced a revival of Protestant Christianity that stressed the infinite qualitative difference between God and humans and refuted the superficial hopes of many liberal Protestants in human evolution toward a perfect society. The spiritual challenge of the Christian believers was to detect the sin in all historical movements and political parties, even when they appeared to be guided by a vision of solidarity and justice. Yet neo-orthodox Protestants were not passive in the face of historical events. Their theological critique of the world prompted them to act in the public sphere—but they did so without any utopian expectations. The mood of neo-orthodoxy in its various forms was sober; it was marked by a certain pessimism, which created a curious contrast to the more optimistic trend in Catholic theology and Catholic social teaching.

It is tempting to interpret this difference as reflecting two distinct doctrinal traditions. Protestants emphasize the sinfulness of humanity and understand the gift of grace mainly as offering divine forgiveness, while Catholics retain a certain trust in human nature, wounded though it is by sin, and look upon God's grace as a transformative divine gift. Yet such an interpretation would be superficial. Both Protestant and Catholic thought are complex traditions, each with significant internal tensions, so quick generalizations are always misleading. We have learned this in the ecumenical movement. This point is dear to me since I think of myself as a Catholic theologian in the Augustinian tradition with a keen sense of the dark side of all human achievements and a (troubled) reliance on unmerited and unexpected divine grace.

The difference between a certain Protestant pessimism and the more optimistic stance of Catholic thought after World War I has to do with the different location of these Christian communities in European and North American society. In the nineteenth century, liberal Protestant theology in Germany, Britain, and the United States—countries that were making enormous strides—supported the idea that the Christian message supported progress and the evolution of culture. Writing in this volume, Douglas Hall shows that World War I shattered the cultural optimism of European Christians, and Donald Schweitzer demonstrates that the Great Depression and the arrival of fascism in Europe undermined the reformist optimism that

Reinhold Niebuhr had at one time shared with the supporters of the Social Gospel. Neo-orthodox theology denounced the error committed by liberal Protestantism by uncritically identifying faith, hope, and love with the optimism and trust in progress characteristic of the dominant culture. With neo-orthodoxy, Protestantism acquired a new sobriety.

By contrast, Catholic thinkers after World War I believed that the moment had come to leave their narrow Catholic circle and engage in a positive way the philosophical and social ideas of the time. Victor Consemius mentions that Romano Guardini spoke of "escaping the Catholic ghetto" and Urs von Balthasar even of "razing the fortress." Why this new sense of freedom? Prior to World War I, Catholics in France had adopted a defensive posture vis-à-vis the dominant secular culture; Catholics in Germany were a minority in a Protestant monarchy, exposed to discrimination; and Catholics in Italy were forced by the popes to define themselves against their recently founded nation. The countries of Europe successful in terms of industrialization, colonial development, and military power were Protestant (Britain and Germany) and secular (France). These countries generated cultural optimism. Catholic Austria was an empire of an older sort, doubtful of its future; the other Catholic countries, resisting the impact of modernity, also lacked confidence in the future. Yet after World War I, Catholics in France were able to shed their defensive attitude, and Catholics in the secular Weimar republic were for the first time citizens on an equal footing. While Protestant theology acquired a new sobriety after war, Catholic theologians were becoming more hopeful, confidently affirming the church's humanizing mission and thus its universal relevance. The church as a divinely appointed agent of humanization became a dominant theme at Vatican Council II (1962-65).

The articles in this volume remind us that neo-orthodoxy in its various forms was not the only theological response of Protestants to the World War and the Great Depression. In his article James Reimer discusses the theology of the religious socialism developed in Germany by Paul Tillich and his theological friends, including Martin Buber. Tillich believed that the 1920s in Germany were a special moment, a *kairos*, when the reconstruction of capitalist society had become a historical possibility. (The South African *Kairos Document*, mentioned above, may well have received its name from Christians who remembered Tillich's radical theology.) In my opinion, Tillich's *Socialist Decision*, published a few weeks prior to Hitler's access to power and then immediately suppressed, is a brilliant book dealing with the relation of identity politics and social justice; it remains relevant to contemporary debates in theology and political science.

In the present volume Donald Schweitzer also tells the story of a Canadian socialist theology, at odds with the liberal Social Gospel and the anti-utopianism of Reinhold Niebuhr's neo-orthodoxy. This theology was created by a circle of Protestant theologians who were actively involved in the newly formed socialist party of Canada and who anticipated the practice-theory dynamics that was further explored, several decades later, by Latin American liberation theology. Ulrich Duchrow's article, moreover, reminds us that the ecumenical movement gathered great strength in the period between the two great wars. The ecumenical movement was carried by Protestant and Anglican theologians of diverse theological tendencies who agreed that the unity of the Christian church was a demand made by the testimony of scripture, the mission of the church, and the new historical situation created by the rapid spread of secularization.

Cautioning against Confident Humanism

After World War II theology underwent dramatic developments. In his article Gary Dorrien makes the bold claim, with which not all will agree, that the Protestant "theological giants" of the decades between the two wars were losing their relevance and were replaced by "theological giants" in Roman Catholicism. The writings of Chenu, Lonergan, de Lubac, Rahner, and Schillebeeckx convinced Catholics that the redemption revealed in Jesus Christ involved the offer of divine grace to the whole of the human family and that this called for a critical openness to secular human wisdom and the world religions. Here fidelity to Jesus Christ implies solidarity and cooperation with all people of good will—since their good will reveals the "always already" of divine grace. Let me add that this new sense of divine immanence uncovered by these theologians has initiated many Catholics to a worldly spirituality, that is, a mystical consciousness of being united to God's will as they act in the world to promote love, justice, and peace.

In his article Robert Schreiter shows that on the basis of this theology Vatican Council II understood the church as the divinely appointed agent of humanization in the world. I remember a conversation with two of the observers at the council, German Lutheran theologian Edmund Schlink and Anglican bishop John Moorman. Schlink was appalled that the council offered a humanistic interpretation of the gospel and the church's mission: "You are repeating the mistake we made in the nineteenth century," he said. By contrast, Bishop Moorman suggested approvingly that the council was taking up the theme of Incarnation as it had been developed at the turn of the century by the *Lux mundi* movement in the Anglican church. The touch of cultural optimism that did mark certain conciliar documents, especially *Gaudium et spes*, was corrected by the Medellín Conference (1968) of the Latin American Bishops' Conference, which looked upon the world from the perspective of the poor, a perspective that was subsequently taken into papal encyclicals such as Paul VI's *Populorum progressio* and John Paul II's *Laborem exercens*.

The Latin American voice was not the only one that cautioned against the confident humanism that now characterized the mainstream of Catholic theology. Johann Baptist Metz and his friend, Protestant theologian

Jürgen Moltmann, asked whether this optimistic interpretation of the world was not, in part at least, a reflection of the successful welfare capitalism that had made the northwestern European countries wealthy and created the illusory hope that this form of capitalism provided the recipe for overcoming poverty in the world. Under the influence of Johann Baptist Metz's political theology, many Catholic theologians acquired a more sober view of contemporary society and recognized that divine grace is not only *sanans et elevans,* as St. Thomas believed, but *sanans, elevans et liberans,* revealing the social sin of society and creating commitment to emancipation.

The turn to liberation found in Christian theology since the 1960s was the result of several other historical developments. As Rosemary Radford Ruether shows in her article in this volume, reflection on the Holocaust forced Christian thinkers to recognize the anti-Jewish rhetoric that had become, almost from the beginning, part and parcel of the proclamation of the Christian gospel. The New Testament itself contains passages that reflect the quarrel of the early Christian community with the synagogue. The presence of the anti-Jewish trend in the Christian tradition, confirmed by a host of historical studies, and the connection of this trend, however indirect, with the genocide of European Jewry, left Christian thinkers speechless and stunned. They recognized that the effort to liberate Christian teaching from the contempt for Jews and Jewish religion would shake the foundation of the Christian faith. And yet it had to be undertaken. Since the Great Commandment revealed in the Bible is the love of God and neighbor, Christians theologically justified subjecting their own religious tradition to a critical review that (1) rejected the elements that sin against love and generate disrespect or even hatred of Jews and Jewish religion, and (2) reinterpreted the teaching of Jesus and the story of his death and resurrection in a manner that encouraged respect for Jews and members of the other religions. In a special declaration Vatican Council II allied itself to such an effort and called for dialogue, cooperation, and friendship with Jews, even if the theological issues raised by this new openness have not yet been completely resolved.

Many years ago I had occasion to write that I had not learned what ideology was—that is, the distortion of truth for the sake of collective interests—from Karl Marx. I had learned it instead through the painful discovery of the church's anti-Jewish rhetoric, an ideology that has marred almost the entire Christian tradition. After World War II, Christians situated in many different locations in the world discovered the power of ideology. Thus Christian communities in the colonies of European empires became aware of the distorted manner in which the gospel had been preached to them. This point is made in Virgilio Elizondo's article. In their struggle against foreign domination and economic oppression, these Christians recognized that the religion they had received from missionaries had legitimated the colonial enterprise by looking upon it as a providential event that had led to the spread of the gospel and brought a superior culture to as yet unenlightened peoples. In the literature of Latin American liberation theology we find testimonies of Christians belonging to the middle classes who came to feel, after the disturbing discovery of the poor, that the God preached by their church and received in their culture was an ideological construct making invisible the massive oppression of the great majority on their continent. Is the God preached by the church an idol of the colonizers? In their article Dwight Hopkins and Linda Thomas tell us that a similar question haunted black men and women in the United States. Is the God of Christianity white? Creative theologies produced in the former colonies and among Afro-Americans have responded to this troubling challenge by purging the ideological heritage of the Christian church and concluding on the basis of scripture and their own religious experience that the God of Jesus Christ is the God of the humble and the poor, eternally intolerant of oppression.

A systematic questioning of the biblical tradition also took place among Christian women. Is God male, they asked, and is maleness, by its proximity to the divine, superior to femaleness? Is patriarchy part of revealed truth? Or can the biblical legacy and the Christian tradition be reread and rescued from their patriarchal heritage? The article of Susan Ross documents the many paths taken by feminist theology to show that the redemption revealed by Jesus Christ is a transvaluation of values, the reversal of norms produced by a sinful world, the overcoming of all structures of inferiorization, and the entry of women and men into the freedom of God's children. Susan Ross and Linda Thomas have demonstrated the richness of feminist theology. They show that feminist concern in church and society is not simply of interest to women, but to women and men together. Feminist thought and practice foster an alternative way of understanding human interaction promoting the emancipation of women and men alike. That feminist theology is usually taught at schools of theology in separate courses reveals the sad fact that this emancipatory approach has not yet been integrated into what passes as theology *tout court*.

An ideology critique of the Christian tradition has also been practiced by theologians troubled by the ecological devastation produced by modern industrial society, with its orientation toward an ever-increasing production of goods. Has the biblical faith in the God of history, in opposition to the cosmic religion that surrounded the people of Israel, encouraged a utilitarian understanding of nature? Is nature simply meant to serve the development of humanity, or does it have a being that demands respect in itself? These questions of ecological theology are discussed in Stephen Scharper's article in this volume.

Systematic "ideology critique" of the Christian tradition from the perspective of Christian faith is a new phenomenon, a theological achievement produced by Christians in various contexts, contexts that revealed to them the harmful ambiguity of the Christian tradition. The articles in this volume demonstrate, I think, that this remarkable contribution of academic theology was for the most part inspired and aided by ordinary Christians committed by their faith to justice and liberation. Yet in my own article in this volume, I suggest that Karl Marx was the first thinker who engaged in systematic ideology critique, that is, a type of reasoning that uncovers the use of texts, ideas, symbols, and rituals to legitimate oppression or other kinds of destructive public policies. The same German philosopher also held that this type of reasoning becomes available only to people committed to emancipation. Here engagement precedes insight, and the love of justice the knowledge of the truth. Of course, Marx and his followers produced an ideology critique of religion from the outside, without having access to its inner meaning, while the theologies of liberation offer an ideology critique of the Christian tradition from within their faith and for that reason are able to follow the *via negativa* by a creative rereading of the tradition—a recovery of its prophetic meaning and power. Negation is here followed by retrieval, a negation of the negation. This method could be traced back to Hegel. It could also, I think, be traced further back to the mystical tradition where the happy possession of the truth (*via illuminationis*) is followed by the dark night of the soul making this truth disappear (*via negativa*) until it is relieved by a new, unexpected, and previously hidden meaning (*via eminentiae*.) The reference to the mystical tradition is appropriate because the discovery of the ideological distortion of Christian teaching is, for the believer, an entry into a dark night, an experience of lostness and pain, from which some never recover.

From Ulrich Duchrow's article we learn that the theology developed by the World Council of Churches has come to interpret divine redemption as God's rescue of humanity from sin, including the social sins of economic, racist and sexist oppression, and the devastation of nature. Echoing the aspirations of all liberation theologies, the World Council now teaches Christians to yearn and struggle for the earthly shalom that is part of the divine promises revealed in the scriptures. Duchrow's article also shows that a conservative current presently flowing through Western society and the churches has weakened the influence of the World Council and reduced its operational base. The most offensive aspect of the theology of the World Council is, for some ecclesiastical bodies, the call for the equality of men and women in the church.

While its Protestant foundation has always made it difficult for the World Council to arrive at a theological appreciation of the world religions, Catholic theology, with its greater trust in human nature and its more recent insistence on the universality of grace, finds it much easier to respect non-Christian religions and recognize in them a reflection of God's saving wisdom. Rome favors respect and dialogue with the world religions but worries about Christians in Asia, Africa, and Latin America who understand the church's mission as an effort, not to convert non-Christians to the Christian faith, but to foster cooperation with them in the practice of love, justice, and peace. Virgilio Elizondo's article in this volume allows these voices from the geographical margin of the church to be heard. They lament a false self-centeredness in the Catholic church in particular. This Catholic church, they claim, still regards its European establishment as its center and expects Catholic communities in other parts of the world to conform to the European model. In matters of liturgy, theology, and canon law the periphery is to follow the directives of the center. More daringly these voices complain that the church is self-centered in another way—by regarding itself as the center of the divine dispensation of truth and grace and hence as superior to other religious communities. What is truly central in this divine dispensation, these voices argue, is the practice of love, justice, and peace, incarnate in the life of Jesus, a practice that transcends religious boundaries and might even be followed in a non-Christian community more faithfully than in a Christian one.

If the remarks I have made on the topic of ideology are correct, then all theologies must be understood as contextual, including those that regard themselves as transcending their historical origin and having universal validity. The classical European-based theology, in which we were trained and which many of us dearly love, must then be understood as an important, brilliant, regional intellectual development that makes the dubious claim of universal relevance, thus failing to recognize its own contextuality. This does not mean, of course, that contextual theologies are confined to regional concerns. To be responsible in today's world, contextual theology must be holistic; that is, it must take into account the location of its context within the global society. European-based theology could become consciously contextual and thus be saved from its ideological taint if it reflected in faith on Europe as the home of the classical tradition and on Europe as the home of the modern empires exercising, with North America, economic and political power touching all parts of the globe. Because our theology is not holistic, we do not recognize that as we celebrate the beginning of the third millennium, we commemorate at the same time the political victory of our calendar over the calendars of other cultures and societies.

Attention to the contextuality of theology makes us aware that the articles of this volume leave out a good number of creative theological movements in response to particular circumstances. I already mentioned the theological development in South Africa. No article in this volume discusses the contextual theology, by David Tracy and other critical theologians belonging to middle classes, responding to the democratic achievements and the social evil of U.S. society. Since I now live in Montreal, I am keenly aware that this volume does not deal with the imaginative theology of Douglas Hall responding to the ethos and historical self-understanding of Canada, or with the contextual theology of francophone Quebecers concerned with social justice and the protection of their collective identity. Left out also are topics of special interest to me—the contextual Protestant theology in communist East Germany (see my book, *The Church for Others*) and the more recent theological reflections on Scotland's self-identity and national aspirations. From the 1960s on, we observe the multiplication of politically responsible theologies that envision the reform or the reconstruction of particular societies, exposed to the globalization of the economy and the consumer-oriented monoculture that accompanies it. These contextual theologies tend to be progressive, that is, they support social justice, unlike the contextual theology of the German Christians under Hitler or the apartheid theology of the Afrikaner church. Through an altogether unique historical development beginning in the 1960s, the emancipatory dimension of divine redemption has assumed, for the first time, a central place in the construction of Christian theology.

Looking to the Future

Do the essays in this volume allow us to make any predictions about the theology of the future? According to Eric Hobsbawm, the twentieth century understood as an historical unit began in 1914 with World War I and ended in 1991 with the collapse of the communist Soviet bloc. If this is true, then the theological wrestling of the 1990s should give us an idea of the issues that will preoccupy theology in the new phase of history that has just begun. Yet the essays in this volume do not agree in their expectations of the future. Lee Cormie focuses on the enormous suffering produced by the globalization of the free-market economy, causing dislocation and hunger among the poor and excluded and undermining the traditional cultures of solidarity. He sees theological creativity in the regional resistances to economic and cultural globalization. This is, in fact, the perspective of the worldwide Christian initiative Jubilee 2000, supported by the churches, which requests the remission of the debt for the poor nations of the South, and of the movement Kairos Europa, which is preparing a massive international demonstration in Berlin in June 2000, demanding the deconstruction of the systems of domination centered in the West. In his essay Virgilio Elizondo also anticipates religious creativity in various parts of the world, expressing pride in the inherited cultural identities and resistance to the powers of the center. In the minds of Cormie and Elizondo, religion and theological reflection will remain in the emancipatory mode. If I read Harvey Cox's article correctly, it suggests that the secularizing trend of the twentieth century is being left behind by an extraordinary revival of religion: a living encounter with the sacred at the edge of the churches and the traditional religions. The religious feeling of contacting the divine is so powerful and spiritually liberating that it makes liberation in the material sense a secondary issue—desirable, yes, but on a lower level than the living contact with the sacred. Michael Scanlon thinks that in Western societies theologians may be increasingly attracted by postmodern thought, which recognizes pluralism and honors otherness. He is not afraid that the linguistic turn of postmodern thought will make Western societies indifferent to mass starvation, a non-linguistic event, or lead them to overlook the economic, non-linguistic forces of oppression and marginalization. While Lee Cormie concentrates on globalization from above through economic domination and globalization from below through movements of solidarity at the base, he also mentions other new developments, especially the power of contemporary science to remake, for better or for worse, humans and their natural environment. We do not know what the future will bring, nor do we know whether the Christian churches will want to face the new challenges, prefer to celebrate the past, or withdraw into otherworldliness. Still, reading the essays in the present volume has greatly encouraged me. They offer their readers hope because they document the intellectual creativity, the rich imagination, and the passion of the heart that moved the theologians of the twentieth century to wrestle with the troubling events of their day and the issues posed by new historical developments—all in order to uncover the contemporary meaning and power of the Christian gospel. Apart from a few betrayals, this history is impressive. The Spirit will continue to speak to the churches in the coming century.

Contributors

Gregory Baum is Professor Emeritus, Religious Studies, McGill University, Montreal. His recent books include *The Church for Others: Protestant Theology in Communist East Germany* (Eerdmans, 1996), *Karl Polanyi on Ethics and Economics* (McGill-Queens University Press, 1996), and *Le nationalisme: perspectives éthiques et religeuses* (Montreal: Fides, 1998).

Victor Consemius is a church historian resident in Lucerne, Switzerland. He is the author of many books and articles on Catholic thinkers and political figures of the nineteenth and early twentieth centuries.

Lee Cormie, theologian, is Professor of Theology at St. Michael's College and theToronto School of Theology. His field of research, teaching, and publishing is the exploration of the church's preferential option for the poor, the theological interpretation of social movements, and the interdisciplinary dialogue between theology and the social sciences.

Harvey Cox is Thomas Professor of Divinity at Harvard University, where he teaches courses on theology, ethics, and religion and society. The author of *The Secular City*, and *Religion in the Secular City*, his most recent book is *Fire from Heaven: The Rise of Pentecostal Spirituality and the Reshaping of Religion in the Twenty-First Century* (Addison-Wesley, 1995).

Gary Dorrien is Professor and Chair of Religious Studies, Kalamazoo College, Kalamazoo. His numerous books include *Social in Society: The Making and Renewal of Christian Theology* (Fortress Press, 1995) and *The Word as True Myth: Interpreting Modern Theology* (Westminster/John Knox Press, 1997). The Barth-Niebuhr debate in the present volume contains material adapted from his forthcoming book, *Theology without Weapons: The Barthian Revolt in Modern Theology* (Westminster/John Knox Press).

Ulrich Duchrow is Professor of Practical Theology, Heidelberg University. His recent books include *Shalom: Biblical Perspectives on Creation, Justice, and Peace* (WCC Publications, 1989), *Europe in the World System: 1492-1992* (WCC Publications, 1992), and *Alternatives to Global Capitalism* (Utrecht: International Books, 1995).

Bernard Dupuis, O.P., theologian, is a former Professor at the Theological Faculty of le Saulchoir and at the Institut catholique in Paris, and presently the Director of the Centre d'etudes oecumeniques d'Istina, also in Paris. He is the author of many books and articles on ecclesiology, ecumenism, and the church's relation to Jews and Judaism. He has promoted ecumenism through his work in several ecclesiastical committees of the Catholic church and the World Council of Churches.

Virgilio Elizondo, founder of the Mexican-American Cultural Center in San Antonio, is a theologian, pastor, and popular writer. His most recent books include *Guadalupe: Mother of the New Creation* (Orbis Books, 1997), and *San Fernando Cathedral: Soul of the City* (Orbis Books, 1999).

Douglas John Hall is Professor Emeritus, Religious Studies, McGill University, Montreal. His numerous books include the three-volume Christian Theology in North America, *Thinking the Faith*, *Professing the Faith*, and *Confessing the Faith* (Fortress Press, 1989, 1993, 1996).

Dwight N. Hopkins teaches theology at the Divinity School, University of Chicago. His most recent books are *Shoes That Fit Our Feet: Sources for a Constructive Black Theology* (Orbis Books, 1993) and *Introducing Black Theology of Liberation* (Orbis Books, 1999).

Joseph A. Komonchak holds the John and Gertrude Hubbard Chair in Religious Studies at the Catholic University of America. Widely known for his writings in ecclesiology, Father Komonchak is co-editor of *The New Dictionary of Theology* (Michael Glazier, 1987), and editor of the English edition of *History of Vatican II* (Peeters/Orbis Books, 1995–).

A. James Reimer is Professor of Religion and Theology at Conrad Grebel College, University of Waterloo, and Toronto School of Theology. He is the author of *The Emanuel Hirsch and Paul Tillich Debate* (E. Mellen Press, 1989) and the editor of *The Influence of the Frankfurt School on Contemporary Theology* (E. Mellen Press, 1992).

Susan A. Ross is Associate Professor of Theology at Loyola University, Chicago, where she has also served as Director of Women's Studies. Her most recent book is *Extravagant Affection: A Feminist Sacramental Theology* (New York: Continuum, 1998).

Rosemary Radford Ruether is Georgia Harkness Professor of Applied Theology at the Garrett-Evangelical Theological Seminary in Evanston. Her numerous books include *Faith and Fratricide: The Theological Roots of Antisemitism* (Seabury, 1974), *The Wrath of Jonas: The Crisis of Religious Nationalism in the Israeli-Palestinian Conflict* (Harper & Row, 1989), and *At Home in the World: The Letters of Thomas Merton and Rosemary Radford Ruether* (Orbis Books, 1995).

Michael J. Scanlon, O.S.A., currently holds the Josephine C. Connelly Chair in Christian Theology at Villanova University. He is a past president of the Catholic Theological Society of America. He teaches and writes on fundamental and systematic theology.

Stephen B. Scharper is currently Assistant Professor of Religious Studies at the University of Toronto and formerly Director of the English-language publications of Novalis Publishing, Toronto. He has taught theological ethics at McGill University and the University of Notre Dame and is the author of *Redeeming the Time: A Political Theology of the Environment* (Continuum, 1997) and co-author, with his wife, of *The Green Bible* (Orbis Books, 1993), an ecumenical, ecological resource book.

Robert J. Schreiter is Professor of Doctrinal Theology at Catholic Theological Union, Chicago. His most recent books include *The New Catholicity: Theology between the Global and the Local* (Orbis Books, 1997) and *The Ministry of Reconciliation: Spirituality and Strategies* (Orbis Books, 1998).

Donald Schweitzer is a member of the clergy team at Wesley United Church in Prince Albert, Saskatchewan, Canada. He holds the Ph.D. in systematic theology from Princeton Theological Seminary and has published several articles in the area of contemporary theology and social ethics.

Linda E. Thomas teaches theology and anthropology at Garrett-Evangelical Theological Seminary, Evanston, and is the Director of the Center for the Church and the Black Experience. She is the author of *Under the Canopy: Ritual Process and Spiritual Resilience in South Africa* (University of South Carolina Press, 1999).

Index